Principles of operations management

D

Principles of operations management

Les Galloway

THOMSON

LEARNING

Australia • Canada • Mexico • Singapore • Spain • United Kingdom • United States

Principles of Operations Management

Copyright © 1998 Les Galloway

The Thomson Learning logo is a registered trademark and used herein under license.

British Library Cataloguing-in-Publication Data
A catalogue record for this book is available from the British Library

First published 1993 by Routledge, reprinted 1994 and 1997
Second edition published 1998
Reprinted by Thomson Learning 2000 and 2002
Typeset by LaserScript Limited, Mitcham, Surrey
Printed by TJ International, Padstow, Cornwall

ISBN 1-86152-378-5

Thomson Learning
Berkshire House
168–173 High Holborn
London WC1V 7AA
UK

http://www.thomsonlearning.co.uk

Contents

List of figures   vi
List of tables   ix
Preface   x
Preface to the second edition   xii

1 Operations management and the operations function   1

2 Operations strategy   15

3 Product design   30

4 Service design   43

5 Capacity investment   57

6 Design of the task   71

7 Planning and control 1 – Capacity planning   91

8 Inventory control   106

9 Planning and control 2 – Batch scheduling   123

10 Planning and control 3 – JIT   136

11 Project planning and control   148

12 The management of quality   163

13 Plant maintenance   191

Appendix 1 Further quantitative techniques   201
Appendix 2 An introduction to control charts   208
Appendix 3 A history of key operations concepts   213
Bibliography   217
Index   219

List of figures

1.1	Production and related organizational functions	5
1.2	Information flow between production and related functions	6
1.3	The operations tetrahedron	7
1.4	Material flow – manufacture supply	8
1.5	Material flow – transport service	10
1.6	Functional layout	12
1.7	Product layout	13
2.1	The product life cycle	18
2.2	Elements of availability	22
2.3	Criterion life cycle	23
2.4	An example of profiling	27
3.1	Where new products fail	31
3.2	Cost of new product	32
3.3	Effect of component number on defect rate	37
4.1	Internal consistency of service operations	51
4.2	Levels of the service structure	51
5.1	Present branch layout	70
6.1	Use of manufacturing technology	75
6.2	Flow chart symbols	78
6.3	Server/customer process chart for ordering a book	79
6.4	Potentiometer schematic	87
6.5	Original layout	88
6.6	Yield and productivity – old method	89
6.7	Revised layout	89

6.8	Productivity and absenteeism – new method	90
7.1	Use of stock with seasonal demand	96
7.2	MPS planning process	99
8.1	Economic order quantity	111
8.2	Variation of EOQ with order cost	111
8.3	Variation of EOQ with holding cost	112
8.4	Sensitivity of the EOQ	113
8.5	Stock movement, no variability	114
8.6	Stock movement, variable demand	114
8.7	Reorder cycle system	117
8.8	ROC system, reduced demand	117
8.9	Pareto curve	119
9.1	Gantt chart, start	125
9.2	Gantt chart, completed	126
9.3	Manufacturing resources planning	132
10.1	JIT implementation sequence	139
11.1	Network symbols	149
11.2	Basic network	150
11.3	Use of dummy activity	150
11.4	New product launch network	151
11.5	Node (activity on node)	152
11.6	Activity on node version of Figure 11.3	152
11.7	New product launch network – minimum time	155
11.8	New product launch network – full analysis	155
11.9	Use of float – network	157
11.10	Earliest start – Gantt chart and labour histogram	158
11.11	Resource smoothed activity chart	159
12.1	Relative costs of quality – reactive and proactive	166
12.2	Ideal operating characteristics	168
12.3	Operating characteristics, single sample schemes	169
12.4	An OC with consumer's and producer's risks	170
12.5	Average outgoing quality	171
12.6	Continuous sampling scheme	172

12.7	Optimal quality level	173
12.8	Control chart	175
12.9	The gap model of service quality	183
13.1	Cost of maintenance	192
13.2	Failure rate	195
13.3	Replacement costs	197
13.4	Kiln: plan view and entrance	199
A1.1	Linear programming	205
A2.1	Trade deficit with time	209
A2.2	Trade deficit with limits	210
A2.3	X chart	211
A2.4	XmR chart	212

List of tables

3.1	Kitchen Components: product range	40
5.1	Process routes	67
5.2	From–to chart	67
5.3	Travel chart	68
5.4	Midport South branch: customer demand	70
6.1	Assembly process	87
7.1	Moving average of demand	93
7.2	Exponential smoothing	94
7.3	Bill of materials data for aspirin manufacture	100
7.4	Electronic Components Ltd: low-voltage product range	105
8.1	Usage of stock items, Company XYZ	118
8.2	National Discount Appliances: stock list	121
9.1	Work content for ten batches	128
9.2	Ten batches ordered by shortest operation time	129
9.3	Structure diagram for portable radio	130
10.1	Kitchen Components: product range	145
10.2	Current stock position	146
10.3	Demand for products	147
11.1	Float analysis – Mega Enterprises	156
12.1	1,000, 50, 2 scheme	169
12.2	1,000, 100, 4 scheme	169
12.3	SERVQUAL dimensions	181
12.4	Electronic Components Ltd: tolerance data	189
13.1	Electronic Components Ltd: burner life	200
13.2	Electronic Components Ltd: tunnel life	200

Preface

The role of the operations function is probably less clearly defined than any other business function. In manufacturing it is assumed to be the production function and there is a view in the UK that this is of no concern to anyone but production management. While most people in management would admit to a need to understand something of finance, marketing, personnel and of course corporate strategy, production is seen as the exclusive concern of the production specialist. This is not an attitude that is found elsewhere in Europe or, more particularly, in Japan where operations is frequently the direct responsibility of the chief executive, and this may go some way to explain the difficulties which seem exclusively to face the UK manufacturing industry. There is some evidence that attitudes are changing, slowly.

Operations is concerned with any productive activity, whether manufacturing or not, and operations management is concerned with ensuring that such activities are carried out both efficiently and effectively. In this way, all managers are operations managers since they are presumably concerned that their departments should be efficient and effective, whatever their function. More importantly, operations is at the heart of all manufacturing and service enterprises, and unless the operations function is carried out effectively, there is little hope that the organization as a whole will be effective. An understanding of operations management principles can thus not only help any manager manage more effectively, it can also contribute substantially to an understanding of the role and function of the organization as a whole. It can facilitate the identification of key corporate strengths and weaknesses and the rational exploitation of the strengths and correction of the weaknesses.

This book has been written primarily for those studying for a Diploma in Management Studies or a Master of Business Administration and is intended to give those not directly involved in operations an insight in the role of the operations function and an appreciation of the issues and techniques which can make a contribution in any area of productive activity. It is hoped that those studying on other business and management courses, as well as the practising manager, may also find it of some interest. The field of operations management is wide, and some specialities have not been addressed, in particular purchasing, warehousing and physical distribution.

The book is structured broadly along the lines of strategic issues first, followed by design and then by planning and control. There are several well established frameworks for teaching operations management and those following a formal course of study may well find a different sequence used. Most chapters are supported by a short case study intended to illustrate some of the main issues raised in the chapter. Since the division into chapters is to some extent arbitrary, the cases are not exclusive and some overlap into other areas will be found. The questions are for guidance only, and other issues may be addressed through the cases. While all the cases are fictional, they are based to a greater or lesser extent upon real situations.

Preface to the second edition

In many ways little has changed since the first edition. The approach variously known as Just in Time, Total Quality or kaizen, continues to advance in both manufacturing and service industries, leading, at least in theory, to leaner, fitter, more responsive and more competitive organizations. Public sector organizations continue to adopt private sector methods and attitudes on the grounds that this will make them more efficient and effective. Quality and service are still claimed to be the main areas of competition.

Yet examples of poor service still abound; customer satisfaction in areas such as banking and financial services fails to improve; even in the leading edge area of motor manufacture, major companies have recently been shown to be plagued by corrosion problems – something which was supposedly solved in the 1970s – and new models are introduced which are apparently unstable when driven hard; in public sector many initiatives seem only to succeed in alienating staff. Many of the problems are operations problems. Poor quality, whether of product or service, is usually a failure of design, delivery or both – its source lies with operations although it is sometimes a failure of will at a more senior level. The lesson is that, despite increasing globalization and competitive pressure, there is still a great deal of room for improvement. The role of operations management is still central.

In this edition the opportunity has been taken to enlarge and develop further a number of key areas, in particular those dealing with strategy, service and quality.

Chapter 1

Operations management and the operations function

An operation can be defined as 'a process, method or series of acts especially of a practical nature' (*Collins English Dictionary*, 1986). This definition covers virtually all human activity of an organized and productive nature. Arising from this it can be argued that all organizational functions are *operations*, and that all management activities involve *operations management*. The terms *production* and *operations* are frequently viewed as interchangeable, and there is a widespread view in industry, commerce and not-for-profit organizations that production management is a separate and discrete field of little concern to anyone outside of production. There are sound historical reasons for this. *Production management* was the first management discipline to be developed and taught, and production managers were, and frequently are still, trained specialists who can be left to get on with the business of managing production. This will be discussed further in Chapter 2, but as long as manufacturing was seen to be the main wealth generating activity of a nation, and as long as the economic situation was characterized by under-capacity (broadly until about 1950), it was a reasonable attitude. We are now in a period of intense, global competition, and the main wealth generating activities in many economies are no longer manufacture but service. *Operations management* can no longer be left to the manufacturing manager alone, and the service sector is too important to be allowed to muddle through.

The view taken in this book is that all productive activities are operations and therefore operations management is relevant to all.

The performance of an organization may be linked to the centrality of its view of operations, and without a clearly articulated operations strategy, and effective operations management, an organization will survive only by chance. Operations management is thus an essential discipline for all managers. Despite this view, it must be admitted that the clearest and most developed applications are still to be found in the area of *production*, and this inevitably leads to bias. Readers from other disciplines should consider how the various approaches and techniques described can be applied within their own function.

In this chapter the nature, purpose and structure of the operations function is described. The sections which follow look first at the operations function itself and then consider its relationship with other functions within the organization. The main areas in which the operations function operates are described and the remaining sections consider the ways in which the function is most commonly organized.

WHAT IS OPERATIONS MANAGEMENT?

A traditional view of operations management is that it is concerned primarily with manufacturing, or the change of state of physical goods. A possible definition is:

> **Those activities concerned with the acquisition of raw materials, their conversion into finished product, and the supply of that finished product to the customer.**

This definition is, however, in some ways too general. It includes the purchasing function and the physical distribution function, which, while closely related to operations are generally considered as disciplines in themselves. More importantly, it is restrictive in that it appears to eliminate any activity not concerned with physical manufacture.

All useful activities are concerned with the conversion of something. This is frequently information, as in financial services, news and, to a degree, entertainment. The conversion process may concern the customer as in hairdressing, the health service, etc. Even within a manufacturing organization, other functional areas such as finance, or personnel, are carrying out operations.

A rather more comprehensive definition of operations management is:

> **All activities concerned with the deliberate transformation of materials, information or customers.**

Operations management is concerned with both the effective and the efficient management of any operation. The degree to which a physical good is involved is largely irrelevant. The theory is equally applicable in a hospital ward or an insurance office as on the shop floor of a factory. The following examples illustrate the core operation of a number of organizations.

Television manufacturer
Transforms pre-manufactured components into televisions. Components are usually purchased from other manufacturers. The manufacturer does not, as a rule, deal with the end customer, but supplies the finished TVs to dealers for onward selling. The transformation is:

   Components $\longrightarrow$ Finished product

Exclusive restaurant
The customer is buying an experience, a complex mixture of gastronomy, entertainment and image building. Hunger is likely to be a small part of the satisfaction but the transformation is:

   Customer seeking satisfaction $\longrightarrow$ Satisfied customer

Fast food restaurant

Generally the customer is only buying a meal so the transformation is:

Hungry customer ⟶ Satisfied customer

but most of the operations effort will be devoted to food preparation:

Raw materials ⟶ Prepared meals

The focus of the operation is therefore mixed.

Self-service supermarket

It is assumed that the customer knows what he or she wants, so the transformation is:

Customer with identified needs ⟶ Satisfied customer

Insurance company

Insurance companies generally maintain that they are selling investment and protection. In fact, insurance does not protect against the occurrence of the insured event, but provides for financial compensation if the event occurs, so protection is perhaps an overstatement.

An investment model of the transformation might be:

Customer with some money ⟶ Customer with more money

while in the case of protection, the truly satisfied customer is the one for which nothing happens, but since that is outside the control of the company an alternative is:

Customer suffering a loss ⟶ Customer financially compensated
for the loss

Both of these transformations are too long-term to be used as a basis for managing the operation, and shorter term transformations of the type:

Customer seeking financial advice ⟶ Properly advised customer

and:

Customer seeking compensation ⟶ Compensated customer

define the operation.

Criminal justice system

Once one moves away from profit making organizations to social, governmental and charitable organizations, problems arise in defining the customer. The alternatives in this case are:

The accused: this hardly makes sense unless the accused is wrongly acquitted, but that would represent a quality failure.

Government: a cynical view might be that since most of the electorate abhor crime, governments must be seen to be tackling crime. The transformation is:

Government ⟶ more popular Government

You must decide for yourself whether this reflects your view.

Society: the general consensus is that crime is undesirable, and the criminal justice system is one aspect of the control of crime. The transformation is:

Society troubled by crime ⟶ Society with less crime

Operations management is concerned with both the effective and the efficient management of any operation.

Effectiveness can be defined as meeting the specified objectives of the system, but more generally this means meeting customer needs. Efficiency is achieving this with minimum use of resources.

At the most basic level profit making organizations survive only by making a profit, which can be expressed simply as:

Profit = Revenue − Cost

Operations management is vital to the success of the organization because of its twofold effect on profit. In seeking to improve effectiveness, the aim is to ensure that the operations carried out are such as to meet customer requirements. The organization is providing a service which the customer wants in a way that meets the customer's needs, or is manufacturing products which the customer wants to an appropriate specification.

Increasing effectiveness will increase revenue by making the organization more competitive. Increasing efficiency will, of course, reduce costs, but this must never be done at the expense of effectiveness.

Without the proper application of operations management principles an organization can only be profitable by accident. It has either quite by chance got things right, or is simply not quite as bad as the competition. Such a situation is unlikely to continue for ever.

The situation is less clear cut in not-for-profit organizations such as local and national government, health services, etc. Such organizations are not profit driven and therefore they are often accused of inefficiency; frequently they are monopolies, by definition not subject to competition, and therefore they are accused of being bureaucratic and indifferent to customer needs. Opinion is often determined by political viewpoint, and facts are hard to come by. The concepts of effectiveness and efficiency are still applicable. Increasing effectiveness ensures that limited resources are not wasted on inappropriate activities, while increasing efficiency ensures that the minimum amount of required resources are used for a particular activity.

An undue stress on efficiency can, however, destroy a service. For example it would probably be more *efficient* if domestic refuse were collected monthly from giant refuse containers, but the problems this would cause householders in handling and storing refuse, together with the health hazards created, would be such that the service would no longer be *effective*.

THE OPERATIONS FUNCTION IN CONTEXT

Most organizations base their structures upon functional divisions, and a typical manufacturing organization may have a structure like that shown in Figure 1.1.

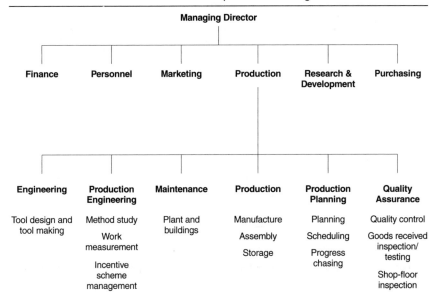

Figure 1.1   Production and related organizational functions

There is wide variation in the precise disposition of responsibilities. Sometimes the Purchasing function is totally subservient to Production. Quality Assurance sometimes reports to Research & Development and sometimes to Marketing. Organizations sometimes have a Technical Services function which includes Research & Development, Production Engineering, Quality Assurance, Data Processing and possibly even Production Control. Despite these variations, Figure 1.1 represents the most common organization.

Figure 1.2 gives a broad overview of the information flow between Production and the other functions. For example Finance is responsible for costing the activities of the production function, providing budget statements, etc. but this can only be done if Production provides accurate and timely information on labour and material usage.

The situation in many service organizations is less clear cut, but in large scale organizations, analogous structures can usually be found.

The operations function is at the heart of the organization, and interacts with all other functions. Personnel and purchasing can be seen as providing a service to operations, while finance is both providing a service and fulfilling a monitoring role. The relationships with R&D and marketing are more ambiguous. Both are more directed towards corporate goals and frequently see operations as being there to serve their objectives.

This conflict is illustrated by the frequently held but incompatible views of sales and manufacturing departments whereby sales believes that the sole function of manufacturing is to make what they are selling while

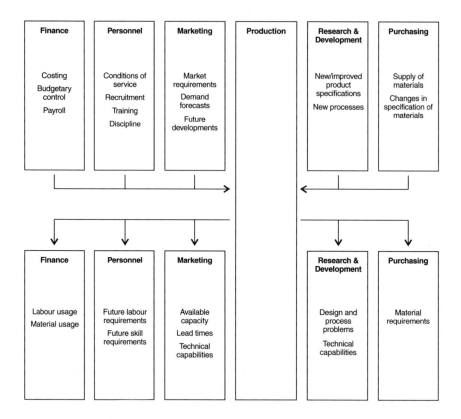

Figure 1.2   Information flow between production and related functions

manufacturing believes that the sole function of sales is to sell what they are making.

In reality both are required to identify and meet market needs, and operations also needs to identify its distinctive competence so that this becomes an input into the marketing process.

OPERATIONS ACTIVITIES

Four distinct types of activity that may be described as operations have been identified.

- **Manufacturing.**   The most obvious operations activity – physical materials are converted into a product which is then sold on to the customer. The customer may carry out further manufacturing operations and the total chain from extraction of raw materials to supply of a product to the end consumer may be quite long.

- **Supply.** Activities which are primarily concerned with the change of ownership of a physical good. Retail distribution is the best known example.
- **Transport.** Activities which are primarily concerned with the movement of goods, or people, from one place to another without any physical change taking place.
- **Service.** Activities which are primarily concerned with changing the condition of the customer. This condition may be physical as in dental surgery or hairdressing, intellectual as in education, or emotional as in entertainment, or more often a complex mix of these and more.

It would be a mistake to consider these as distinct and separate activities. All manufacturers supply their end product to a customer; this may also involve transporting the product, and there will be some element of service involved in the handling of enquiries and provision of information. A convenient way of representing the relationships between these activities is through the operations tetrahedron, shown in Figure 1.3.

The operations tetrahedron demonstrates that an organization can be seeking to provide one of an infinite range of possible mixtures of any two or more of these elements. No organization lies at an apex of the tetrahedron, since there is an element of service in every manufacture, supply or transport transaction, and no significant venture has been identified which can be classed as pure service.

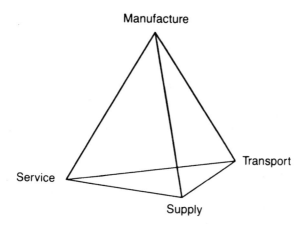

Figure 1.3 The operations tetrahedron
Source: Armistead and Killeya, 1984

MATERIAL FLOW

Operations systems can be classified according to the way in which material flows through the system from supplier to customer. There are two basic categories of system, one covering manufacture and supply where the customer is the final recipient of a good, and one covering transport and service where the customer is an input to the process.

Manufacture and supply

The basic model is one where material flows into the system from a supplier, is processed and then flows on to the customer. Models differ in terms of their treatment of stock.

   They are illustrated in Figure 1.4.

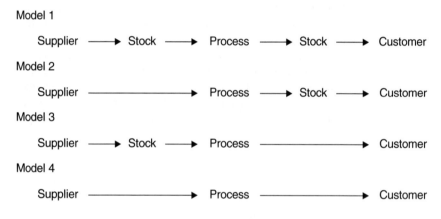

Figure 1.4 Material flow – manufacture supply

- **Model 1** This is a very widely used system. In manufacturing it has the advantage that the production function can operate to maximum efficiency since supplies of raw materials are guaranteed, and there is no requirement to react quickly to customer demand since this will be supplied from stock. The stock operates as a buffer isolating production from the vagaries of both supply and demand. The same model applies to retail distribution where stock is held in a warehouse, then brought forward for display as required and held as stock on display until purchased. The use of stock to isolate stages from each other greatly simplifies the management task, but it also introduces constraints and penalties. The most obvious penalty is the cost of holding stock, which is discussed further in Chapter 8. Such an approach can only be used in situations where there is demand for a standard product range. Stock of finished products cannot be held in any situation where customization is required.

- **Model 2** The high cost of stock has led to a number of organizations seeking to reduce or eliminate raw material stocks by arranging supplies to match exactly the demand from production, and such a situation is represented by model 2. Production is now critically dependent upon the reliability of supply, and this reliability is often achieved by the supplier holding larger stocks than would be the case otherwise. Unless very carefully managed, this often results in both stockouts and stockholding in the manufacturing organization, caused by failure in communication. There is also no overall reduction in stockholding costs since they are now being born by the supplier. There are situations where the raw material is too perishable to stock, and the whole purpose of the processing is to increase its storage life. For example peas must be frozen within a few hours of harvesting. Model 2 applies to much of the food processing industry.
- **Model 3** This model applies to any situation where the customer is prepared to wait for supply, where the process is very short, or where the product is produced to the customer's specification and cannot therefore be stocked in finished form. Much heavy and civil engineering conforms to this model although the extent to which raw material stock is held varies. Other examples include bespoke tailoring, or the manufacture of hand made solid timber furniture. In the latter case the raw material stock is almost part of the process since the timber must be held in stock to season before being used.
- **Model 4** There are mail order companies who advertise a product, accept orders, pass these on to a manufacturer who then manufactures and delivers the product. The mail order company simply handles the administration of the order and, if cash is paid in advance, collects the interest on this during the period between the receipt of the order and the payment of the manufacturer's invoice. Model 4 would fit this activity. More generally the model applies to most custom manufacturing activities where raw material stock is not held. For example civil engineering projects usually obtain materials as required rather than holding substantial stocks and the finished product is never stocked.

The pressure to reduce stockholding costs, and to increase responsiveness, has led to the development of the Just in Time approach to manufacturing. The end aim of this approach is zero stock at all stages and model 4 reflects this exactly. This is considered further in Chapter 10.

Transport and service

Transport and service operations differ from manufacturing and supply in two important respects: the customer is an input to the process, and service cannot be stocked. In order to cope with variability in demand spare capacity can be held, or a stock of customers can be held in some form of queue. Both are perishable in that surplus capacity today cannot be used to satisfy additional demand tomorrow, and customers are liable to leave queues if kept waiting too long.

Queues of customers can take the form of a physical queue as at a bus stop, supermarket check-out, passport control desk, etc., or an appointments system, or some combination of the two. The three possible configurations of service activities are shown in Figure 1.5.

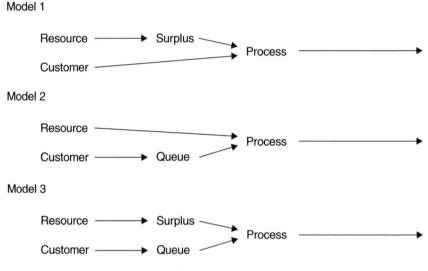

Model 1

Model 2

Model 3

Figure 1.5 Material flow – transport service

- **Model 1**   This is a model of almost any premium service. Customers receive an immediate service, but this is achieved by maintaining a surplus of capacity. Premium service is of course more expensive because this surplus must be paid for.
- **Model 2**   This model represents a low cost service. Resources are fully utilized hence the great efficiency, but at the expense of waiting customers. The contrast between models 1 and 2 is illustrated by the contrast between private and public health care. While private health care does not give an instantaneous service, waiting times are usually much shorter, and appointments are usually appointments to be seen rather than appointments to join a queue in the waiting room. Courier firms frequently offer a two-tier service: a guaranteed next day delivery, and a rather less clearly specified service possibly quoting an average delivery time rather than a maximum. The same facilities are used for each service, so it is unnecessary to hold surplus capacity to allow for variation in demand for the premium service. If demand for the premium service increases, capacity can be released by

increasing the waiting time for the standard service. If demand for the premium service falls the standard service performance will improve again.

- **Model 3**   This could be viewed as a model of management inefficiency, idle resources and waiting customers, but it models most service operations in the medium term. Most services are characterized by rapid and large variations in demand. Public houses, restaurants, and hospital accident departments show much higher demand at weekends, public transport shows dramatic variation in demand between 8.30 am and 9.30 am, etc. Since capacity cannot be varied with sufficient speed, management have no option but to operate some sort of queuing system at peak demand times and tolerate some overcapacity at other times. Cheap off peak fares and discounts for pensioners at off peak times are attempts to increase the utilization of this surplus capacity.

WORK ORGANIZATION

Regardless of the material flow pattern adopted, there are various ways of organizing the physical and control structure of the operations function. The distinctions are not clear cut, and the number of different systems identified by different authorities varies between three and six, but a division into three broad groups is adequate for most purposes.

Job/project organization

A civil engineering contractor building an airport or bridge does not at first glance seem to have much in common with a design consultancy producing a brochure for a client, but very small and very large scale operations share certain characteristics which lead to common structures. The term 'job' is usually applied to small scale operations and 'project' to large scale.

The tasks undertaken by a civil engineering contractor, while broadly similar from project to project, will differ considerably in detail. No two building projects are the same. Contracts are negotiated with the client and the product or service is produced to the client's specification. Each product is a one-off. Because of this variability from job to job or project to project, information gained from completed work is only of general application to new contracts. In order to complete work on time and at a profit an engineering organization depends very heavily upon the skill of its estimators. The precise volume and timing of future work cannot easily be determined so the organization needs to adopt a flexible structure and needs to tolerate some under utilization. This flexibility can be achieved by having a multi-skilled work force, or by subcontracting. Equipment is usually owned but may be under utilized since the organization will need equipment to satisfy every likely requirement. Equipment which is utilized infrequently may be hired when required if it is readily available. The planning and control system depends heavily upon subjective estimating for its targets, while the monitoring of progress is based upon the completion of discrete stages.

Batch organization

If demand for a particular resource, function or skill is great enough, it can be fully utilized to reduce unit costs. A batch organization applies this principle in situations where a limited range of products or services is made. Batches of several, or several thousand, of the same item are processed together as a single unit. A particular product will always follow the same process sequence and the actual operations will usually be carried out using the same pieces of equipment. Because these are standard products, the precise requirements in terms of machines, labour, materials and time are all known from past experience, giving a sound basis for planning and control. It is customary to use a process layout of the workplace in batch operations.

To give a simple example, in producing tablets, whether aspirin, indigestion or even mint sweets, the process might consist of three stages. Mixing, where the ingredients are blended together; pressing, where the tablets are formed; and finishing, where the tablets are inspected and packed. The factory would be laid out as shown in Figure 1.6. All mixing plant is grouped together, operated by a fixed labour force and controlled by a single supervisor, and the same applies to forming and finishing.

This organization offers several advantages. The definition of discrete process areas with common skills, techniques and problems gives a convenient basis for planning and control. Work is allocated to the process area, and its progress is

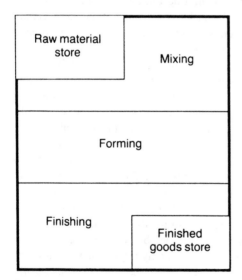

Figure 1.6 Functional layout

monitored by recording its passage from one process to the next. Quality control can also take place at the process area boundaries and a batch may be held back from the next stage until deemed satisfactory. One individual can be given responsibility for both management and technical oversight of the area. Labour is usually flexible within a given process area (i.e. a mixing operator can operate any machine within the mixing section) which enables high labour utilization. There may, however, be a lower plant utilization because particular products require particular machines but are not made in sufficient quantity to use the machine fully.

Flow/mass organization

The term 'flow' is used by some authorities specifically to identify continuous processes such as are found in the petrochemical industry, while others apply it to operations involving flow lines. As the term 'mass production' implies, if the scale of demand for a particular product becomes great enough, it may be possible to dedicate both equipment and labour solely to that product. This allows the design and layout of the workplace and equipment to be optimized for that product alone which gives a considerable increase in efficiency, but at the expense of flexibility. The result of this process is usually a flow line, where consecutive process stages are physically adjacent and may be linked by a conveyor system. The layout of the workplace is product based, and the management structure often follows this with a supervisor being responsible for the whole process for an individual product. Figure 1.7 shows how such a layout might look.

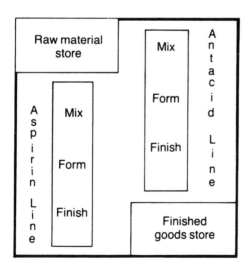

Figure 1.7 Product layout

Because of the degree of specialization involved, a flow line is usually unable to tolerate significant variation in the product or its components, and any reduction in demand will lead to unused capacity.

SUMMARY

This chapter has introduced the concept of the operations function, and briefly described its relationship with the other functional areas of a business. The operations tetrahedron has been introduced as a means of describing the main function of the organization, and several alternative ways of organizing the operations function have been introduced. The success of the enterprise is critically dependent upon matching the design, organization and control of operations to the main function of the organization, and then ensuring that it operates efficiently. Chapters 2, 3 and 4 are mainly concerned with achieving this match, while the remainder of the book is concerned with the details of efficient operation.

Chapter 2

Operations strategy

Effective and efficient operations management is totally dependent upon an appropriate operations strategy. If the operations function does not have well specified, consistent and achievable objectives, then it is self-evident that it will, on occasion, fail to meet expectations.

Unfortunately many organizations have no specified strategy at all, and even those organizations with an overall strategy have frequently given little thought to the operations function.

There are manufacturing organizations who behave as if their operations strategy is to make whatever the customer wants, in whatever quantity, at the lowest possible cost, and highest possible quality. This is, of course, an impossible objective, but sales departments often assume that manufacturing departments can achieve it. When manufacturing fails it is seen to be manufacturing's fault. Operations managers all too often see themselves as purely reactive, there to satisfy the demands of the market place (as interpreted by sales) and so busy dealing with the crises generated by this impossible task that they have no time to develop a coherent strategy for themselves.

Chapter 1 demonstrated that the operations function is the key to successful competition.

Without an effective and efficient operations function no organization can hope to retain market leadership, since it will fail on delivery, price or quality, or, more probably, on all three.

In this chapter the essential elements of a consistent operations strategy will be considered. The chapter will look at the elements of corporate and marketing strategy which influence operations, while considering the development of the operations strategy from these elements. Finally the use of profiling to identify areas of mismatch and the merits of the operations function taking a proactive stance towards corporate strategy will be considered.

CORPORATE INFLUENCES

The corporate influences directly relevant to operations are those related to basic function or focus, those related to product/service development and those related to investment and labour.

Focus

The basic function of the organization is a matter of defining precisely what the organization is doing. It is meeting a market need, but, particularly when supplying a product, the organization could be concerned with all stages of manufacture and distribution. At the other extreme, it may only be concerned with design and promotion, subcontracting everything else. There are very few organizations which own the whole process from raw material to finished product, although there are food manufacturers who control the manufacturing, packaging and distribution of their products. At the other extreme, particularly in consumer electronics, there are organizations which subcontract design and manufacture and concentrate solely on marketing and distribution. The total chain of manufacture can be broken into the following stages:

- design;
- raw material extraction;
- manufacture (the creation of components from raw materials);
- assembly (the association of components into a finished product);
- distribution (the shipping of the finished product to wholesalers, retailers, or the end user).

Any of these stages can be contracted out. It is a matter of corporate policy to determine what is to be the core business and the degree of vertical integration to be adopted.

There are two main arguments in favour of integration:

- **Having everything under central control**.   This is intended to improve reliability and responsiveness. Unfortunately the system frequently becomes too cumbersome and bureaucratic for effective management. Also the absence of competition at a functional level can lead to a deterioration in service and quality.
- **Subcontractors require to make a profit**.   So it is assumed that they will inevitably be more expensive. Here integration should lead to cost savings, but this presumes that a large general operation can be as efficient as a small specialist operation.

Against this, there are strong arguments for developing a high level of competence in the core activity of the organization and subcontracting areas which, although important, are not what the business is about. This focusing of effort enables the organization to avoid the distraction of peripheral activities and to utilize the core competence of its subcontractors. Two examples illustrate this.

> Transport is a major activity for national supermarket chains. Large volumes of goods have to be moved quickly throughout the country to tight deadlines. Failure to deliver to a store on time will result in lost sales, and possibly un-saleable goods. However, early delivery is equally unacceptable due to the pressures on storage space. Distribution is, however, peripheral to the core activity of sales, and supermarket chains tend to subcontract their transport activities to transport specialists.
>
> A major manufacturer of industrial equipment uses large numbers of fastenings (nuts, bolts, clips, etc.). Their value is low, although they are vital to the assembly process, but their volume and variety are high. This imposes a great load on the purchasing and stock control functions. The company subcontract the provision of fastenings to a specialist supplier who sets up and maintains stock points on the shop floor. The sourcing and management of over 1,000 items has been replaced with one contract.

Concentrating on the core business and subcontracting the peripheral aspects increases efficiency and effectiveness by allowing both manage-ment and labour to concentrate on the important elements without allowing peripheral issues to dilute their effort and expertise.

Subcontracting, or out-sourcing, peripheral activities, if done well, allows the organization to benefit from the efficiency and effectiveness achieved by the supplying organization, for whom this is a core activity.

Product development

Product development policy is concerned with the position of the organization's portfolio of products in the product life cycle. It is also concerned with the degree to which the organization is an innovator or an imitator, and the degree to which the organization has focused its product range. The product life cycle is illustrated in Figure 2.1 which shows a product moving from introduction through maturity to decline.

From an operations management viewpoint, there are important differences between the introduction and early growth stages, the later growth and maturity stages, and the decline stage.

In the early stages of its life a product is produced in relatively low volumes, and the product design is relatively fluid. Lack of agreement on design can occasionally extend a considerable way into the life of the product, as was shown by the various conflicting video tape standards which survived for several years. Since the detailed design of the product is likely to change, and volumes are

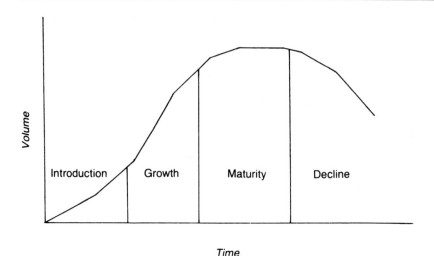

Time

Figure 2.1   The product life cycle

likely to be unpredictable, considerable flexibility is demanded of the operations function. In the stages of late growth and maturity, the product and its market are relatively stable, and the emphasis tends to move towards market share. The demands placed upon operations are now for consistent, high quality, low cost output, which tends to emphasize predictability rather than flexibility. Since the product and market are stable, operations can now afford to invest in improvements in working methods to achieve these aims.

Innovative organizations would generally seek to abandon products before they reach the decline phase, but imitative organizations may well not enter the market until this stage is reached. An example of this behaviour is given by the Eastern European car manufacturers who manufactured and sold out-dated Fiat models, manufactured using redundant Fiat tooling. These manufacturers competed solely on price.

Investment and labour

Operations, whether manufacturing or service, require equipment and labour. The degree to which processes are automated or labour intensive depends upon a number of factors, but an important element is the organization's willingness to invest in either. There is a continuum from labour intensive operations through to full automation, and while the full range is not usually available to any particular organization, a substantial part of it is.

This will be considered further in Chapter 6. It is enough for the present to note that a clear corporate policy towards automation and labour, backed up by the necessary resources, greatly simplifies the task of the operations manager.

MARKET INFLUENCES

A common view of the operations function is that it is there to meet market needs, and there are many operations managers who would accept this. In order to meet this objective effectively and efficiently it is necessary for market needs to be clearly identified. The market can be defined in many ways and broken down into many elements. The following are those which are important to successful operations.

Service content

There are probably no situations in which pure manufacturing, or pure service, arise. It is a mistake to consider manufacturing and service as distinct, or indeed as the only, alternatives. There is a continuum which also includes transport and distribution as discrete activities. A convenient way of representing this is through the operations tetrahedron, shown in Figure 1.3 (Chapter 1). This demonstrates that an organization can be seeking to provide one of an infinite mixture of any two or more of these elements.

It is important that the organization clearly identifies the position of the market that it is dealing with, and then sets up the operations function to provide an appropriate balance.

Too little stress on the service element will lead to customer dissatisfaction; too much will lead to inefficiency.

The service component is often misunderstood in manufacture and supply both by the provider and the customer. Both sides find it easier to respond to tangible elements of the transaction, and this can lead to quite inappropriate behaviour. For example, car retail sales probably comprise about 80% supply and 20% service. What is important is the acquisition of a suitable vehicle in acceptable condition. There are a large number of peripheral activities associated with this transaction, including provision of information, test drive facilities, negotiations over finance, part exchange, etc. One of the difficulties facing suppliers in this type of field is the tendency of the customer to express dissatisfaction in terms of the tangible elements of the transaction even when these are not the principal cause. A customer who is mildly dissatisfied with the way in which they have been treated by the salesman is likely to be more critical of the vehicle. Dissatisfaction will show as complaints about noise, performance, cleanliness, etc. A good car retailer, faced with this sort of customer feedback will put more effort into vehicle preparation and still less into the intangible elements of the transaction, thus causing a further deterioration in service.

The operations function needs to provide an appropriate balance between the four elements, and needs to monitor performance in a way that reflects that balance. The balance is determined not by what the providing organization thinks is required, nor even by what the customers think they want, but by what the customers actually want. This is rather more difficult to define.

Variety

How wide and variable is the product range the market demands? At one extreme there are single product markets with little scope for variation such as those represented by the utilities. A reliable and continuous supply of electricity at 240 volts is all that most customers require, or indeed could use even if there were a choice. Low variety markets may be a result of lack of need, or lack of choice. Whatever the cause, the organization must beware of complacency.

> The Ford motor company standardized on the model T, and its production process became so specialized that, while it was superbly efficient, it could not be changed. The assumption was that no one could want more from a car than the model T provided. The competition, unable to compete on cost, successfully introduced variety into the market, a move that Ford barely survived.

Markets change and the operations function may be required to change with them. The other extreme is the market where everything is custom made, for example, bespoke tailoring, prescription spectacles at an optician, a great deal of civil engineering, etc. Most organizations lie between the two extremes. The implication of this for operations is profound.

A custom market precludes the use of stock, and reduces the scope for standardization of process, plant and materials, all of which are important elements in achieving efficiency.

Volume

Volume is the inverse of variety. A low variety market is by definition high volume. Operations can be set up to produce a single product or service, or a range of very similar products, very efficiently. There is no need to allow for variation in material, specification or process.

Quality

The importance of quality is often taken to be self-evident, but not all markets are concerned about high quality. Quality needs to be adequate, but quality higher than that required may simply increase costs without giving any competitive advantage. The issues of matching design quality and manufacturing quality will be taken further in Chapters 3 and 4. At this stage it is enough to stress that design quality must match market needs while manufacturing, or the service supply system, must be capable of meeting design quality standards.

Price

Price is only relevant to operations in as much as it is related to cost. A very price competitive market will increase pressure on operations to minimize cost and maximize efficiency. This may well be at the expense of quality and flexibility. A market which is not price competitive allows operations to concentrate on other elements such as quality, variety and responsiveness.

Availability

There are two elements to availability: the speed with which the good or service is made available, and the reliability with which this is achieved. Markets which require a rapid response usually demand that orders are supplied from stock.

Retail grocery is an example of a market which requires an immediate response – the customer is not prepared to order a tin of beans in advance – but reliability is perhaps less critical. We would forgive the grocer who occasionally ran out of beans.

The demand for blood in a hospital accident and emergency department also requires an immediate response, but here reliability is also critically important.

Furniture sales is an example of a market which is prepared to tolerate some flexibility in supply. The customer does not usually expect to be supplied with a new dining room suite from stock, and would probably consider a promised delivery of six to eight weeks as quite acceptable. Some slippage on this would probably be tolerated.

In heavy engineering long lead times are quite common. A contractor building a steel rolling mill can probably order the required electric motors twelve months before they are required, but reliable delivery is vital. If the motors are late, an investment of several million pounds is lying idle. Penalty clauses are often used to encourage reliable performance in this sort of contract.

The various elements of availability are expressed graphically in Figure 2.2.

Qualifying criteria and order winning criteria

In considering the relative importance of market requirements, it is useful to distinguish between those requirements which the product/service must satisfy in order that any sales at all are achieved, and those which, while not essential,

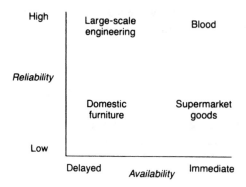

Figure 2.2 Elements of availability

confer a competitive advantage. The former are sometimes known as qualifying criteria, and the latter as order winning criteria.

Unless an organization has correctly identified, and is satisfying, the qualifying criteria, it will fail.

Having satisfied these, the organization is in a position to seek competitive advantage by improving its performance with respect to the order winning criteria. Markets change, and criteria which were not previously relevant may become important.

> When domestic television was first introduced on a large scale to the UK, sets were not reliable. The public accepted this as the penalty to be paid for using 'high technology', and manufacturers apparently decided that reliability was not an important issue. It was only when reliable sets were imported from Japan that the customer realized that reliability was possible. It then very rapidly moved from being irrelevant to becoming a qualifying criterion. The long-term effect of this on the UK television manufacturing industry is well known.

In general, order winning criteria tend to age towards qualifying criteria, and as this occurs so new bases for competition develop. These might arise from the market place, or they might be created by organizations seeking to establish a competitive advantage.

Figure 2.3 illustrates the life cycle of a criterion, and shows the way in which an issue might develop from a weak order winning criterion through a more powerful order winning criterion to a qualifying criterion.

In the quasi-competitive environment established through state regulation of monopolies, as for example the public health service and the utility providers in the UK, qualifying criteria may even be imposed, directly or indirectly, by

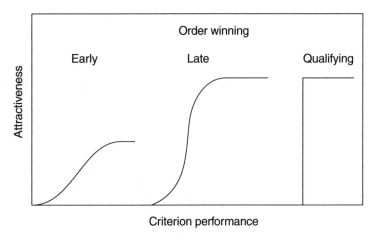

Figure 2.3 Criterion life cycle

government. In such circumstances there is no reason to suppose that there will be an intermediate stage as an order winning criterion.

The message for operations is that constant vigilance is required. Issues of minor or even no concern may rapidly become issues of survival.

OPERATIONS STRATEGY

Careful consideration of corporate and market strategy issues should lead to a clear specification of the following operations strategy issues.

Make or buy

The issue of what the core business of the organization is was discussed earlier in this chapter. The choice of core business is essentially a corporate decision but operations has an important input into this. The extent to which operations is seen as manufacturing, assembling, distributing or providing a service has important implications for all other operations decisions. Equally important are decisions on the extent to which the core business skills are to be retained in house. A manufacturing concern may choose to buy in components which it also makes itself in order to maintain flexibility, but if quality and consistency of manufacture are important to the market, this may be inappropriate.

Pre-judgement is impossible. For example the main asset of computer consultancies might reasonably be assumed to be the technical competence of their staff. This would suggest that the core element of the business is the staff who should therefore be retained at all costs, yet many successful companies rely heavily on subcontracting.

Process choice

This is probably the most important decision since an inappropriate choice guarantees poor performance. If the error is enshrined in substantial capital investment then it becomes very difficult to correct even if recognized. There are three broad categories of process, which lend themselves to particular market requirements as follows.

- **Job/project** based organizations are particularly suited to the one-off job. It is relatively inefficient, but allows for a great deal of variation in the product specification. The process is so flexible that it can be adjusted to meet almost any variation to the final specification, or to the raw materials. A particular merit of this type of organization is that it can allow work to continue until the output is right. Given appropriate skill, equipment, material and time very high quality can be obtained. The disadvantages are the relatively high costs associated with this approach, and the uncertainties of both cost and time.
- **Batch** processes lend themselves to a moderate output of a range of products. By permitting some standardization they allow for some economies of scale and therefore lead to lower unit costs. The flexibility preserved in the process layout does allow substantial variations in volume and even in specification without serious cost penalties. A batch organization could satisfy an order for 500 units as easily as 5,000, and would be able to cope with minor changes in specification without undue difficulty. Despite this batch processes are best at producing standard products within well-defined volume constraints. Batch processes lend themselves well to formal quality control procedures, and batches which fail to meet the specifications can usually be reworked without disrupting the process.
- **Flow/mass** processes are very efficient but quite inflexible. The flow line can only make one product, with minor variations in specification, at one rate of output. It requires standardization in materials, process stages and output. A hold up at any stage in the line leads to lost capacity for the whole line. Its advantages lie in predictability and low cost. It will produce consistent quality output only to the extent that the raw materials input, operator skills and equipment are consistently good. Attempts to rework errors during processing will disrupt the whole line.

An organization need not restrict itself to only one alternative. In a manufacturing organization, components could be manufactured on a batch basis, but the final product may be assembled on a flow line. An insurance company may deal with requests for insurance or claims from clients on a jobbing basis as they arise, but the resultant paperwork can then be assembled into batches for processing. The objective of the operations strategy is to achieve the correct mix of processes.

Location

Location is perhaps more important in service industries than in manufacturing. It interacts with customer service – does the customer actually need to visit the site? However, labour policy, material management policy, risk and political attitudes are all relevant to both. A high-technology automated production process located in a third world country is unlikely to be successful because of the lack of supporting infrastructure. Locating a low cost labour intensive process in an area of high employment will be equally unsuccessful, since it will fail to attract the necessary labour force.

Equally relevant are strategic decisions on whether or not to operate from multiple sites, and how the organization should be divided between such sites should be arranged.

European Airbus production is spread across several countries as a matter of political policy. Because output is numerically small each country had to be given part of the process rather than a proportion of the finished products. While the operations system works well, the design was the result of corporate policy acting as a constraint on operations policy.

Automation and labour

At the extremes an organization can be fully automated or labour intensive. This applies to the service sector as well as in manufacturing. There are restaurants where the customers discuss their requirements with the staff and the meal is then prepared and there are restaurants where pre-prepared meals are dispensed from vending machines. It is possible to carry out banking transactions from home using a computer terminal or over the counter at the bank branch.

There are various risks and costs associated with any policy and these need to be evaluated at corporate level before operations is called upon to implement them. Having made the decision, corporate policy on labour needs to be explicit. Of particular importance are such things as pay rates and payment methods, terms of employment, training policy, policy with regard to part time labour, overtime, etc.

Planning and control

The planning and control systems must be appropriate to the operations organization adopted. Systems which work well in a project organization are inappropriate for a flow line. Systems which work well in a highly automated environment with skilled staff are unlikely to succeed in a low skill, labour intensive operation even if the basic process organization is the same.

The systems must be matched to the type of process, the level of technology, the capabilities of the staff and the expectations of the customer. In multi-site operations systems must also interface between sites even when the site requirements differ.

MATCHING OPERATIONS AND MARKET STRATEGY

In an ideal world, careful definitions of corporate and market strategy would lead to the development of appropriate facilities, processes and control structures. In practice this rarely happens. Organizations already exist and facilities will be more or less well matched to requirements. While expansion into completely new facilities is not unusual, progressive development is much more likely.

Too often operations management decisions have been purely reactive in this situation. They have tried to satisfy the often conflicting demands of marketing with the facilities available. Change has been undertaken on instruction from above, or piecemeal as funds have become available or as a result of a consultant's report, but often without any coherent plan or real commitment. The result is something which works, but not well, and an organization that is very vulnerable to competition.

Operations management can make two major contributions to the development of a coherent and implementable strategy. Firstly they can identify their distinctive competence: whether they are best at quality, volume, maintaining low cost, responding to changes in customer requirements, etc.

If a distinctive operations competence can be identified then it should be promoted and cultivated.

Marketing should focus on what operations are good at and the organization as a whole should seek to foster and improve this (always assuming there is a market for it).

Secondly operations management should compare their own strategy, as expressed in what is actually done, with the requirements of the market they are actually dealing with. This will lead to the identification of any mismatch in process, equipment, location, labour and control systems which can then be prioritized for rational correction as and when opportunities arise.

The technique of profiling is frequently used to facilitate this process of identification. The important characteristics of the operation and of the market are modelled using a matrix such as the one shown in Figure 2.4. This procedure highlights gaps, and where operations lag behind market requirements it can lead to the rational development mentioned above.

Where operations exceed the market requirements, two alternatives arise; either the operations process can be reduced to an appropriate level, hopefully with some cost saving, or the performance can be developed as an order winning criterion.

The example shown in Figure 2.4 is based on a clothing manufacturer struggling to come to terms with changing market conditions. Caught between

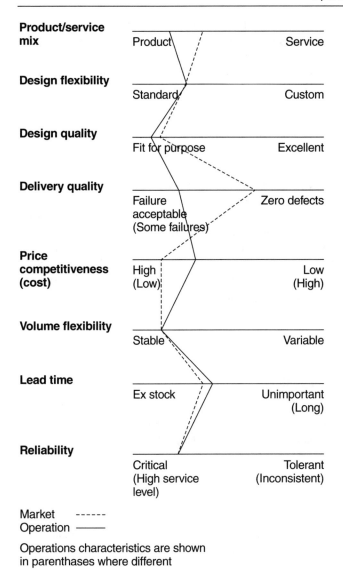

Product/service mix — Product / Service

Design flexibility — Standard / Custom

Design quality — Fit for purpose / Excellent

Delivery quality — Failure acceptable (Some failures) / Zero defects

Price competitiveness (cost) — High (Low) / Low (High)

Volume flexibility — Stable / Variable

Lead time — Ex stock / Unimportant (Long)

Reliability — Critical (High service level) / Tolerant (Inconsistent)

Market   ------
Operation ———

Operations characteristics are shown
in parenthases where different

Figure 2.4   An example of profiling

the demands of major customers for a greater design input, and the increasing competitiveness, on price and quality, of developing countries such as Bangladesh, its survival is in some doubt. The profile clearly shows the need to increase service (through offering a design facility) and improve quality and cost. It does not, regrettably, show any distinctive competence that the organization could develop.

Profiling can give a clear lead to the organization on marketing policy and act as a brake on uncoordinated opportunism even if it does not lead to the release of funds for development. At worst it should stop further deterioration, at best profiling will lead to a comprehensive and funded development programme.

SUMMARY

This chapter has given a broad overview of the main issues involved in developing an appropriate operations strategy. The relevant elements of the corporate and marketing strategies of the organization have been identified and linked to the options open to operations in developing its own strategy. The need for continuous vigilance in monitoring market changes has been identified, and the use of profiling to produce a better match between operations and the market has been described. Finally the advantages of operations taking a more proactive stance than is customary have been considered. Chapters 3 and 4 look in more detail at some of the issues concerned with the market and what is being provided, while the remainder of the book considers the detailed implementation and management of the operations function.

CASE STUDY: Beazer Boilers

Beazer Boilers are a division of a large multinational engaged in the manufacture of industrial steam generators. The company has a number of plants all of which manufacture a complete range of steam generators.

The product

The industrial steam generator is essentially a cylindrical steel vessel capable of holding steam under pressure. Water is fed into the vessel where it is heated either by gas, oil, electricity or solid fuel depending upon the requirements of the customer. A limited range of generators is manufactured, specification depending upon steam output required and heating method. Construction is modular so that a generator of a given capacity will consist of the pressure vessel and a bolt on heating unit. As a result of this, the company can offer a wide range of products built from a small range of standard sub-assemblies.

The market

The steam generator market is fairly static, and is about 70% replacement and 30% new plant. Replacement plant is usually required quite quickly, and the most important competitive issues are speed and reliability of delivery and price.

The market is highly price competitive. The actual specification of the steam generator is relatively unimportant, provided it is adequate. Beazer Boilers have established a good reputation for keen pricing and fast delivery.

The organization

All Beazer factories are based upon flow line principles, with one line making the pressure vessels and leading into final assembly and separate lines for the assembly of the different heating elements. In line with the policy of competitive pricing, the main management effort is devoted to minimizing cost. Beazer pay one of the lowest rates in the industry and have established a reputation for hard bargaining. Although this does not lead to good industrial relations, strikes are rare because it is well known that the firm will sit out a strike rather than concede increased costs. Indirect labour (supervision, inspection, etc.) is kept to a bare minimum.

The opportunity

As nuclear power generation developed Beazer identified a new opportunity in the growing market for nuclear reactor pressure vessels. These were seen as larger versions of the existing steam generator pressure vessels and management felt that their proven track record would guarantee success in this growing and potentially lucrative field.

Since the nuclear reactor pressure vessel is very much larger than the largest steam generator a new purpose designed facility was set up on a green field site. The proven flow line organization was adopted, and experienced managers and supervisors brought in from other plants. Labour was recruited from the largely agricultural communities in the area. From the outset management was determined to implement the tried and tested methods used elsewhere in the group. For example, when the labour force discovered they were being paid even less than employees in other Beazer factories they went on strike. Beazer refused to negotiate, and eventually the strike collapsed, although thereafter staff turnover remained a serious problem.

Beazer's experience with this new venture was far from satisfactory. The plant was designed to produce 20 vessels a year when fully operational, but a cautious start up was planned and in the first two years of operation orders were taken for the delivery of 28 pressure vessels. At the end of two years only three had been delivered and the remaining 25 were all late, many to re-negotiated delivery dates. At this point major customers removed 16 part completed vessels and shipped them to other manufacturers for finishing.

Questions

1 Why were Beazer so unsuccessful?
2 How might they have made a success of the venture?

Chapter 3

Product design

Unless a product is designed to meet market requirements it will not sell. While this is of great concern to design and marketing, it is of rather less interest to the operations manager whose main concern is that the product can be made to specification at an acceptable cost. In other words, design for manufacture.

It is far easier and less expensive to produce a design that is easy to manufacture from the outset than to try to modify an established design to accommodate manufacturing constraints during the later stages of the process.

It is relatively rare for a product to be designed for a completely new production facility. More frequently, products are designed to be manufactured alongside an existing product range, or existing product designs are modified to take account of new developments. In this situation it is important that the design process takes account of the limitations and opportunities provided by existing plant, labour and management.

The following section gives an overview of the product design and implementation process, while the remainder of the chapter considers specific issues of relevance to operations including the question of standardization and variety control, quality and reliability and value analysis and value engineering.

PRODUCT DESIGN

There are various views of the role of product design. The most limited and short sighted view is that the process finishes when a feasible design which meets market needs has been produced. It is then up to manufacturing to produce this at an acceptable price.

This approach is often evident in the personal computer field where new models have been known to be late, unreliable and to fail to perform to specification. The design is logically sound, and the prototype works but the design does not stand up to the realities of mass manufacture.

One of the causes of this particular problem is the pressure to get new models on the market quickly in the light of intense competition and rapid technological change.

More realistic is an approach which takes full account of manufacturing, and considers the design process to continue on into successful selling. Recent developments prompted by environmental concerns have led to the design process considering the whole life of the product including disposal, and it may well become necessary to consider such things as energy costs and pollution costs in the future. Most authorities agree that the design process should follow, with iteration, the sequence:

- Market needs;
- Specification;
- Conceptual design;
- Detailed design;
- Manufacture;
- Sell.

The logic of this approach is demonstrated by Figures 3.1 and 3.2. Figure 3.1 shows the rejection rate of new design ideas through this sequence, while Figure 3.2 shows the cumulative cost. The cost increases dramatically once real resource consumption arises from detailed design onwards, hence the earlier

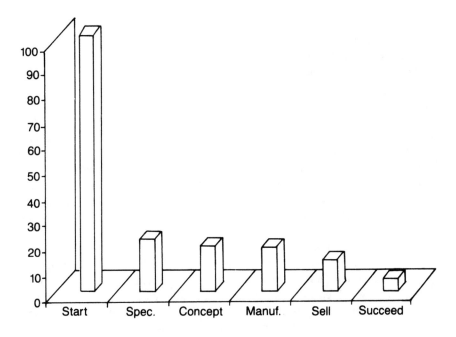

Figure 3.1   Where new products fail

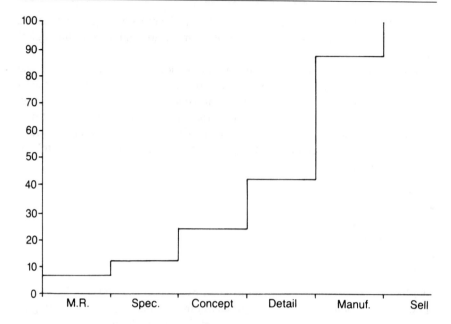

Figure 3.2 Cost of new product

stages are important because they eliminate potential failures before substantial costs have been incurred.

In cases of doubt market research, specification and conceptual design can be further extended without excessive costs being incurred.

Market needs

The market needs stage of the process is intended to ensure that there is a demand for the product, and to determine precisely what characteristics the market demands. New products often arise from market pull, where market research has identified customer needs which are not currently being satisfied. Since the needs already exist, they can be fully researched and moved on with confidence, always bearing in mind that competitors are probably also aware of them.

Technology push frequently gives rise to new products where a pre-existing market need has not been identified. Here the technical capability to provide a new product, or new facilities on existing products, is being promoted. Examples include wrist watch calculators, where the technology of miniaturization for its own sake is being sold, through to odour eliminating detergents which most consumers did not realize they needed until they were advertised. The failure rate is higher in part because the need must be created, and in part because the risks of premature exposure which arise with extensive market research may reduce the amount of research carried out.

Occasionally the opportunity for development arises internally. A decision to re-equip production brought on by the wearing out of existing plant, or the need to move premises, can give an opportunity to update designs and manufacturing technology. This does not lead to new products, but it may lead to upgrades and style changes which enhance competitive advantage and extend product life.

Specification

The design specification links market needs to organizational and technical capabilities. It specifies those features which market research has identified as being required not only for the prime function of the product, but also for peripheral issues such as size, degree of standardization, aesthetics, price, life expectancy, etc. It should also specify those characteristics which have a bearing on organizational capabilities such as volume, quality and reliability, and likely technology. It is at this stage that operations should become involved so that the degree of convergence between the proposed product and operations capability can be specified and the implications of divergence recognized. If new manufacturing techniques are required these must be planned for from the outset.

Design

Conceptual design is perhaps the most creative stage of the process. The object is to develop a number of possible approaches to satisfying the requirements of the design specification. Like brainstorming, this is best carried out in an uncritical atmosphere, and only later are the designs appraised in terms of their feasibility. The selected winner goes on to the detailed design stage which in its turn produces detailed drawings, parts lists, assembly sequences, test specifications and so on.

Manufacture

Initially manufacture may well be on a fairly small scale. As the market expands, or simply as a result of manufacturing experience, both the design and the manufacturing methods are likely to change.

Small scale assembly of electronic equipment will use standard components, and the way in which these are assembled on the circuit board will determine the function of the equipment. As the scale increases it will become more cost effective to use purpose designed integrated circuits. This will reduce the number of components in the equipment, increasing reliability and changing assembly patterns, but it may also lead to a reduction in power consumption and hence a smaller power supply unit. These changes in turn may lead to a redesign of the case.

It is necessary for manufacturing to be flexible in the early stages of a new product.

VARIETY CONTROL AND STANDARDIZATION

The fewer components, processes and techniques that are used in operations, the more cost effective the operations will be. A few processes common to all products lead to high utilization of both plant and labour, high levels of skill in the labour force and the potential for investing in process design to maximize efficiency.

Where a large number of different processes are used for different products plant utilization is likely to be low and frequent changes will lead to lower labour productivity and lower levels of skill.

It is not economic to invest in improving the efficiency of processes which are used infrequently.

Similarly, fewer components and materials lead to smaller stockholding, fewer suppliers to deal with and less frequent deliveries compared with an organization spending the same amount on a large number of different components. The savings can be substantial.

If company X spends £10,000,000 a year on raw materials and components, and has 10,000 stock items with an average stockholding of three months' usage, then £2,500,000 is tied up in stock, and the cost of stockholding will be about £600,000 a year. If company X were able to halve the number of items stocked (while still spending £10,000,000 a year) the stockholding would be reduced by about 30% with the release of about £1,000,000 capital and a cost saving of £250,000 a year.

It is for reasons such as this that organizations embark upon variety reduction programmes.

Variety reduction

The object of a variety reduction programme is to reduce the number of different stock items held by the organization. Because of the risks associated with discontinuing rarely used but essential items, or reducing the number of variations of the same item without properly considering the implications, it is usual to set up a variety reduction team with representatives of design, engineering, sales, production, quality assurance and purchasing. Obtaining the agreement of all of these functions is usually difficult and variety reduction programmes are expensive and time consuming.

Consider the variety implicit in the simple wood screw. Without considering variations in diameter and length, there are at least four materials (brass, mild steel, chromium plated, zinc plated), two types of head (domed and flat), and three types of slot, giving a total of twenty-four possible varieties for each size. It is likely that many applications could be met equally well by several different specifications but habit and tradition are sometimes very difficult to overcome. Cost must also be considered. Almost all requirements could be met with chromium plated screws but these are the most expensive.

Normal practice is to start with slow moving stock and consider whether any of this could be discontinued, and then to move on to classify stock according to its use. If two or more stock items serve the same purpose then the potential exists for eliminating one or more of them. It is during this process that care needs to be taken to ensure that the interests of the customer, quality of the product, and cost are all taken into account. The retail trade in particular is frequently concerned with meeting the market's demand for variety. Life would be much easier for the decorating shop if the public were prepared to buy paint only in 2 litre tins.

In manufacturing, variety tends to creep up if not carefully controlled. The cost, both financially and in terms of interdepartmental relations, of variety reduction is high so control of variety from the outset is more effective. This is best done by adopting a policy of standardization.

Standardization

The object of standardization is to ensure that wherever possible new products and further developments of old products use existing components, materials and processes. It begins with design, since this is the most likely source of increased variety. A designer must be required to justify the use of a component or material which is not currently stocked, or a process which is not currently available. This requires first that clear and up to date specifications of all approved stock items are readily available. The organization's own approved stock list must be at least as accessible to the designer as suppliers' catalogues otherwise the temptation is to choose something known to be available and to argue the case later.

Standardization is often resisted because it restricts freedom and it is argued that this leads to sub-optimal designs. It often fails because of the problems of ensuring up to date specifications of approved parts are available. However the most serious problem is that of technological obsolescence. A rigid policy of standardization in a firm manufacturing electromechanical cash registers led to a failure to follow the market into electronic cash registers and finally to the failure of the company.

QUALITY AND RELIABILITY

Issues of quality are addressed in more detail in Chapter 12 and only a brief review of some of the more important issues is presented here. It is assumed that the design specification is appropriate for the market needs: in other words it is assumed that if it is correctly made from good quality components the final product will be of the required quality.

If the product design is not good enough there is no possibility of manufacturing producing a good quality product.

The product design can contribute substantially to the ease with which manufacturing can achieve the required level of quality, although there will always be applications at the frontiers of technology where the only way to achieve high quality output is through rigorous inspection and testing.

> In the early 1990s the latest developments in active liquid crystal display screens, required for high speed high resolution colour displays, were manufactured by a process which gave less than 4% acceptable output. This has improved over time, but a limited market was prepared to pay for this very high loss rate.

There are three areas where design can make an important contribution to quality manufacture.

- The specification and sourcing of bought in materials and components should be carried out together to ensure that there is a reliable supply of acceptable quality.
- The specification of components manufactured in house should take account of process capability. There is no point in specifying a tolerance of $+/- 0.1$ mm if the machinery available has a machining tolerance of $+/- 0.2$ mm. Either the specification must be changed, or the process, and acquiring high tolerance process equipment and training operators in its use is expensive and time consuming.
- The number of components in an assembly, and the number of stages in a process both influence error and failure rates. If there is a 0.1% chance of an operator making an error, then the error rate in a 10 stage process will be 1% and in a 100 stage process it will be 9.5%. The impact of number of components is much more obvious.

A computer memory chip consists of a large number of transistors, two per bit of storage. Even a 64 Kbit chip contains 128,000 transistors while a 1 Mbit chip contains over 2,000,000. If these functions were taken over by individual transistors then the failure rate would be such that personal computers could not exist. If transistors suffer a failure rate of 1 in 1,000,000, then 64 Kbits of memory would suffer a failure rate of 12%, while 1 Mbit of memory would suffer a failure rate of 86%.

Figure 3.3 shows the effect of number of components on reliability.

In summary, products should be designed with the minimum number of components and process stages, all manufactured components should be specified to tolerances which are within process capabilities and all bought in components should be specified so that a reliable high quality source is available.

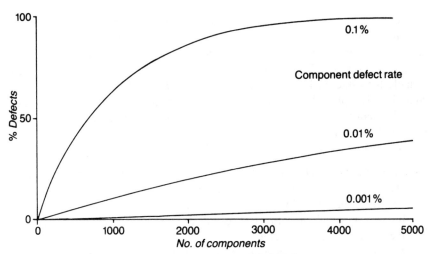

Figure 3.3   Effect of component number on defect rate

VALUE ANALYSIS AND VALUE ENGINEERING

The only difference between value analysis and value engineering is the stage at which the technique is applied. Value analysis is an approach to cutting the cost of an established product or service without causing any reduction in its value. Value engineering is the application of exactly the same principles and procedures during the design stages of a new product.

Value analysis begins by identifying the function(s) of the product and then carrying out a detailed analysis of the design and construction of the product with a view to eliminating those elements which do not contribute to function.

It is important to clearly identify all the functions which a product serves and to link these into price, and value analysis has identified two components which together give the value of the product.

Exchange Value = Useful Value + Esteem Value

Exchange value is a measure of what the market is prepared to pay for the product, while useful value is a measure of how valuable the main function of the product is. Esteem value is an attempt to measure the value of other attributes of the product which do not directly contribute to its usefulness.

> For travelling to work in an urban area, a reliable second hand 2CV car, costing about £3,000 fulfils all the required functions. Despite this many people use cars costing £15,000 or more almost exclusively for this purpose. The esteem value of such a car must therefore be £12,000.

In order to ensure that esteem issues are not missed, and that function is not compromised, value analysis is always a team task. Since a large team is unwieldy, a core team of five or six members, who can call on others when required, is preferred. The composition suggested for variety reduction is equally suitable for value analysis. It is usual to target the products, services, or even administrative procedures which have the potential for the largest savings. Complex multi-component products obviously yield more potential for saving than products consisting of very few components.

Value analysis is usually carried out following Gage's twelve steps:

1 **Select the product** Products which are likely to yield the greatest returns are those which are complex since there is considerable scope for simplification; for which there is large usage since the total savings will be greater; which are old since technical development will have increased the potential for improvement.

2 **Extract the cost** An accurate marginal cost is required, since this is what value analysis seeks to reduce. Overheads should not be included. Many organizations find this very difficult to specify.

3 **Record the components**

4 **Record all the functions** This involves the whole team, and brainstorming may well be used to overcome prior assumptions. The object of the exercise is to identify the functions which the customer may be looking for, not the functions which the manufacturer thinks are appropriate.

5 **Record present and future demand**

6 **Determine the primary function** This involves eliminating functions identified in step 4 which can be classed as secondary until only one function is left.

7 **List other ways of achieving the primary function** Again a whole team activity involving brainstorming.

8 **Cost the alternatives** This should be done as soon as possible after brainstorming, but not *during* brainstorming since it would then inhibit the generation of ideas. At this stage only broad brush costings are required.

9 **Investigate the three cheapest alternatives** Three is an arbitrary cut off, but is usually found to be adequate. A detailed study of feasibility, performance and cost is carried out.

10 **Choose the best alternative** And continue its development.

11 **Identify the additional functions which need to be incorporated** Functions identified at step 4 and not already incorporated by step 10 can now be introduced if required. If necessary further work to produce a detailed design is carried out.

12 **Ensure acceptance** As with variety reduction, inertia and vested interest can be substantial obstacles to successful implementation. The value analysis team must be prepared to sell their proposal within the organization, and a strong case including detailed costing and cost savings, implementation plans and models or prototypes may well be required.

Value analysis is a widely used cost reduction technique, although some designers maintain that it should not be used since it encourages bad design, i.e. if the design were correct in the first place, value analysis would have nothing to contribute. This ignores the fact that both designs and technology change, and after a time a design is likely to have become sub-optimal even if it was perfect in the first place. Rear view mirrors in cars used to be screwed to the roof panel, an expensive process involving several fasteners and the drilling of holes. It was only with the development of reliable adhesives that it became possible to glue mirrors to the windscreen with a substantial saving in cost and no reduction in value.

SUMMARY

The field of product design is large, and this chapter has given a brief overview of the procedures involved. More attention has been devoted to those aspects of product design which have a direct impact on manufacturing. Consideration has been given to the impact of variety control and standardization in simplifying procurement, stockholding and manufacture, as well as the negative aspects of inhibiting development leading towards stagnation. The contribution of number of components, and number of process stages to reliability has been considered, with the almost self-evident conclusion that simplicity leads to reliability. Finally the contribution of value analysis to the process of product cost reduction, and of value engineering to cost avoidance, have been discussed.

Many of these approaches and techniques are equally applicable to the design of services, but services possess a number of characteristics which cause particular problems for the operations manager. In Chapter 4 these specific issues will be considered in the context of service design.

CASE STUDY: Kitchen Components

Kitchen Components are a well established manufacturer of plastic kitchenware. Their existing product range is shown in Table 3.1. Because people tend to re-equip their kitchens when they move house, a downturn in the housing market has led to a reduction in the demand for general housewares, leaving the firm with some spare capacity.

At present the standard range of kitchenware is available in four basic colours with contrasting trim. The premium range is similar except that six colours are available, and the plastic mouldings are 10% thicker. The Sales Director believes that there is a market for a deluxe range which would offer an even wider range of colours and a 25% increase in thickness over the standard range to give a greater feeling of weight and substance. In order to distinguish this range from the others, and from the competition, all items would be colour matched rather than using contrasting trim. Preliminary market research suggests that demand for this range would amount to 20% of current output at a price premium of 40%. In the light of this the company decides to conduct a feasibility study.

Table 3.1 Kitchen Components: product range

Item	Number of components
1 Pedal bin	4
2 Swing bin	3
3 Rectangular bowl	1
4 Round bowl	1
5 Dish drainer	1
6 Cutlery drainer	2
7 Small vegetable rack	3
8 Large vegetable rack	4
9 Bucket	2
10 Soap dish	2
11 Small plastic box	set of 4
12 Large plastic box	set of 3
Sets	
13 Drainer set	one each of 5 and 6
14 Sink set	3 or 4 plus 5, 6 and 10
15 Small kitchen set	1 and 7
16 Large kitchen set	3 and 8

The process

All products follow the same process. A batch of plastic is mixed with the addition of an appropriate quantity of pigment. The mix is then transferred to an injection moulding press already fitted with the appropriate moulds. The press setter carries out a trial pressing and checks the dimensions of the moulding. If necessary adjustments are made to the press before it is handed over to the operator to complete pressing of the batch. The batch then proceeds to trimming and inspection before going into store. Typical batch sizes are 100 components. Finished products are assembled by drawing the appropriate components from store, labelling them, assembling them into sets and packing them. The present equipment consists of two 50 kg capacity mixers and two 25 kg capacity mixers. There are eight presses available, in two sizes. While the capacity of the presses is expressed in terms of the maximum pressure they can apply, the company rates them in terms of the surface area of product. Three presses are able to produce up to 3 square metres per cycle and the remaining five up to 1 square metre. Process times and costs (pence) for a typical product (rectangular bowl) are:

Mix

	50 kg at 190 p/kg	9,500
	0.15 hours at 1,700 p/hour	255
Press		
	Setting 0.50 hours at 2,000 p/hour	1,000
	Pressing 1.45 hours at 1,100 p/hour	1,595
	Yield Standard 96	
	Premium 86	
Finish		
	1.35 hours at 700 p/hour	945
	Total Cost	13,295
	Cost per unit	
	Standard	138
	Premium	155

The feasibility study

Early trials demonstrated that the existing plant and tooling could cope with the increased thickness but with a 5% loss at finishing due to bubbles and surface defects. The additional thickness and the presence of defects also reduced the rate at finishing to one third of its previous level. Despite these problems, the project seemed profitable and it was decided to proceed with manufacture and test marketing on a small scale.

Soon after starting, operators at final assembly and packing began to report problems with colour matching at final assembly. This was particularly noticeable in assemblies such as pedal bins which had traditionally been made with contrasting trim, but were now made as a single colour, but were also more noticeable in such things as matched sets of washing-up bowl, dish drainer and cutlery drainer. Investigation revealed that all the new shades and three of the existing shades were showing this problem.

At first mix quality was suspected but tighter control of weighing at the mixing stage, and extension of the mixing time had no observable effect. Further investigation revealed that there was as much variation within batches as between batches, and that the problem had always been present, but had been less noticeable because of the thinner walls, and the presence of contrasting trim. The new colours all accentuated the problem.

The problem was finally traced to minor variations in the age of the mix and the temperature of the press, and it was found that colour matching could only be guaranteed if all the components in a set were pressed simultaneously on the same press.

Future developments

Pressing complete sets was found to be technically feasible, but only if press capacity was increased to 5 square metres. Composite moulds would also be required containing all the components of the set i.e. the three components of a swing bin, the four components of a pedal bin, the three components of a dish draining set, etc. The cost of a 5 square metre press was found to be £45,000 and the cost of new moulds £15,000. Press setting time would be doubled, as would setting losses. A further complication would be the need to keep sets together through to final assembly and packing.

Question

Identify the alternative courses of action open to Kitchen Components and evaluate them.

Chapter 4

Service design

Pure service does not exist, so this chapter is concerned with issues which do not arise in product design, but do arise when the service component of the transaction with the customer is significant. This chapter is not an alternative to Chapter 3 but a supplement, and much of the substance of Chapter 3 is equally relevant to service design.

Service activities provide the operations manager with a whole range of problems which either do not exist, or are far less important, in manufacturing activities. Most of these are concerned with the presence of the customer during the process. Manufacturing operations managers prefer to keep the customer at arm's length since this allows them to get on with managing the operation efficiently and also allows them to keep any mistakes to themselves. Neither of these options is available to the service operations manager.

In this chapter the most important differences between manufacturing and service operations will be considered in more detail. The 'industrialization' approach to the design of service operations whose main emphasis is increased efficiency, will be considered, this will be followed by a discussion of some of the more recent approaches which concentrate upon developing service for competitive advantage.

SERVICE CHARACTERISTICS

Manufacturing operations can be described simply as the process of transforming materials into finished product and then, possibly after a delay, supplying that product to the customer. The important characteristics of this are that the customer is not usually involved in the transformation process, and that the finished product may be stocked prior to supply.

A service on the other hand, is defined by the American Marketing Association as:

Activities, benefits or satisfactions which are offered for sale or provided in connection with the sale of goods.

Such a definition applies equally to public sector and not for profit organizations if the concept of sale is removed. The provision of the service, to a greater or lesser extent, involves the customer's participation.

The view that this has nothing to do with manufacturing is also being increasingly challenged. As long ago as 1941, Morris (*The Theory of Consumer's Demand*, Yale University Press) was able to say,

> The emphasis . . . is upon the services of the goods, not upon the goods themselves.
>
> Goods are wanted because they are capable of performing services – favourable events which occur at a point in time.

Service is increasingly becoming the order winning criterion in areas of manufacture where competition on price, quality, and reliability is no longer possible because all manufacturers have committed themselves to the same high technology approach. Service operations show the following significant differences from manufacturing operations.

Customer involvement

In all service operations the customer is a more or less active participant in the process. For example the service component of a transport or supply operation involves the customer in communication with staff and in working within the operating environment. The customer is actually part of the labour force in a self-service supermarket and customers have to find their own way to the correct train or bus in a railway or bus station.

The operations system has to accommodate their needs and capabilities. If it does not, then the immediate perception is one of poor quality. The customer who cannot find the sugar in a supermarket, or cannot understand the public address announcements in a railway station may well be incompetent, but they still become a dissatisfied customer, and their dissatisfaction is likely to be communicated to others. A seriously dissatisfied customer is likely to inform at least ten other people. Since the cost of obtaining a new customer can be more than five times the cost of retaining an existing customer, the importance of customer satisfaction is self-evident.

In personal services, the retail store, hairdressers, restaurant, hospital, the issues are more those of personal interaction and environment. Again it is the customer's perception that is important.

The key differences that the customer's presence makes are first that the service cannot be checked for quality before being supplied since production and consumption are simultaneous, and second that the customer is likely to be untrained and unpredictable.

In manufacturing the mistakes do not leave the factory, and the work force is hopefully both trained and predictable.

Services cannot be stocked

Since production and consumption are simultaneous, services cannot be stocked. If a bank teller who can serve 20 customers an hour has no customers between 10.00 am and 11.00 am s/he cannot as a result serve 40 customers between 11.00 and 12.00. Service capacity is sometimes described as volatile since if it is not used it is wasted.

Service demand is variable

All demand is variable, but service demand is characterized by large, complex and rapid variations. Demand for all services is seasonal (varies in a more or less fixed pattern over a period of one year), but shorter term cycles are also observed. Demand for public transport can vary by a factor of ten between 9.00 am and 10.00 am. Demand for restaurant services peaks between midday and 2.00 pm and between 8.00 pm and 10.00 pm. Demand for most entertainment facilities rises towards the end of the week and demand on hospital accident and emergency units peaks on Saturday night.

These variations may be predictable – the electricity generators, whose product is like a service in that it cannot be stocked, use television programme schedules as part of their forecasting process – but the difficulty facing the service providers is that of meeting peak demand without the inefficiency of spare capacity at other times and without the option of using stock.

Intangibility

The issue of the balance between tangible and intangible elements in any transaction has been discussed in Chapters 1 and 2. The intangibility of the service component of the transaction gives rise to the following problems:

- Clear specification, and agreement, on the precise nature of the service is frequently difficult to achieve. People differ in their perception of what is appropriate. Some customers welcome the immediate attention of an assistant when they enter a shop while others perceive this attention as an unpleasant intrusion designed to pressure them into spending. Maximum waiting times are often used as performance indicators in service design but people's perception of acceptability is very variable.

A survey of patient perceptions in a hospital accident and emergency department found that some patients felt that a waiting time of 15 minutes was excessive while others were perfectly happy to wait an hour or more.

- Some people welcome a friendly greeting from service personnel while others reject this as artificial and unnecessarily obsequious. Overall a clear understanding of the customer's needs, while essential, is difficult to achieve.
- Feedback on performance from the client is more likely to stress the tangible elements of the transaction and lead to an unbalanced picture of the service and its performance.
- Measurement of performance is difficult. There is a tendency to measure what can be measured rather than what is important. It is relatively easy to measure client waiting time, but difficult to be sure that this is really important.

These problems lead to two main areas of difficulty in designing services which are not apparent, or at least far less important, when designing tangible products.

Efficiency

Because the customer is involved in the production of the service, the design of the service operation and the design of the service itself are often indistinguishable. A critical aspect in the design of any operations system is utilization, and hence cost. The wide and rapid variation in demand and the inability to use stock to buffer the service operation makes the design of efficient, high utilization services very difficult.

Quality

It is difficult to define quality without a clear specification of the good or service. The high intangible content of services makes clear specification difficult and there may be considerable differences in their perception of the service between the customer and the service provider. This is complicated by the tendency of customers to express dissatisfaction about the tangible elements of the service whether or not these are the prime cause.

Because the customer is part of the process, traditional quality control procedures are not applicable. The service cannot be quality assured before supply. The act of inspection also interferes with and distorts the provision of the service.

INDUSTRIALIZATION IN SERVICE DESIGN

Early approaches to service design have tended to concentrate on the issues of utilization and efficiency. The issues which these approaches address are those of demand variability, which leads to low utilization, and customer participation, which makes demand variability more difficult to manage and also adds a large element of unpredictability. This has led to three approaches:

- Remove the customer from the process as far as possible and adopt industrial process design strategies for that part of the process not involving the customer.
- If the customer's presence is unavoidable, use the customer as labour.
- Increase the flexibility of staffing so that capacity can match demand.

Front office/back shop

This approach seeks to identify the irreducible minimum involvement of the customer, and assigns these activities to the 'front office'. All other activities are carried out away from the customer in the 'back shop' where conventional manufacturing principles can be applied.

A simple example of this approach can be seen in the contrast between the meat section of a supermarket and a conventional butchers shop. In the supermarket the customer is presented with a selection of pre-cut pre-weighed and pre-packaged material prepared out of sight in a meat packing factory by specialist process workers. The customer selects the nearest equivalent to his/her requirement. The service content of the transaction is low but the efficiency is high since the preparation can be done in advance and the prepared meat stocked. In the butchers shop the customer can discuss requirements with the staff, receive advice and have the meat cut to his/her precise requirements. The service content of the transaction is high, and the staff require far more skill both in interpersonal relations and in meat preparation, which is frequently carried out in the presence of the customer. There is little scope for pre-preparation, therefore the whole system is subject to demand variation.

There is no doubt about the efficiencies achieved by the front office/back shop division, but the cost in terms of service content, and in terms of de-skilling and reducing the job satisfaction of staff can be high. It is interesting to note that new supermarkets are increasingly tending to include in-store butchers.

Customer as labour

The whole concept of the self-service operation is based upon using the customer as labour so that capacity varies in proportion to demand. It is frequently combined with a rigid front office/back shop division. As technology advances so does the concept of self service. The self-service supermarket still requires staff to fill shelves and collect payment, although a number of chains are experimenting with systems which allow customers to carry out their own bar code scanning and charge the items directly to their own account, thus eliminating the check-out operator. Self-service banking is fully automatic, and recently self-service filling stations have appeared where automatic payment is made by bank card rather than needing a cashier. This type of automation has advantages for the customer in that services are frequently available for longer hours, as in banking and filling stations, and both waiting times and costs are reduced. The disadvantages rest in the relative absence of help and advice and the problems caused by unskilled customers. The customer unsure of procedures required of him or her may avoid the facility altogether.

Labour flexibility

Service industries tend to rely heavily on part time staff. This allows them to vary capacity to meet demand rather than carry excess capacity during off peak periods. This imposes substantial management problems. The total labour force may be five or more times the equivalent full time labour force. Staff loyalty tends to be low and therefore turnover is high (as high as 15 times per year in some parts of the licensed trade). Substantial investment in training is not justified because of the few hours worked and the high staff turnover. The overall effect of this can be an unskilled and uncommitted labour force which is hardly likely to encourage customer satisfaction. An alternative approach is to use the same staff for front office and back shop activities. During peak demand times all customer service points can be manned and back shop activities reduced to a minimum, while at other times the majority of staff can be engaged in back shop activities leaving a minimum on customer service. The success of this approach depends upon the availability of sufficient back shop activities, which are not time sensitive, to allow a proper balance to be achieved. It also depends upon the availability of a suitably skilled labour force willing to work flexibly.

Automation

Automation is, perhaps, merely an extension of self service to the point where there is no interaction with service personnel, but it is worth considering separately. The automation of services has a number of advantages. It avoids the problems of staffing a service at hours which most people find uncongenial. It introduces a high level of consistency and reproducibility by eliminating the unpredictability of the human operator. It often enables a more widespread network of service outlets to be provided because, although the capital cost may initially be high, an automatic service outlet usually occupies much less space than a manned outlet (an ATM terminal is much smaller than even the smallest bank branch).

Automation is not new – vending machines are automated retail outlets – but as technology advances, the economics of automation become more favourable.

Centralization

Centralization is one aspect of the front office/back shop divide, but again it is important enough to be worth considering separately.

A centralized service not only gives economies of scale, but also reduces variability. When demand from a number of sources is combined, there is always some cancelling out of peaks and troughs, and the overall variability of demand is reduced, thus centralization gives greater efficiency. Many banks have centralized decision making about loans, insurance, etc. The customer still deals with the branch they are registered with, but the branch staff have little discretion and must refer all requests to the central organization. This ensures standardization and reduces the opportunity for fraud, at least in theory.

An important disadvantage of centralization of decision making on service offerings in this way is that it complicates the process by introducing additional stages. Each additional stage increases the risk of error and of delay.

A retail bank introduced centralized processing for all loan, mortgage and insurance decisions. The various central offices were supposed to give a same day decision on at least 90% of enquiries, but branch staff soon noticed that this target was not being achieved. More importantly, the decisions were often in error and had to be referred back by branch staff, increasing the delay. In order to protect customers, and to avoid the need for frequent apologies, branch staff quickly learned to tell customers that a decision would take two or even three days.

Demand management

Since service cannot be stocked, and varying capacity to match demand is always expensive, attempts are frequently made to control the demand. Customers can be stocked through queues and appointment systems. This leads to loss of custom through people leaving queues and missing appointments, but generally improves utilization. Alternatively pricing policy might be used to alter customer behaviour. The practice of offering off-peak discounts is a widespread example of this.

SERVICE QUALITY

Quality, measured by customer satisfaction as indicated by retained customers, has generally been found to depend very heavily on the intangible elements of the service package. From this point of view most of the steps taken to improve productivity through industrialization have reduced quality.

- Industrialization and standardization reduce consumer choice and minimize the intangible elements which the customer may well value.
- The use of part time labour and labour flexibility tends to lead to a less skilled and trained labour force in an area where labour skill is a key determinant of quality.

- Obviously self-service reduces skill and training to a minimum, but the incompetent customer not only suffers a poor quality service experience themselves, but may reduce the quality of the experience for other customers.
- Automation eliminates interpersonal contact, and this is valued by many service customers. It can also be seen to increase risk, and many bank customers, particularly among the elderly, refuse to use ATMs because of this. Customers are less likely to be forgiving of automatic facilities, and in the event of a failure there is no opportunity for recovery. It has been found that ATMs need to achieve at least a 95% success rate – it takes very few failures for customers to conclude that the system never works.
- Centralization disempowers the customer contact staff which may well lead to a less skilled and motivated work force. More importantly it leads to delay. This may be manageable if it is consistent, but when information has to be passed from department to department, unpredictability and error both creep in and quality falls off.
- Demand management does not necessarily lead to perceptions of poor quality, even though it means that the customer does not get the service when they want it. In areas which might be considered 'fashion sensitive' the fact that demand outstrips supply will be seen as an endorsement of the service – a restaurant that is difficult to book, or a show for which it is impossible to get tickets must be 'good'. Despite this demand management should be treated with caution.

In a service operation more than any other quality costs are high, both in terms of the cost of providing the service and the cost of failure, but it is obviously important that once the level of quality for which the market is prepared to pay has been identified, that the expenditure on providing the service is properly directed to those elements of the service which the market values most highly.

An important issue in determining customer perception of service quality is customer confidence. Poor service will be perceived in situations which generate uncertainty in the customer, either because the customer is not sure how to behave due to conflicting or inadequate information, or because the customer perceives uncertainty and lack of co-ordination in the service provider. Galloway and White (1989) identified the internal consistency of the service providing system as being important in achieving high quality through maximizing confidence. Figure 4.1 shows the four linked elements of service personnel, service management, service package and process time.

Consistency is achieved by ensuring that each of these elements is appropriate to customer needs, and that there is agreement between service personnel and management as to what those needs are and how they should be achieved. If the needs are not clearly defined, or if management and service personnel do not have a consistent view of how they are to be met then customer uncertainty is inevitable. The service must, of course, function adequately at all levels, and the relationship of those levels in the service structure is shown in Figure 4.2.

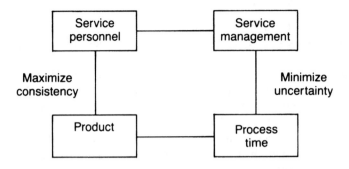

Figure 4.1   Internal consistency of service operations

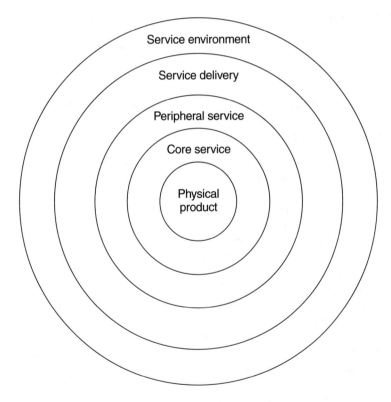

Figure 4.2   Levels of the service structure

In more detail the five levels are:

- **Product**   The core of the transaction; the good which is changing hands. It may be absent in pure service industries, and of greater or lesser importance in mixed transactions.
- **Core service**   The specific features of the service incorporated in the service. For example a bank current account might include a cheque book, a cash card, free overdraft facility and service through a branch network. Alternatively it may depend upon ATMs and a centralized telephone service.
- **Peripheral services**   Aspects of the service which might be valued by the customer, but are not their main purchase intention. A coffee-shop in a department store is a peripheral service, as is 'free' insurance with a credit card.
- **Service delivery**   The manner in which the service is provided; the script adopted by service personnel. This is often highly standardized, giving a predictability which is comforting to customers and re-assuring to management, but it must be appropriate to the service.
- **Service environment**   The external environment includes: location, the premises, ease of access, ambience, etc. The internal environment is the atmosphere and structure within which the service personnel operate. It includes employee support, reward, training and control systems.

While this structure identifies aims, and the areas in which they must be achieved, it does not identify the means. The following procedure is based upon the nine steps described by Lyth and Johnston (1988) and is designed to ensure that the service provides the requisite quality efficiently.

1 Ensure that the service concept is defined clearly and in detail. Unless this is done there is little chance of producing an appropriate design for the service package.
2 Develop a clear understanding of the image that the service concept will project in the market place. This is essential for an understanding of the customer expectations that are going to be generated. A good service will still be judged poor if it fails to meet customer expectations, and if those expectations are inappropriate then the fault lies in the way in which the service is presented.
3 Develop an understanding of the abilities and workings of the operation from the customers' viewpoint, and how customer expectations and perceptions are managed during and after the provision of the service. Designers and providers often have great difficulty in seeing a service from the customers' viewpoint since their perception is coloured by their familiarity with the system and its purpose.
4 Get top management commitment to service quality, with clearly identified corporate objectives. Quality ultimately depends upon the customer contact staff as it is their behaviour which governs the customers' perception of the

service. If top management is not committed to quality there is little point in asking such commitment from customer service staff.

5 Define standards of functional and technical quality. This is one of the most difficult areas. Quality standards for the tangible elements are fairly straightforward, since we are dealing with physical products, but quality standards for the intangible elements are less so. The condition of the service environment can be specified, together with such things as frequency of cleaning; maximum and average waiting times can be specified and measured; competence, manner and appearance of service staff are more subjective and probably more important. Quality standards need to be matched, as nearly as possible, to customer expectations, and recruitment, training and remuneration policies arranged appropriately.

6 Develop appropriate procedures and systems to support the service-providing activities in meeting the defined standards. The necessary infrastructure must be present to ensure that facilities are provided and maintained.

7 Develop appropriate procedures to deal with predictable events, train staff to deal with unpredictable events. The service encounter is by its nature unpredictable so procedures cannot be implemented to deal with every eventuality. Service personnel must be trained to deal with the unexpected, as must those further up the hierarchy if this means referring problems on.

8 Develop all systems to facilitate the provision of good service. In particular treat customer service staff as if they are internal customers to ensure their continued support. If the customer service staff are not treated as though the organization values them, they are not going to behave as if the organization values its customers.

9 Define inspection procedures. Performance will drift unless it is monitored and maintained, so procedures for monitoring quality and acting to restore it if necessary are essential. Methods depend upon what is being measured: sampling is adequate for tangibles. Methods used for measuring the quality of intangibles range from *ad hoc* customer feedback through questionnaires and customer panels to the use of the professional customer.

This approach addresses most of the problems associated with service design, by directing attention to the need to specifically identify intangibles and their contribution to the overall service package; to the need to consider the customer viewpoint; to the critical role played by the customer contact personnel and the support they require; and finally to the need for explicit and relevant performance monitoring. Carefully implemented the nine point approach should also ensure that the resulting service-providing system is internally consistent.

SUMMARY

This chapter has considered the issues which distinguish services from products and the impact these have on the design of efficient and effective services. In particular, customer presence, intangibility and variability of demand have been identified as major issues. Two broad approaches to dealing with these problems have been described: the industrialization approach with its stress on efficiency characterized by reducing customer contact and moving as much as possible of the process to the back shop, and an approach based upon identifying the characteristics of the service which determine quality. The two are not incompatible. The industrialization approach taken to extremes tends to destroy valuable elements of the service, but stressing quality alone is likely to lead to too high a cost. A balance needs to be struck and where this lies will depend upon the precise circumstances. It should be remembered that pure service does not exist and the techniques described in Chapter 3 for product design are frequently applicable to the design of the service package.

CASE STUDY: Bolthorps Brewery

Colonel Bolthorp, chairman of Bolthorps Brewery, returned from a golfing holiday on the Algarve full of enthusiasm. The mission of Bolthorps Brewery was to be 'Excellence in Customer Service'. He had played several rounds with Frank Fielding, the UK Sales Director of International Car Rentals, who had described in glowing terms the transformation that their Customer Care programme had made to repeat business. He was totally convinced that Bolthorps Brewery could achieve the same results, and lost no time in calling a board meeting to implement the scheme.

As a result of this meeting Michael Bolthorp, Sales Manager and the Colonel's grandson, was given the task of setting up and leading a small group to investigate the matter further and make recommendations to the board in three months.

The group first investigated best practice elsewhere, and in particular, following an introduction from the Colonel, the procedures at International Car Rentals. They then gathered relevant information on Bolthorps Brewery operations prior to carrying out an analysis and drawing conclusions.

Summary of best practice findings

Meeting customer expectations was identified as the most important issue. This required that they first be determined and if necessary modified through the development of image and publicity.

Factors relevant to customer expectations included:

- customer mix;
- physical environment;

- choice;
- waiting time;
- attitude and skill of customer service staff.

The group were particular impressed by the evidence on the role of customer service staff. At International Car Rentals they found that customer service staff were recruited via a programme of interviews and tests which took three hours. Applicants were usually qualified above GCSE level, but were required to have a good GCSE grades in Maths and English as a minimum. Following recruitment they were sent on a three-day residential customer care course, which was followed up by a one-day refresher course once a year. Staff were paid 30% more than the average for the industry and were given considerable discretion in dealing with customers. Staff turnover, which had previously been a problem, was now very low.

Bolthorps Brewery background material

The brewery owns 74 public houses in a variety of locations, and of varied size. While 17 are operated by tenants, the remainder have managers employed by Bolthorps. It was decided initially to concentrate on the managed houses where the brewery have more direct control. The breakdown by size (square metres of public space) and location of the 57 managed houses is:

| | | Location | |
Size	Town centre size	Suburban	Rural
70–100	1		2
100–200	18	14	5
>200	1	6	

Most of the public houses served food, but the variation was considerable, with 18 serving lunch only and eight of those serving sandwiches but not full meals.

| | | Location | |
	Town centre	Suburban	Rural
Lunch only	13	5	
Lunch and evenings	4	6	
Evenings only		3	4
Dining room	3	3	2

Customer service staff

Most of the staff have some contact with the customer, but the following were discounted from consideration: cleaners, cooks, kitchen staff.

Total full time staff	83
Total part time staff	274

Part time staff hours per week

<5	32
5–10	65
10–15	120
15–20	48
>20	9

Analysis of staff records showed that over the past year 32 full time staff and 295 part time staff had been replaced.

Demand

No detailed analysis on demand was carried out, but general observations suggested that urban public houses were full on most weekday lunch times but relatively quiet in the evenings except at weekends. The suburban and rural public houses were busier at weekend lunchtimes as well as weekend evenings, while those which served meals, as opposed to snacks, were busiest on Friday and Saturday evenings and Sunday lunchtime. In general, all the public houses could be described as full, if not over full, at peak times. A rough estimate of the overall capacity utilization suggested 35%.

Question

What recommendations would you make to the board?

Chapter 5

Capacity investment

Cost effective operations depend upon achieving a proper balance between demand for goods and services and the resources required to provide those goods and services. Although this is the central issue, decisions are required not just on the capacity of the facilities planned, but also on their location and their layout. In the short term it is sometimes possible to vary capacity to meet variations in demand, for example by introducing overtime working, and these issues are addressed in Chapter 7. However the scope for such variation is usually small compared with the total capacity, and the initial capacity investment decisions are expensive and long term. They set an upper limit on the total output possible and a lower limit on operating cost.

Decisions on location and layout also impose limitations on the efficient operation of the organization. If these decisions prove to be incorrect then not only will the organization be unable to operate with maximum efficiency and effectiveness, but even when the errors are identified it may not be feasible to correct them.

In this chapter the necessary preliminary decisions on total output and operations focus will be briefly considered, together with the determination of optimal location for the organization. The issues relevant to the use of single or multiple sites and the problem of facilities layout will also be discussed.

PRELIMINARY DECISIONS

Before any decisions on location and layout of facilities can take place, the exact focus of the organization must be agreed and the total volume of capacity determined. The issue of focus was addressed in Chapter 2: is the organization a manufacturer, an assembler, a distributor or a service provider?

Capacity decisions arise from corporate policy and if this is not clear a satisfactory outcome is unlikely.

The issues which dictate the location of a manufacturing facility are different from those which dictate the location of a distribution centre or a service outlet. If an organization is embarking upon more than one function, it may well be appropriate to treat them separately from a facilities location viewpoint.

Overall capacity is also a matter of corporate policy. Long-term forecasting using economic modelling or scenario construction is beyond the scope of this book, but the output of the corporate planning process must be a clear statement of the maximum capacity required together with some indication of the flexibility required.

In the service sector, where demand is highly variable, and stock is not available to provide a buffer, the overall capacity investment decision must take into account the fact that whatever capacity is chosen, it will always be possible for demand to exceed this. In other words, queues will form. The overall service capacity must be greater than the overall demand otherwise queues will simply extend infinitely, but even when the available capacity is significantly greater than the average demand the variability of both arrival rate and service time means that queues will sometimes form.

Policy decisions are required on the magnitude of queues that will be tolerated, the idle capacity that will be tolerated, and the management of the queues.

Queuing theory is a well established operational research technique designed to optimize the balance between customer waiting times and idle service capacity. Queuing theory is applicable to any situation where a variable demand meets a fixed capacity. It applies in situations where obvious queues form, such as shops, bus stops, waiting rooms, but it is also applicable in such areas as receiving telephone calls, capacity of ports, airports and even roads.

Queuing theory addresses the cost function:

Cost of customer waiting time + cost of idle capacity

and seeks to minimize it. It should be easy to determine the cost of idle capacity, but the cost of customer waiting time is less obvious and much more dependent on the circumstances. At the simplest level the cost of customer waiting time may be the cost of maintaining a suitable waiting area, but it will almost certainly be necessary to include an allowance for goodwill, since customers kept waiting too long will leave, and may permanently withdraw their custom.

The most common situation is one in which arrivals at the service point are random, i.e. follow the Poisson distribution, and service time follows the negative exponential distribution. It is not appropriate to go through the derivation of the formulae here, but given that

A = mean arrival rate
S = mean service rate per service channel
N = number of service channels

then

T (traffic intensity) $= A/(SN)$

T must be less than 1.

Where N is 1, i.e. a single service point then

Q (average number in queue) $= T^2/(1 - T)$
U (utilization of service facility) $= T$

Where N is greater than 1 the mathematics become somewhat more complex. A general formula is given in Appendix 1, together with some discussion of other queuing problems, but the formulae for $N = 2$ and 3 are as follows

$N = 2$

$$Q = \frac{T^3}{4(1 + T)(1 - T/2)^2}$$

$N = 3$

$$Q = \frac{T^4}{18(1 + T + T^2/2)(1 - T/3)^2}$$

In all cases $U = T$

In arriving at a specification of capacity, it is necessary to consider the relative costs of waiting customers and idle resources for each relevant number of service facilities, and choose that number which gives the lowest total cost.

There may well be two levels of decision: capital and operational. In planning a supermarket, the number of check-outs and the amount of queuing space are fixed and these decisions would be taken at the planning stage on the basis of the maximum demand the supermarket is expected to accommodate. During actual operation the number of check-outs to be manned would be determined by the average demand expected at particular times of the day and particular days of the week.

FACILITIES LOCATION

A large number of factors influence the choice of an ideal location. The most important are:

- **Market** Location near to the market for the product or service helps to ensure a prompt and responsive service. This is particularly important in transport and distribution where the whole function of the operation is to bring a resource to the customer. In other services this may or may not be important. Where the service requires the participation of the customer (health care, entertainment, recreation) then a reasonable proximity is required, but banking and financial services can be carried out satisfactorily by telephone or by the use of representatives. Even retail distribution in the form of mail order shopping does not require that the outlet be near the market.

- **Raw materials**   Where large quantities of bulky raw materials are to be processed there may be a case for locating the processing plant near to the source of that material i.e. in extracting metal from ores, sugar from sugar cane, etc. but in practice this is rarely a serious constraint and is likely to be the least important consideration.

- **Labour**   A source of labour with the appropriate skill or at least the potential to be trained is an obvious prerequisite for a successful operation. Labour can of course be imported, as it is regularly for large scale construction projects where location is determined entirely by the project, but a local source of labour is always less expensive and easier to manage. Labour cost is frequently a determining issue in location decisions, hence the use of Taiwan and Korea for many assembly tasks in the past. However low cost labour on this scale tends to lead to the industrialization of the country, increasing wealth and expectations, and therefore its availability is often short lived. This is demonstrated by the fact that the role of low labour cost economies has moved on to other south and south-east Asian countries. In information processing, efficient telecommunications means that labour availability can be the dominant factor in determining location.

    There is some evidence that attempts to introduce new working methods are more likely to succeed if areas where the labour force already has experience of the product are avoided. Nissan chose to build cars on Tyneside, where there was no history of car assembly, in part to avoid the problems of changing previously learned working practices.

- **Transport**   In manufacturing and wholesale distribution the transport of materials and goods is a major consideration. The mode of transport must be decided first and if rail, water or air transport is to be the main method this may well be the single most important factor in determining location. Where road transport is used much greater flexibility is possible but proximity to a motorway junction is an important consideration. In retail distribution and services, access for the customer is important and this will usually mean road access. If the customer is likely to be a car owner then an important consideration is adequate car parking, however if a significant proportion of customers are likely to use public transport then the choice of location is limited to areas well served by public transport. Substantial demand may of course persuade transport companies to introduce a service.

- **Infrastructure**   The relevance of the availability of roads, services, etc. depends upon the scale of the enterprise. A small unit will most probably look for a factory, warehouse, or shop in an existing trading estate or retail development. A large unit, for example a new car assembly plant, can justify the use of a green field site and absorb the cost of providing services.

- **Technical support**   Commercial ventures tend to be social and cluster together. In medieval markets different crafts were grouped together, and the same tends to be found today, with, for example, the majority of shoe shops, banks or estate agents in a town centre being in the same street. This is sound marketing since an outlet off the beaten track is more likely to be overlooked by the customer. In manufacturing, and particularly high technology manufacturing, the same tends to happen as exemplified by silicon valley (or silicon glen in Scotland). Proximity to common specialist services and to centres of expertise, for example a university, is the main reason for this.

- **Political policy**   Governments, both national and local, frequently offer inducements to organizations to locate in particular areas. These inducements are usually financial in the form of grants, subsidized premises, etc.

It is frequently found that these factors are contradictory, for example what is convenient for the customer may not be convenient for the labour force; a good location for labour and transport may be more expensive than an alternative which attracts lucrative subsidies. A short list of feasible sites is usually drawn up and each one evaluated according to how well it meets the specified criteria. Where financial values can be attached to the various considerations the decision is relatively easy, but more often it is necessary to use subjective judgement. If rapid occupation of new premises is important, then the overriding consideration may be availability.

SINGLE OR MULTIPLE SITES

The nature of the market, particularly in the service sector, frequently dictates the need for multiple sites. Retail distribution, transport, financial services and catering are all examples of operations where sites are located in centres of demand, and where particular sites usually provide a full range of services. Even here there are exceptions: for example mail order shopping and home banking. Many financial services companies deal through home visits, but for most service organizations this possibility does not arise.

In manufacturing the same constraints on location do not arise since the goods are usually transported to the customer, so a manufacturing organization has the choice of a single large site or several smaller sites. If several smaller sites are chosen, then a further decision is required on how the work is to be divided between the sites. The alternatives are:

- Each site could carry out a full range of operations on the full product range. This is often done to overcome trade barriers which are sometimes based upon the proportion of total value generated in the host country. In the absence of such constraints dispersed plants often only carry out assembly, the actual manufacture being done in the home country.
- Different sites could be devoted to particular products or groups of products. A food manufacturer might make ice cream in one location, and meat pies in another.
- Different sites could be devoted to different processes. This may be combined with product differentiation, for example meat pies and ice cream are made by different processes, but it is also found in single product organizations.

The motor industry frequently carries out body panel manufacture, engine manufacture and final assembly at quite different locations, and the different components of the European Airbus are manufactured in different countries.

Advantages of single site operation

The main advantage of single site operation is that associated with economies of scale. Compared with any form of dispersion, the infrastructure necessary to support operations on a single site is greatly reduced. Functions such as personnel, purchasing, storekeeping, engineering, etc. do not need to be duplicated. Centralized purchasing and delivery lead to better terms from suppliers.

When compared with multiple sites manufacturing the full product range, a single site can offer larger batch sizes and hence lower set up costs, and can provide the same level of service with substantially lower stocks. If perfectly operated, stocks should be proportional to the square root of the number of sites for a given level of service, thus a single site could operate on half the stock of four separate sites.

When compared to sites manufacturing part of the range, the single site can offer greater flexibility as it is easier to transfer under-utilized capacity from one product to another if they are made in the same place. When compared to sites concentrating on particular process stages, the single site overcomes the problems and costs of transportation and in principle confers greater reliability. Communication and co-ordination should also be easier and more reliable, although this is not always the case.

Advantages of multi-site operation

The usual reason for dispersal of the whole range of products over several sites is the satisfaction of local market conditions. This applies in particular to multinational operation where individual countries may prefer, or even demand, that goods are made locally. As organizations grow through acquisition they may find themselves with dispersed plants producing the same goods, and while this might not be advantageous, the costs of rationalization may outweigh the benefits. Another merit of having the whole operation dispersed is that the smaller sites may be easier to manage effectively. Economies of scale are in any case not always realizable, and above a certain size, the problems often outweigh the advantages. Vulnerability of the organization to political, industrial, or even natural, forces is reduced by dispersion. Flexibility is increased in as much as it is easier to close down one small site than to reduce output permanently at a single large site, and it is also easier to experiment with new working practices.

Dispersion on the basis of particular product groups is frequently easier to justify. The advantages of easier management accruing from smaller size are increased further by the reduction in the product range being manufactured. If different product groups also use different process types then this separation is even more desirable since there is rarely any advantage in housing different process types on the same site. The potential thus arises for the optimal location of a particular factory according to proximity to raw materials, the market, skilled labour and/or infrastructure without compromising other products. Scale is an important indicator of the need for dispersion. Jobbing activities and flow line production are generally considered incompatible, requiring different technologies, labour skills and management attitudes, and an organization which manufactures for markets which vary in their demands for volume and customization would be well advised to disperse on this basis.

Dispersal on the basis of process stage also simplifies the task of local management in that they not only have a smaller unit to manage but that unit is highly focused on particular processes and technology. Again location can be based upon the availability of skills and support services without compromising other issues. It is usually only considered for the large scale manufacture of a limited product range, for example cars, aircraft, electronic consumer goods, etc.

The development of the Just in Time (JIT) approach, discussed further in Chapter 10, has led to an increasing interest in the development of dispersion within a single site. JIT tends to lead to relatively small, highly focused production units which may well be incompatible in the same way that jobbing and flow production are. In order to accommodate this, a large production unit may be broken down into several small separate units occupying the same site, but operating more or less independently.

Dispersion imposes demands upon the communication and control system of the organization which centralization, at least in theory, avoids. Where there is a need for co-ordination between units, as when dispersion is based upon process stage, then a failure of communication can be catastrophic, but even when the production units are independent the need for centralized control cannot be avoided. Reporting systems are rarely perfect and it is not unknown for local management to pursue their own objectives rather than those of the company while manipulating the reporting system in order to maintain their independence.

A gold mining company in South Africa had a very simple and direct control system. Mines had to exceed a minimum yield of gold in the ore extracted or face closure. A small and remote gold mine had one rich seam of gold, but was otherwise worked out. The cost effective strategy was to strip this seam as quickly as possible then close the mine, however local management, with the active support of local labour, continued to extract low grade ore. This was blended with high grade ore to maintain the target yield, and the mine continued in operation for several years after its useful life should have ended.

FACILITIES LAYOUT

A good layout can have a substantial effect upon safety, efficiency and staff motivation, whereas a poor layout will at the very least lead to wasted space and time and could well constitute a serious hazard.

Issues and constraints

The issues and constraints which a layout needs to take into account include:

- **Available space**   The limitations of existing buildings must be taken into account except in the relatively rare event of a completely new building. Space should always be considered as three dimensional. Some processes require height, but vertical space is frequently more readily available than horizontal space and can be used for transport and storage through the use of conveyors, ducting, cranes and racking.
- **Safety**   Sufficient space needs to be allowed for plant to be operated and maintained safely. Access ways need to be large enough and clear enough to be useful and to give good visibility. Processes which are intrinsically dangerous must be segregated.
- **Access**   First and last stages are sensibly located near goods received and finished goods stores which should themselves be located at the edges of the building. Where customers are involved customer service points should be located near to access points. The location of processes which require dust or fume extraction, or which require daylight may be determined by the need to be near the edge of the building.
- **Space**   The space required for the operation and maintenance of each machine, together with its immediate storage requirements must be determined. Space is also required for access by both goods and personnel. The space required by intermediate storage areas must be defined if required.
- **Organization**   Layout should help to cultivate a sense of identity both to encourage motivation in the work force and to ease the task of supervision by close association of the plant for which a supervisor is responsible and also for ease of oversight.
- **Flexibility**   Changes in demand or technology are easier to implement if the layout has been designed with flexibility in mind.

While not all of these issues will necessarily apply in any one situation, layout is inevitably a compromise. An optimal layout for a particular situation is unlikely to be flexible, and could be almost unworkable if circumstances change. Where there is conflict, safety should generally take precedence.

Layout options

There are three commonly used layouts.

- **Functional or process**   Functional layouts are typically used in job and batch manufacture. Plant performing similar tasks is grouped together. In batch manufacture a section would contain all the plant concerned with a particular type of process as well as all the labour and would form a single unit for supervisory purposes. When optimizing layout it is usual to seek to maximize use of space and minimize transport of goods. The functional layout lends itself to control on a functional basis, and sections are used as the unit of scheduling and of costing. Quality is often controlled at section boundaries, with work being inspected before being allowed on to the next section. Functional layouts give a degree of flexibility in as much as labour is usually able to carry out any activity within the section. While changes in total demand may affect labour utilization, changes in product mix should not.

- **Product**   In a product layout both plant and labour are devoted exclusively to a particular product. This typically gives rise to a flow line system, whether powered or unpowered. Workstations are arranged in a process sequence and are usually closely coupled with only sufficient space for interstage buffer stocks between them. On a powered flow line the interstage buffer is sometimes created by extending the line between stages. The management structure reflects the operations layout, with supervisors being responsible for particular lines rather than particular functions. The product layout gives little flexibility since the line is designed around a given rate of output for a particular product. Marked changes in demand for the product will lead to low utilization, or an inability to meet demand. The output of a flow line is determined by the speed of the slowest operation, hence an efficient flow line must be balanced so that each process stage is achieving approximately the same output. Because the plant is to be devoted exclusively to one product it is worth devoting substantial effort to designing the process for maximum efficiency. A broad brush design will give the approximate total work content for the planned weekly output.

> **If an output of 1,000 units a week requires 800 hours per week then, on the basis of a 35 hour working week, the process would require 23 operators. This would suggest that the line should be designed on the basis of 23 process stages. Since the total work content per item is 800/1,000 hours or 48 minutes, then the average work content per stage should be 48/23 or 2.09 minutes.**

The efficiency of the line will be determined by how closely each stage approaches the ideal. It may be feasible to double up a stage which cannot sensibly be broken down, so that an operation which takes 5 minutes could be carried out by two operators in parallel giving an output of one item every 2.5 minutes, but further multiplication usually complicates the process to an excessive degree.

Since the process stages are so heavily designed very high productivities can be achieved with flow lines because non-productive work is largely eliminated. This contrasts with process layouts, or jobbing organizations, where flexibility is important.

- **Group technology**   It is often found that while the volume of output of any one product is insufficient to justify the use of a product layout, products can be grouped into families based upon their process requirements. Issues which are considered include precise process sequence, though this need not be absolutely identical for each product in the family, type and size of machines used. The total output for a particular family group may well be great enough to justify a product organization. Group technology usually results in small self-contained work cells rather than extensive flow lines, and it may be applied for only part of the process. The work centres are not usually as highly designed as those in a true flow line. The advantages claimed for group technology include reduced set up times, reduced storage space, reduced travelling space and time. More significantly the close association of operators and supervision with a small family of products leads to greater expertise and awareness. Operators frequently comment that the fact that they can see their work proceed on to the final stages and emerge as a finished product increases their motivation. This rarely happens in process or flow line layouts.

Layout techniques

In designing a layout, the ideal approach would be to express all the factors identified above in a cost function and then seek to minimize this. In practice this is usually impossible, and it is more usual to define those issues which are fixed constraints such as the building itself, the location of goods inwards and outwards, etc. and then to seek to minimize the costs of unused space and the time wasted in transport.

All layouts start with a plan of the available space which must show fixed doors and windows, and internal structural walls and pillars. Non-structural partitions can be ignored. If the floor strength varies this should also be noted since heavy equipment may not be located on light duty flooring. The plan may be a scaled drawing on squared paper, in which case scaled cut-outs of the floor space required for each piece of equipment should be prepared. Alternatively plastic construction kits are available which have the advantage of including height. As a further alternative a computer based graphics package may be used.

The usual emphasis is on transport, so it is important to identify those routes which will carry the greatest traffic so that the layout chosen can minimize these distances. The from–to or movement chart is a convenient way of identifying the most important routes. Its use is illustrated in the following example.

A company manufactures six products using a total of eight process stages. Table 5.1 shows the process routes of the six products and the relative number of batches made.

Table 5.1 Process routes

Product	Route	Batches
1	A, B, C, D, E, F	15
2	A, B, C, E, G, H	20
3	A, B, C, E, D, F, H	10
4	A, C, D, F, H	5
5	A, B, F, D, G, H	20
6	A, C, D, F, G, H	30

The from–to chart is a table showing each stage as both a source and a destination, so that each cell becomes a route. The number of batches following a particular route is entered into the appropriate cell. For example, products 1, 2, 3 and 5 follow the route A to B and in total they represent 65% of all batches so 65 is entered into the cell from A to B. Table 5.2 shows the from–to chart for this example.

Table 5.2 From–to chart

		To A	B	C	D	E	F	G	H
F	A		65	35					
r	B			45			20		
o	C				50	30			
m	D					15	10	20	
	E				10		15	20	
	F				20			30	15
	G								70
	H								

From the point of view of optimizing layout, the direction of travel is of no relevance, so those batches which travel from E to D are equivalent to those that travel from D to E. The travel chart, shown in Table 5.3 shows the number of journeys independent of direction of travel.

Table 5.3   Travel chart

	A	B	C	D	E	F	G	H
A		65	35					
B			45			20		
C				50	30			
D					25	30	20	
E						15	20	
F							30	15
G								70
H								

Now all that is required is to rank the routes in order of importance with the following result:

Route	Batches
G/H	70
A/B	65
C/D	50
B/C	45
A/C	35
C/E	30
D/F	30
F/G	30
D/E	25
B/F	20
D/G	20
E/G	20
E/F	15
G/H	15

Using templates defining the shape of the various departments an optimal layout can be determined by trial and error. The object is to minimize the total distance travelled, and this will usually be achieved by placing the departments between which there is the greatest traffic most closely together. This must obviously be done within the various other constraints identified.

Optimality is difficult to achieve given the number of constraints which may have to be satisfied, and in a situation with a large number of departments, products and process routes, the trial and error approach outlined will give a more or less satisfactory route rather than an optimal one. There are a number of computer packages available for generating layouts, most of which concentrate on the proximity of sequential operations, which are likely to reduce the labour involved in producing a satisfactory layout in a complex situation.

SUMMARY

This chapter has considered some of the issues which need to be taken into account in deciding the location and layout of operations facilities. The determination of total capacity as a necessary prerequisite was considered, in particular the use of queuing theory to identify the balance between idle capacity and waiting customers in service operations.

The various factors which influence decisions on location were discussed, among the most important being transport costs, proximity to customers and availability of labour. The need to rely on subjective judgement, because of the difficulty of quantifying many of the issues, was identified. The issues involved in deciding on single or multiple sites were considered, together with the basis of such a division. Sites focused on both products and processes were identified as options.

Finally layout was considered, identifying the three main options of process, product and group layout, together with their advantages and disadvantages. The criteria and constraints operating on layout decisions were identified and the from–to chart as an aid to layout decisions was described.

Chapter 6 will continue this by looking at the design of the work itself.

CASE STUDY: Midshires Bank

Midshires Bank, one of the few remaining small independent banks, does not expect to remain independent for much longer but the board are seeking to maintain or even increase market share so that, in the event of a take-over, the terms will be as favourable as possible.

In common with other financial institutions, this will involve a move away from a simple transaction based approach to one founded on customer service and customer choice. The bank is thus actively promoting its role as financial advisor and seeking to tie in existing customers more firmly by providing investment, insurance and pensions advice and services. It is hoped that by providing a 'good' service it will also attract more new custom.

The move into personal financial services requires substantial retraining of staff, and the bank is anxious to obtain as high a utilization from its new 'financial consultants' as is consistent with good service.

The situation

Branches are being modernized as financial resources and trained staff become available, and the Midport South branch is now due for refurbishment. Figure 5.1 shows the present layout of the branch.

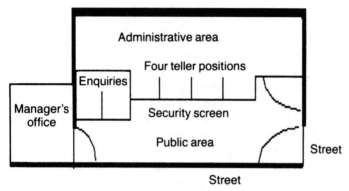

Figure 5.1   Present branch layout

The intention is to create a more open and welcoming environment where the customer can sit in comfort and discuss his/her requirements with a trained member of staff. There will still be a need for standard teller services, but a substantial part of this demand will be taken over by cash dispensers and automatic paying in points. The cash dispensers will also be able to handle balance enquiries.

The projected demand figures for the branch are shown in Table 5.4.

Table 5.4   Midport South branch: customer demand

Mean demand	Teller	Cash dispenser	Auto pay-in	General enquiries
Morning	18.00	27.00	12.00	3.00
Lunchtime	28.00	54.00	19.00	5.60
Afternoon	16.50	29.00	10.00	2.70
Mean service rate	19.35	42.86	35.29	9.68
Financial services				
Mean demand	1.80			
Mean service rate	2.22			

All figures are transactions per hour; Lunchtime is 12.00–14.00 pm; 80% of financial service transactions are expected to be by appointment. This business often arises out of general enquiries.

Questions

Make recommendations on the following;
1 Layout of the refurbished branch.
2 Number of cash dispensers and automatic paying in points.
3 Number of staff.

Chapter 6

Design of the task

The design of the actual tasks involved in producing a product or service is almost as important as the design of the product or service itself. The task must be designed in such a way that it can be carried out efficiently and effectively by whatever resources are devoted to it. The choice of resources is an important preliminary step. Automation may be used to a greater or lesser extent, the extent that is feasible is of course changing as technology develops, but the operations manager's task tends to be easier if tried methods are used rather than methods at the frontiers of technology. Where full automation is not used the capabilities of the labour force become an important consideration.

Trouble free operation depends very strongly upon the design of the human/machine interface, and the degree to which this leaves the human component of the system with a meaningful and integrated task which is within his or her capabilities.

The availability of skills within the work force, the susceptibility of the work force to training, and the availability of appropriate training facilities must all be taken into account. At one extreme the task could be designed to be carried out entirely manually by largely unskilled labour while at the other it could be fully automated. Usually the correct solution lies somewhere between these extremes.

In this chapter the criteria for allocating tasks to human or machine labour will be briefly considered. There is an overview of the options currently available when automation is considered, and the circumstances in which their application might be appropriate. Approaches to the design of the task from the point of view of the human operator are also considered, looking briefly at the human relations and the ergonomic approaches, and finally the approach adopted by work study is considered.

TASK ALLOCATION

The determining factor in task allocation will always be human capability. There are tasks which cannot be carried out unaided by human operators because the environment is too hostile, for example inspection of the interior of nuclear reactors, or because the scale is too small or too large. The relevant human capabilities that must be addressed include physical strength, reach, precision and reproducibility of movement, perception and discrimination, attention and fatigue.

Capabilities vary enormously, obviously in such areas as physical strength and dexterity, but also in perception and discrimination. Some people possess perfect pitch, which means that they can identify the frequency of a tone without artificial aids, but an electronic frequency analyser would usually be considered more appropriate if this measurement were an important part of a process. The author has heard of the case of a female process operator who could identify at a glance whether the diameter of tins and lids on parallel conveyors were within tolerance so that the lids would correctly fit the tins, but this is a rare skill and no designer would expect a human operator to carry out such a task. Tasks must be allocated to the human operator on the basis of normal skills and capabilities given appropriate qualifications and training.

In the event of the task being unsuitable for either human operator or machine operation then the first step should be to redesign the process to render it more compatible. If this fails, automation is usually recommended on the grounds that human capabilities have evolved slowly over millions of years and are unlikely to change, while machine capabilities have developed very rapidly and may well embrace the task in the near future.

The human operator is more likely to be suitable for tasks involving flexibility and judgement, whereas machines are more suited to tasks involving repetition and precision. Generally the endurance of machines greatly outweighs that of the human operator, so tasks requiring uninterrupted performance for prolonged periods are best automated. In safety critical applications, it should be born in mind that the failure of machines is usually sudden and dramatic, while human operators show a more gradual deterioration in performance.

Generally, better performance is obtained from a human operator if the task is designed as a rational and integrated process. Disconnected fragments of activity give rise to difficulties of attention and comprehension which lead to errors and lack of motivation.

Particular difficulties arise in tasks where the human operator is present as a backup to an automatic system, usually being required to respond quickly and correctly to an emergency. Since emergencies are, hopefully, rare this means that the operator, highly trained and skilled, may spend many hours doing little or nothing. The effect of this on morale, and on attention, can be substantial and may result in the operator failing to perform well when the need arises. If the human operator is required to be alert then the task should be designed to encourage alertness even at the expense of not automating elements which could reasonably be automated. Tasks which require a continuous high level of alertness are very taxing, and where safety critical, staff should be rotated onto other duties fairly frequently.

In general the human operator is preferred where flexibility and judgement are required, while automation is preferred where reproducibility and consistency are required.

Automation requires a very detailed specification of the task whereas the human operator is able to tolerate a degree of vagueness and even inconsistency. In reality of course the determining issue is often that of cost.

AUTOMATION

The development of automation is accelerating at about the same rate as that of information technology, and it is conceivable that at some future time it will be possible to automate almost any task. The technologies involved at present differ between manufacturing and service, so these sectors are considered separately.

Automation of services

Automation of the interface with the customer has a number of advantages, in particular greater consistency and wider availability, both of which are seen as improvements in service quality.

Automation can also reduce costs, particularly when compared to the costs of operating a 24 hour service with human operators. In the case of ATMs, for example, the cost of maintaining manned premises 24 hours per day, seven days a week would be prohibitive. Much of this cost would be an ongoing revenue expense whereas the greatest cost in setting up the ATM network is capital. The question of whether automation is cost effective at any one time depends upon the relative state of development of the technology, however technology inevitably becomes cheaper while labour costs seem only to rise.

The main difficulties with service automation were addressed in Chapter 4. These centre on the customer's perception of the service and the customer's skill in operating the interface. If the customer perceives interpersonal contact as being an important element in the service then full automation is inappropriate; though an organization may install and use service contact personnel, for example virtually all lifts are self-service, some organizations still employ lift operators. Customer skill is related to customer selection, and also to the flexibility of the service offered. It is necessary for the service designer to know the customer, and to design an interface which the customer will find easy to use. The presentation of too many options frequently only causes confusion and fully automated service interfaces are best when only a few facilities are offered.

Manufacturing automation

The history of manufacturing automation is long and complex. The first numerically controlled processes were probably developed in the weaving industry, for example the jacquard loom in the early nineteenth century was operated by punched cards and can be seen as the first example of numerical control. In general textile production (spinning and weaving) and chemical processing have been heavily automated for some considerable time.

More recent developments in automation have been in the fields of metal cutting and simple assembly. These areas have the advantage that the materials tend to be rigid and predictable. While automation is developing rapidly in these areas, the unpredictability of such materials as fabrics and timber has delayed its cost effective implementation in others.

The development of automation has proceeded rapidly, with many technologies overlapping and being used simultaneously. The main developments, in more or less chronological order, are as follows:

- **Numerical control (NC)**   Machine tools controlled by a pre-written program. This may be supplied on punched paper tape or magnetic tape. At its simplest, the program requires that an operator loads the workpiece onto the machine and fits the correct tools. More sophisticated models will locate and fit the required tooling from an attached tool store.
- **Computer numerical control (CNC)**   The machine tool is directly linked to a computer, thus it does not need an operator to load the program tape.
- **Flexible manufacturing cell**   A computer controlled workstation able to carry out a number of different operations on a variety of different components. Such a system will include a tool store, and probably tool condition sensors so that the rate of working can be linked to the quality of the material and the sharpness of the tools. Tool breakage will lead to automatic replacement of the tool. The cell identifies the component from machine readable coded data on the pallet holding the component. The cell may include automatic inspection sensors which check tolerances and surface condition while the process is in operation.
- **Transfer line**   An automated materials handling system which moves work pieces between workstations in a fixed sequence. Work pieces are normally secured to pallets to facilitate automatic handling. The movement may be effected by conveyor, overhead conveyor, or automatic guided vehicles.
- **Flexible transfer line**   A computer controlled transfer line which moves work between workstations according to the requirements of the workpiece and the availability of workstations.
- **Flexible manufacturing system (FMS)**   A combination of flexible manufacturing cells and a flexible transfer line, able to produce a variety of components and simple assemblies in any quantity and any sequence.
- **Automatic assembly**   Automated assembly is available in a wide variety of industries for a wide variety of materials. The best known are perhaps the automatic welding equipment used in car assembly, and automatic component insertion and soldering used in the electronics industry.
- **Automatic inspection and test**   Again a wide variety of equipment is in use for measuring weight, physical dimension, surface characteristics, and electrical characteristics. The development of sophisticated sensors for monitoring and matching colour and pattern made it possible for the clothing industry to offer two piece suits as two separate items rather than always as a

matched pair. The advantages of this in enabling retailers to offer a wider range of fittings while actually holding less stock are self-evident.

In selecting automation the usual consideration is the trade off between capital cost and revenue cost. Automatic processes will usually give higher output and more consistent quality, at the expense of a greater initial investment. The effectiveness of the investment is closely linked to the volume of individual products as illustrated in Figure 6.1.

The disadvantage of investment in high volume automatic production facilities is of course the lack of flexibility which results.

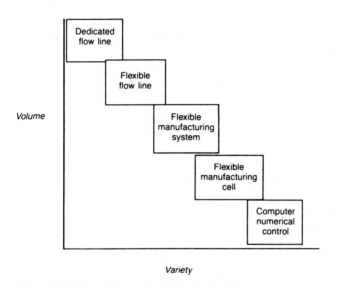

Figure 6.1   Use of manufacturing technology

DESIGN OF WORK

Whatever balance between human and machine is designed into the process, there will usually be some demand for the human operator. Three well established disciplines have developed which contribute towards the optimal design of the work of the human operator; *ergonomics* which is the science of human capabilities, the *human relations* school, which concentrates on the needs of the worker, and *work study* which adopts a fairly pragmatic engineering approach to the issue. Detailed consideration of ergonomics and of the human relations school are beyond the scope of this book so they will only be briefly discussed.

Ergonomics

Ergonomics is the scientific study of the capabilities of the human operator both as a mechanical and a sensory device. Its main contribution in operations design is in optimizing the design of workstations to minimize unnecessary movement and to maximize the comfort of the operator. It also has a contribution to make in the design of displays in order to maximize information transfer and minimize confusion. It is a specialized field best left to experts.

The human relations school

This approach concerns itself primarily with the idea that the well motivated worker will work harder, faster and better, resulting in higher productivity, higher quality, lower absenteeism and better industrial relations. This is undoubtedly true, the difficulty lies in identifying motivating factors. The approach of job enrichment, for example, identifies job satisfaction as an important motivator and seeks to make jobs interesting, challenging and complete, so that the operator can feel a sense of achievement. Unfortunately this is often seen by the operator merely as an unnecessary complication of the task and may result in even lower motivation. The most successful applications of this approach are those which result in the operator developing an identity with a group of fellow employees, when loyalty to the group can give rise to higher and better output, but the outcome is unpredictable, and such changes are on occasion recognized by the work force as devices for increasing output and are resisted on those grounds.

The reasons why people work are complex, and beyond the scope of this book, but their correct identification does assist in the design of tasks which will be done well. They include financial reward – though this is rarely as important as is often assumed – job satisfaction – a complex issue which can apply at any level but can never be assumed to be relevant – esteem and social status, and time structuring, or the need for something to do. This variety of factors renders predictable motivation very difficult to achieve.

WORK STUDY

Work study developed out of the scientific management approach developed in the nineteenth century. It is based upon the scientific analysis of tasks, and tends to treat the human operator merely as another component. It has been tempered by the human relations school, but is still largely mechanical/engineering oriented. It is, nevertheless, the best established approach to the design of the task in operations management.

Work study consists of two distinct disciplines, that of *method study* which is concerned with the way in which the task is carried out, and *work measurement* which is concerned with the time and effort required to carry out the task. When considering administrative tasks rather than manufacturing tasks, the term *organization and methods* is usually used.

While the two disciplines differ in detail, their basic approach to the problem is identical.

Method study

Method study is a systematic approach to the design and improvement of the way in which tasks are carried out. A well established approach has been developed which is embodied in the mnemonic SREDIM: Select; Record; Examine; Develop; Install; Maintain.

1 Select

Selection of the area to be studied may be based upon the presence of a new process or piece of equipment which self-evidently requires the proper design of working methods, or upon the identification of problems. In the case of the former the investigation proceeds immediately to step 4, Develop. In the case of the latter, the selection stage is rather more important. It consists of a preliminary investigation of the problem area with a view to determining the true cause of the difficulty. This may be poor methods, inadequate plant, poor training, poor supervision, or inadequate procedures elsewhere in the process. Difficulties often arise as a result of problems elsewhere in the system.

The selection process is designed to ensure that the problem really exists and that it is appropriate for method study to tackle. A problem that really lies elsewhere will lead to an investigation of the appropriate area, while a matter of inadequate training or supervision may be more appropriate for the personnel department to tackle. The outcome of the selection process should be a report to management confirming that the problem exists and should be investigated by method study, or identifying the appropriate route for further investigation. Organizations with work study departments frequently carry out investigations on a periodic basis even in the absence of obvious problems to protect against procedural drift.

2 Record

It is sometimes argued that a good designer should be able to design an optimal process from scratch and that investigation of existing practices prejudices optimal design. This may be true, but good designers are not that common, and improvement to existing practice, while not necessarily leading to perfection, is frequently more cost effective than starting again from scratch. Detailed recording of existing practice does tend to ensure that the proposed improvement is at least feasible. Existing procedures are closely observed over several work cycles.

Where more than one operator is involved, a representative sample of operators is observed, the object being to build up a representative sample of observations of the way in which the task is carried out, including variations in conduct and in circumstances. This observation is always carried out with the prior agreement of the process operators and where appropriate, the trade unions.

While recording is occasionally carried out using video, the most common method is detailed observation by work study engineers using flow charting techniques to record the process. The most common symbology used in method study charting is illustrated in Figure 6.2.

Charts may either follow the flow of material through the system, the *material flow* chart, or may concentrate on the actions of a particular operator. Where an operator is being studied, the chart may well record the actions of each hand separately, the *two handed* chart. The type of chart and the level of detail is selected to suit the situation. It is likely that both types will be used at various levels of detail in any given study. Such charts are particularly useful in the design of services, where the contrast between the function of the service provider and the customer can be highlighted. Figure 6.3 shows an example of the attempt to purchase an obscure book. The chart clearly highlights the difference in activity between the customer and the service provider. *Movement* charts (see Chapter 5) may also be used.

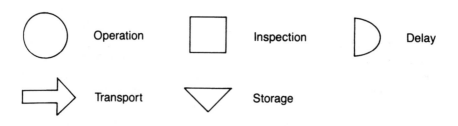

Figure 6.2 Flow chart symbols

3 Examine

The record of the existing procedure is examined in detail with a view to identifying areas for improvement. While delays and transport operations are the most obviously wasteful, the greatest potential for improvement lies in the productive operations, since changes in these may completely eliminate some delays and transports. A standard questioning technique has been developed, and these questions are asked of each operation in the following sequence:

- **Purpose**   – What is being done?
                  – Why?
                  – What alternatives are there?
                  – What should be done?
- **Place**   – Where is it being done?
                  – Why?
                  – Where else is possible?
                  – Where would be best?
- **Sequence**   – When is it done?
                  – Why?
                  – When else is possible?
                  – When would be best?
- **Person**   – Who does it?
                  – Why?
                  – Who else could do it?
                  – Who would be best?
- **Means**   – How is it done?
                  – Why?
                  – How else could it be done?
                  – How best should it be done?

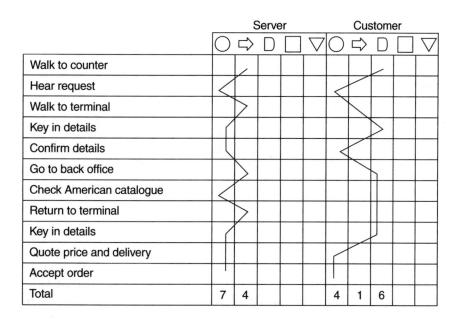

Figure 6.3   Server/customer process chart for ordering a book

The result of this process is that every aspect of the task is critically appraised, alternatives identified and the best feasible alternative selected. By applying this approach first to operations in the flow chart, unnecessary transports and delays should be automatically eliminated. Remaining transports and delays can then be investigated.

4 Develop

The examination process described above leads directly to the development of improved methods. Once these have been formalized, usually in the form of flow charts, they are subjected to the same critical examination to ensure that they are feasible and better.

5 Install

The revised methods are submitted for approval, first to budget holders where expenditure is required and then to those who will be required to carry them out. It is important that operators and first line supervision are convinced that the proposals are sound, since no procedure will work well if those carrying it out do not believe in it.

Clear specification and presentation are essential together with a willingness to listen to comment and criticism. Only when acceptance has been gained can capital expenditure be undertaken and training commenced.

6 Maintain

Maintenance is necessary to deal with events and circumstances not anticipated during stages 4 and 5, develop and install, and to deal with the drift in operating practices which inevitably occurs. Day to day maintenance is best carried out by shop floor supervision using comprehensive procedure manuals. Over time, drift plus piecemeal approaches to new circumstances may lead to the whole process deteriorating, hence the use of regular method studies – despite the absence of overt problems, by some organizations.

Work measurement

Work measurement is not strictly concerned with the design of the task, though it may be used to evaluate alternative methods. Its principal use is in establishing the necessary data for capacity planning, by establishing the elapsed time required for the conduct of productive operations. It provides the factor which allows demand, in terms of quantities of goods to be produced, to be converted into the only useful direct measure of capacity, time.

While the most important use is in providing the database for capacity planning and control, work measurement is also used for the following:

- **Costing**   Some costs such as labour and machine time are obviously time based, and other costs such as supervision and indirect materials are often recovered against operator or machine time. While time based costing is not always the best approach, no product costing system can produce accurate costs without process times being known.
- **Payment**   Bonus and incentive payment schemes depend upon an impartial and reproducible way of measuring the amount of work involved in a task. Work measurement provides this.
- **Evaluation**   Evaluation of new equipment, new methods, or even new recruitment and training schemes can all be carried out by measuring how long the task takes.

Work measurement adopts a similar methodology to method study.

1 Select

As with method study, selection of the area to be studied may be due to the presence of a new process or piece of equipment. Difficulties with scheduling, costing, or bonus schemes would all indicate the possibility that work measurement is required, but it is important that the selection process should identify that the problem is caused by inappropriate time standards rather than inappropriate working methods. The introduction of some form of output related payment system would usually require a work measurement investigation. Organizations with work study departments frequently carry out investigations on a periodic basis even in the absence of obvious problems to protect against drift. Since work measurement is concerned with establishing the work content of tasks as carried out, it is often desirable to carry out a method study first to ensure that the methods are correct.

2 Record

The process to be measured is recorded in exactly the same way as that described for method study.

3 Measure

Measurement of work is a difficult task. The first step is obviously to measure the time taken for a particular operation, but this is complicated by issues such as how consistent the operation is, how hard the operator is working, obtaining a precise definition of the start and finish of the operation, and the effect of observation on the performance of the operator. On the shop floor consistency of operation is usually fairly high, and the start and finish of the operation are well defined, the use of method study charting ensures this.

In administrative and service operations the situation is less clear cut. How does the work measurement engineer distinguish between constructive thought about the task, constructive thought about another issue altogether or simple daydreaming on the part of an office worker? The traditional hostility to the stopwatch shown by shop floor operators is even greater in office workers and the stopwatch is rarely used in such situations. There are several approaches to these problems and these are described in more detail later in the chapter.

4 Publish

The results of the exercise are published in a form appropriate for their final use.

5 Maintain

As with method study, periodic review is necessary to ensure that the standards remain appropriate.

Time study

The most obvious method of measuring work is to measure the actual time a task takes. This is the basis behind time study. Once the task has been broken down into clearly defined elements, each element is timed using a stopwatch. Where several operators are involved in the same task, then several are observed over a period of time, the object being to obtain a representative sample of normal working practice. The fundamental difficulty with this approach is that operators will be working more or less hard, and how hard they are working will be influenced by the knowledge that they are being observed. Time study overcomes this problem through the time study engineer forming a subjective estimate of how hard the operator is working (the process of *rating*) while carrying out the time study.

There are several scales used for rating, but the most common, adopted by the British Standards Institute is the 0–100 scale. Zero represents no work, while 100 represents the rate of work which a skilled and motivated operator could reasonably keep up through a normal working shift. It has been compared to the effort required to walk at 4 miles per hour. Time study engineers learn, and maintain, their (subjective) rating scale by the frequent study of films in which operations are performed at various rates. The engineer observes the film, rates it and then compares his or her rating with that of the film. A high degree of consistency is usually achieved.

The procedure for carrying out a time study is best illustrated by an example.

The Observed Time is the time actually recorded, say
  10 seconds

The *Rate* is noted at the same time, say
  110

The Basic Time is obtained by adjusting this for the observed rate
  $10 \times 110/100 = 11$ seconds

The operator cannot be expected to work continuously throughout the shift so a Relaxation Allowance is added, to allow for tea breaks, visits to the lavatory, etc. This varies with the industry and must be higher in conditions which are particularly noisy or suffer extremes of temperature, but 12.5% is quite common. A further allowance, 2.5% in this example, may be added to cover the occasional need for extra work due to faulty tooling or materials. The Work Content is the basic time plus these allowances.
  $11 + 0.125 \times 11 + 0.025 \times 11 = 12.65$ seconds

In a perfect world the operator should be able to achieve an average of one operation every 12.65 seconds throughout the shift, but other circumstances intervene and must be allowed for if a realistic standard is to be achieved. Processes may not be perfectly co-ordinated which may result in idle time while machines are slowing down, or while waiting for a second machine involved in the task to complete its cycle. When appropriate allowances are added, 5% in this example, the result is the Standard Time.

In summary:

  Observed Time is measured
  Basic Time = *Observed Time* + rating adjustment
  Work Content = *Basic Time* + *Relaxation* and *Extra Work* allowances
  Standard Time = *Work Content* + *Process* allowances

Predetermined Motion Time Systems (PMTS)

Time study is expensive, requires a high level of skill and continuous training, and is frequently resisted by operators who have a universal aversion to the stopwatch. PMTS methods overcome some of these problems by breaking the task down into very small basic units for which times are then published. The units of movement are so basic that any task can, at least in theory, be broken down into a sequence of predetermined movements and the standard time calculated.

These are proprietary schemes and the purchaser is supplied with tables classifying various movements and listing the time required for them. The

Method Time Measurement (MTM) system uses the TMU (time measurement unit) equal to 0.00001 hours (0.036 seconds) as its basic unit. The advantage of PMTS systems is that they do not involve the stopwatch or rating, however they do still require a considerable amount of skill and training in breaking down the task into the small and precisely defined units and identifying the correct units in the tables. The time required to carry out work measurement using PMTS is probably about the same as that required by a time study, so it is unlikely to save cost.

Synthetic methods

If an organization correctly codes and files its time study measurements, these can form the basis for a simplified form of PMTS. A clear classification and retrieval system is essential but the result is that standard times for new or short run tasks can be estimated quickly and easily. Unlike commercial PMTS systems, tables of synthetic times are not usually transferable.

Activity sampling

Activity sampling is widely used in administrative and service tasks where the stopwatch would be intrusive or unacceptable. It does not concern itself with the time taken by individual tasks, but rather with determining the proportion of available time used by various activities. The activities need to be identified and clearly defined in advance, but having done this the observer simply notes which activity is taking place at each observation by placing a tick against that activity on a prepared form. At the end of the exercise the number of ticks against a particular activity divided by the total number of observations gives the proportion of time devoted to that activity. It is normal to classify only the main activities and have a catch-all class for anything else. Obviously if the proportion of time spent on these unidentified activities becomes too great a re-analysis will be required.

Activity sampling has several advantages. It does not involve stopwatches, or rating, or careful and detailed analysis of the tasks. It does not require a particularly skilled observer, the observations themselves are instantaneous and the observer is usually fairly unobtrusive. It does however lack the precision of other methods.

The number of observations to be taken is determined by the formula:

$$N = \frac{4P(100 - P)}{L^2}$$

where N = number of observations
$\quad$ P = percentage occurrence of the activity in question
$\quad$ L = maximum acceptable percentage error.

A preliminary study can be undertaken to estimate P for the most frequently occurring activity, but a value of $P = 50$ could be assumed since this is always the worst case.

If the most frequently occurring activity occupied about 30% of the time, and an accuracy of 1% was required (i.e. true result within 29–31%) then the required number of observations would be:

$$N = \frac{4 \times 30 \times (100 - 30)}{1 \times 1} = 8{,}400$$

If the required accuracy was reduced to 2.5% (27.5–32.5%) then N would become 1,344 and at 5% N would become 336.

The actual sampling must be carried out in such a way as to be fully representative. Where periodicity exists in the pattern of work at least one and preferably more full cycles must be included. For instance in sampling the work of the accounts department at least one month's activity needs to be sampled since accounting activities tend to follow a monthly cycle. Care must also be taken that the frequency of observation does not correspond with any natural cycles in the work. For example if a task takes 55 minutes with a further 5 minutes set up time then sampling once per hour will either not detect set up at all or show set up as the only activity.

SUMMARY

This chapter has considered some of the issues and techniques involved in the design of the production task and its allocation to human operator or machine. The basic criteria for task allocation have been considered, and the need to design tasks within the capabilities and comprehension of operators identified.

The current state of automation was described and the various categories of machine from simple numerical control through to fully fledged flexible manufacturing systems were considered. The relationship between the type of automation used and market requirements was briefly considered. In considering the design of human work, three approaches were identified. Ergonomics treats the human operator as a mechanical and sensory device and seeks to optimize the conditions for its efficient performance. The human relations approach directs attention towards the reasons why people work and seeks to influence the design of the task to maximize motivation. The shortcomings of this approach centred around the problems of identifying motivating factors were outlined. Method study is the most widely used and most pragmatic approach and seeks to design efficient and effective procedures by the careful analysis of current practice. The well established methodology of Select, Record, Examine, Develop, Install and Maintain was described, together with the process charting methods used.

The planning and control systems require a sound database linking demand, in units, to capacity, measured in available time. Work measurement provides these data, and the various methods adopted for measuring work were described. These are time study which measures the actual time taken by observation while rating the operator to allow for variations in rate of work, synthesis which uses an established time study database to establish the work content of new tasks and predetermined motion time systems which require that the task be broken down into very small standard elements whose work content can then be looked up in proprietary tables. Somewhat different from these approaches is that of activity sampling which seeks to determine the proportion of time spent on various activities using an instantaneous observation statistical sampling technique.

In Chapters 7–10 the function, requirements and operation of the operations planning and system will be considered.

CASE STUDY: Electronic Components Ltd. 1

Electronic Components Ltd. is a well established manufacturer of components for electrical and electronic assembly industries. It has a number of factories, each one specializing in the manufacture of a particular range of products. The factory in question manufactures low voltage resistors and potentiometers. This case concerns potentiometer assembly.

The product

All potentiometers are structurally similar. They consist of a central brass or steel spindle which rotates within an aluminium can. Rotation of the spindle moves an electrical contact over the surface of an electrically conductive strip of resin, thus varying the electrical resistance of the device. Figure 6.4 shows a drawing of the basic potentiometer. Products vary in their power rating, nominal resistance, tolerance and on whether the resistance variation is linear or logarithmic. The power rating influences physical size, otherwise the only variable is the electrical specification of the resin conductive strip.

The process

All the products follow the same process sequence. The sequence, together with material requirements and standard times is shown in Table 6.1.

Assembly takes place in a self-contained area of the factory, which is relatively quiet and well lit both with daylight through roof lights and windows in one wall and with artificial light when required. The plant is laid out as shown in Figure 6.5. There is no automation, all stations being operated by unskilled

Table 6.1 Assembly process

Operation	Materials	Standard time (seconds)
Fix conductive track		45.00
	Plastic moulding Conductive track 2 rivets 2 contacts	
Insert spindle		34.00
	Spindle Circlip	
Fit contact carrier		39.00
	Contact carrier Circlip	
Fit case		33.00
	Case	
Test		36.00
Label and Pack		32.00

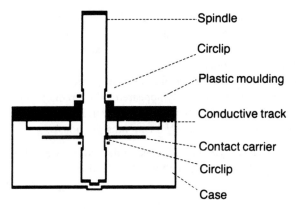

Figure 6.4 Potentiometer schematic

- Spindle
- Circlip
- Plastic moulding
- Conductive track
- Contact carrier
- Circlip
- Case

Figure 6.4 Potentiometer schematic

female labour. Part completed work is simply passed along the workbench from station to station.

Standard working hours are 8.30 am to 16.45 pm with two 15 minute tea breaks and a one hour lunch break.

The situation

Management had observed that both yield and productivity had been declining for some months. Figure 6.4 shows the figures for the past year.

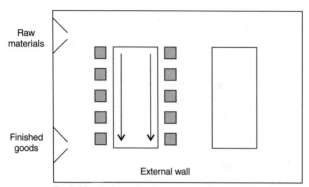

Total of four independent lines, each staffed by five operations

Figure 6.5 Original layout

Method study were called in to investigate the situation and reported the following:

1 The main cause of falling yields was loss or damage to components when being passed between stages. At certain stages the product was particularly vulnerable to damage to the moving contact or the track, and careless handling could lead to damage or even to components falling off.

2 Damaged components were slowing down the assembly process when noticed, but the general cause of lower productivity appeared to be a reduction in motivation. A time study confirmed that operators were working at a rate approximately 15% lower than the last time study 14 months previously.

It was concluded that both the reduced yield and reduced productivity were due to a reduction in motivation, though no cause for this was identified.

The solution

Following discussions between work study, management and unions, it was decided that lack of motivation was almost certainly due to the very slight opportunities for job satisfaction offered by the work. Since losses seemed to be almost exclusively associated with the transfer of part completed work between stations it was decided that a programme of job enrichment should both increase motivation and reduce interstage transfers. The outcome was the production of individual workstations designed to allow an operator to carry out the complete assembly process. The stations were carefully designed so that component storage bins, large enough to hold one batch of components, were arranged in the correct order around the operator, with the necessary assembly and testing equipment to hand. The revised layout is shown in Figure 6.7.

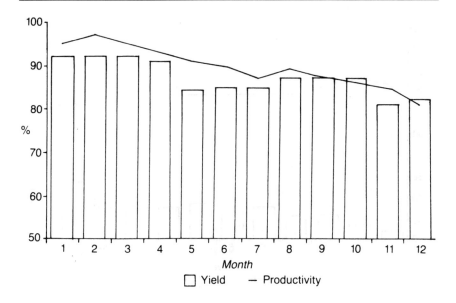

Figure 6.6   Yield and productivity – old method

The outcome

The equipment was installed over a weekend, and the operators given one week
of formal training on the new process. Management anticipated a gradual return
to previous output levels over a period of six weeks or so, followed by a further
increase in productivity at least to the levels prevalent before the recent decline.
The actual results are shown in Figure 6.8.

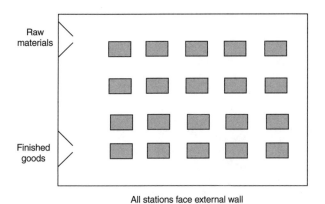

All stations face external wall

Figure 6.7   Revised layout

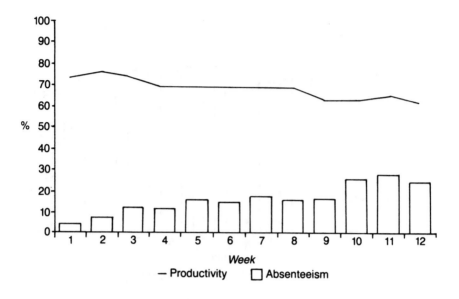

Figure 6.8   Productivity and absenteeism – new method

Questions

1 Identify the reasons for the failure of the scheme.
2 How could the company have avoided the situation?
3 What should be done now?

Chapter 7

Planning and control 1 – Capacity planning

The objective of the operations manager is to meet customer requirements as efficiently as possible. This means supplying the correct quantity of goods or service at the correct time with the maximum utilization of the resources available, i.e. balancing capacity with demand. The task is complicated by the fact that demand is frequently unpredictable and capacity is usually fairly inflexible.

The capacity planning process is usually divided into three stages: long-term, medium-term and short-term. While the time scales may vary from months to years for long-term and hours to weeks for short-term depending upon the industry, the principles governing them remain much the same.

Long-term capacity planning is concerned with the overall capacity of the organization and investment in facilities and has been covered in Chapter 5. Medium-term capacity planning is concerned with achieving the best overall balance of demand and capacity, while the short-term is usually concerned with what is actually going to happen in the next hour, day or week.

This chapter deals primarily with the medium-term and considers the nature of demand and the problems of demand forecasting. Alternative strategies for accommodating demand variation are considered, and as no planning system can operate without appropriate data, the planning system and its data requirements, and some of the methods of obtaining these data, are also looked at.

Most of these approaches assume that if demand exceeds available capacity either additional capacity will be made available or that the customer will wait. Where demand for a variety of products exceeds capacity and that excess demand is bound to be lost, the technique of linear programming can be used to calculate the best mix of demand to meet. This is described briefly later in the chapter.

DEMAND AND DEMAND FORECASTING

If a manufacturing company receives an order to supply 1,000 widgets in six months time, and the raw material supply and manufacturing lead time is less than six months in total, then the widgets could be manufactured ready for delivery in six months, and the required materials could be ordered so that they were available for use when required. In this case demand is known as 'dependent' – demand for finished products depends on orders, and demand for raw materials depends upon demand for finished products.

If demand for finished goods or services is unpredictable in that the required delivery lead time is less than the manufacturing lead time it is referred to as 'independent' and a forecasting method must be used to determine manufacturing output.

In manufacturing, demand for raw materials is always dependent since the planning process must start from the required output of finished product, but if the supply lead time is long compared with the process lead time (i.e. if it takes two weeks to make the product but six months to obtain the raw material) it must be treated as independent. However, such is the convenience of independent demand systems that the demand for raw materials is frequently treated as if it were independent even when it is not.

Dependent demand planning is driven by known advance orders, and independent demand planning is driven by demand forecasts. Demand forecasts can be subjective or objective, and the commoner methods are briefly described in the following. Those interested in taking the matter further should seek out specialist texts. It should be remembered that the only criterion for choosing a forecasting method is that it gives results that are sufficiently accurate while being cheaply, reliably and quickly available. There is no requirement that the success of the method should be explicable.

There are three broad classes of forecasting methods in use:

- **Time series** methods which seek to extend past quantitative data into the future.
- **Causal** methods which endeavour to construct mathematical models linking causes to effects.
- **Subjective** methods which depend upon opinion as much as quantitative data.

Time series

This is probably the area of forecasting with the greatest number of alternative techniques. All of them are attempts to distinguish between trends in the data and random variations or 'noise'. By definition random variations cannot be forecast so a good technique ignores it.

A difficulty which all techniques share is that of distinguishing between random variation and changes in trend. A single figure which is off the main line of the trend may just be noise, two consecutive figures may indicate a change. Techniques which are sensitive to change tend to be too sensitive to noise, while techniques which give a smooth forecast are usually slow to respond to a change in trend. The skill in choosing a forecasting method frequently lies in getting the sensitivity right.

The *moving average* is the simplest mathematical forecasting technique available. It balances smoothing and sensitivity by averaging the data over the immediate past and using this average as the forecast. Table 7.1 illustrates a 3 month and 6 month moving average on the same set of data.

Table 7.1   Moving average of demand

Month	Actual demand	Moving average 3 Month	6 Month
Jan	100		
Feb	103		
Mar	120	108	
Apr	112	112	
May	111	114	
Jun	109	112	109
Jul	132	117	114
Aug	133	125	119
Sep	126	130	120
Oct	144	134	126
Nov	135	135	130
Dec	139	139	135

The three month average is obtained by summing the previous three months' sales and dividing by three and the six month average is derived by summing the previous six months sales and dividing by six. Each month the oldest figure is dropped from the total and the newest added, continuously updating the forecast. At its simplest the latest moving average is the forecast for next period.

A potential disadvantage of the moving average is that it gives equal weight to the oldest and most recent figures in the average, and no weight at all to figures older than the time period of the average. The exponentially weighted moving average, or exponential smoothing, gradually reduces the contribution that a figure makes to the forecast as it gets older, so that the most recent information has the greatest effect. The formula for the exponentially weighted moving average is:

$$F_{t+1} = \alpha A_t + (1 - \alpha)F_t$$

where F_{t+1} is the forecast for period $t+1$
F_t is the forecast for period t
A_t is the actual figure for period t
and α is the exponential coefficient, $0 > \alpha < 1$.

The larger the value of α the more sensitive, and less smooth, the forecast. α is usually kept below 0.1 in practice. Table 7.2 shows the use of exponential smoothing on the same set of data used in Table 7.1.

Table 7.2 Exponential smoothing

| Month | Actual demand | Forecast | |
		$\alpha = 0.05$	$\alpha = 0.10$
Jan	100	100	100
Feb	103	100	100
Mar	120	101	102
Apr	112	102	103
May	111	102	104
Jun	109	102	105
Jul	132	104	107
Aug	133	105	110
Sep	126	106	111
Oct	144	108	115
Nov	135	110	117
Dec	139	111	119

These methods are of direct use in forecasting only if all variation is random. If there is a rising or falling trend, or any seasonality in the data these must be allowed for.

Demand often shows a pattern of variation which may be repeated from day to day (demand for electrical power, or public transport show clear peaks and troughs at the same times each day), week to week (a great deal of general consumer demand is concentrated on Fridays and Saturdays), or year to year (holidays, new cars, etc.). If any underlying trend can be separated from the seasonal effects then a forecast can be produced for any time period. The term *seasonal* is reserved for patterns which repeat on an annual basis, and the term *cyclical* is used for patterns which repeat over other time periods.

The extraction of trend and seasonality – called decomposition because the overall pattern is being decomposed into its component parts – requires data covering several cycles. One of several possible approaches is illustrated in Appendix 1.

Causal methods

Causal methods rely upon identifying some measurable factors which have a clear and consistent influence on demand, with a sufficiently large lag to allow a forecast to be produced. For example, interest rates are believed to have an influence on demand for consumer goods, and there is a substantial lag between the cause, a change in interest rate and any change in demand. Unfortunately the number of other influences involved in consumer demand make it virtually impossible to produce forecasts of sufficient accuracy to be useful.

Causal forecasting is usually based upon regression analysis but is little used in operations since it is rarely possible to produce a model of sufficient accuracy.

Subjective methods

When hard information is not available, the planner must fall back upon opinion. This sometimes amounts to a simple assumption that demand will be much the same as last year, or may be a more sophisticated attempt to gather and collate a variety of opinion. The opinion of the sales team may be sought or that of overseas agents, or even trade associations.

A structured method of obtaining and evaluating opinion which is sometimes used in low volume high value capital goods manufacture is scenario construction. A panel of 'experts' prepares a number of alternative scenarios, assesses the likely effect of each scenario on demand and evaluates the probability of each scenario arising. This is obviously not a precise forecasting technique but it is sometimes the best available.

DEMAND VARIATION

Demand variation takes two forms, variation in total demand and, in a multi-product environment, variation in demand between products. The latter, provided the total demand remains more or less constant, can be managed through the scheduling systems adopted. The former causes far more difficulty. Because of this attempts at demand smoothing are frequent. Global marketing helps to even out seasonal effects as does seeking out complementary products. The greetings card industry has been very successful in introducing cards for all occasions to offset the demand peak at Christmas.

The service sector, with its much greater demand variation, frequently adopts differential pricing in an attempt to smooth demand, for example the use of off peak fares. These attempts are rarely totally successful so the operations manager continues to be faced with the problem of satisfying variable demand. Two strategies are available, though usually a combination of the two is used.

Level capacity

Level capacity is certainly the most efficient of the two methods. The total capacity of the system is set at the average demand, perhaps with a small surplus as a contingency allowance, and a steady output is maintained. In effect, demand variation is ignored. This strategy will only work if customers are prepared to wait, or if stock is used to buffer operations from demand variation. Figure 7.1 illustrates the use of stock as a buffer in a seasonal market. Goods are manufactured for stock during the trough in demand and sold from stock during the peak.

This option is only available to manufacturing since service cannot be stocked. In addition it depends upon the product having a great enough shelf life – it is not possible to build up stocks of ice cream in the winter for sale in the summer. The advantages of this approach, where it is applicable, lie in the lower

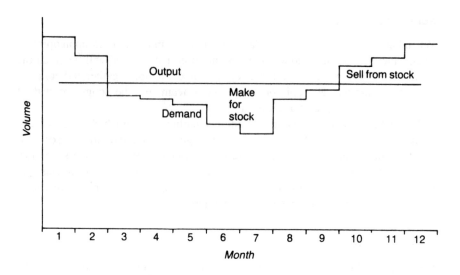

Figure 7.1   Use of stock with seasonal demand

costs associated with the efficient use of operations resources. The disadvantages are also associated with cost, the cost of promotion and discounting in the case of demand management and the cost of stockholding (see Chapter 8) where stock is used as a buffer. The disadvantages can outweigh the advantages hence the second approach is often used even when level capacity is feasible.

Chase demand

The exact opposite of level capacity, the chase demand strategy attempts to vary capacity in line with demand, thus maintaining a high utilization without the penalties of stockholding or demand management. To be effective this needs to be done quickly and without substantial cost penalties. It is only useful if costs are reduced as capacity is reduced. Capital capacity is difficult to vary in the short term, and a capital intensive operation is best viewed as having a fixed capacity. Varying the full time labour force can also be difficult. A hiring and firing policy carries substantial cost penalties in the form of redundancy payments and recruitment and training costs, while laying labour off is almost as expensive. Neither approach encourages good industrial relations.

The following methods are commonly adopted.

- **Overtime working**   By planning overall capacity on the basis of say 10 hours overtime per week on a basic 40 hour week, output can be varied by $+/-10$ hours per week ($+/-20\%$) without laying off or taking on additional labour. There is a cost premium associated with overtime working, but the chances are that a higher basic rate would be demanded if overtime was not available. Overtime also gives rise to better capital utilization since the facilities are used for 20% longer than would otherwise be the case. The Japanese policy of jobs for life depends on very substantial overtime working.

- **Flexible labour**   This is useful in the service sector where there is an appropriate balance between front office and back shop activities. The front office capacity can be increased at peak demand times by transferring the majority of the labour force to the front office, while at other times back shop tasks can be carried out.

- **Part time labour**   Overtime working gives limited flexibility and is best suited to modest seasonal variations in demand. In the service sector, substantial short-term variations in demand require a different solution and this is usually achieved by the use of part time labour. A supermarket may require three check-outs to be operating on a Monday morning, and twenty on a Friday afternoon. Since there is little useful back shop work that a check-out operator can undertake at off peak times, the best solution is to employ part time staff. Many service sector operations depend upon staff who work less than eighteen hours a week.

- **Casual labour**   Industries which have substantial seasonal demand variations, for example holiday resorts, depend upon seasonal casual labour to meet demand. Fortunately there appears to be a sufficient pool of labour willing to take on seasonal jobs.

- **Make or buy**   In times of peak demand in manufacturing operations, the option of buying in components that are normally made in house might be invoked. This obviously requires an available source of components of an appropriate quality. The bought in components will cost more than those made in house.

- **Subcontract**   The ultimate in flexibility since it involves both capital and labour. Civil engineering depends upon subcontracting for efficient operation, the main contractor mainly carrying out a coordinating role. Labour and plant are hired as necessary. This approach is successful because the industry has evolved in this way. It requires ready availability of subcontractors and plant hirers. A variation of this is found in the clothing industry with the use of outworkers. These are self-employed subcontractors who work from home, thus supplying premises and equipment. A clothing company may vary its production capacity very rapidly within the whole range of available outworkers with no cost penalties.

Mixed strategies

Very few organizations are successful in meeting demand variation with only one strategy. In manufacturing in particular the same organization may use overtime, stock, and demand management, and still fail to maximize utilization. Service operations will have idle capacity at off peak times and queues or appointment systems at peak times despite demand management and the use of part time labour.

The perfect match of capacity and demand is probably unattainable, and the task of the operations manager is to obtain a satisfactory balance most of the time.

In achieving the optimum balance any appropriate combination of the above strategies might be used.

THE PLANNING SYSTEM

Medium-term planning, often called aggregate planning, is concerned with ensuring that capacity is matched to demand on a time scale usually measured in weeks or months. Demand is usually expressed in terms of units shipped, or customers served, whereas capacity is concerned with machine, labour, and material availability. For successful planning both must be accurately measured in compatible units. In single product manufacturing there is no real problem, a sugar refiner can measure the capacity of the plant in terms of tonnes output per week, or in working hours available per week, knowing that the whole plant has been designed to produce sugar at a given rate.

When a factory is making a multiplicity of products the problem is more complex. Different products may occupy different processes for different lengths of time and there is no simple relationship between output and capacity. Despite this, many multi-product organizations express their aggregate plan in terms of total financial value and assume that the product mix will remain constant. As long as the product mix, and the process methods, do remain constant this is acceptable.

Where product mix is variable a more sophisticated approach is necessary to ensure that the plan is attainable.

The only common measure of capacity that can apply to all products and all processes is that of time.

An operator has a capacity of 40 hours per week, or 60 with maximum overtime. The capacity of a piece of plant will depend upon the work patterns adopted but may be 40 hours with single shift working, 60 hours with overtime, 80 with two shifts, etc. In order to produce an attainable aggregate plan data must be obtainable on the available capacity of each machine/operator, and on the required time for each operation on every product.

Too much detail could make the system unworkable. Aggregate planning overcomes this problem by taking fairly substantial time units, i.e. output on a monthly basis rather than on a daily basis, and by grouping products that make similar demands on the production facilities. Both time and products are aggregated.

To give a simple example, a particular model of car might have four engine variations, four trim variations and 25 different colour schemes. This gives a total of 400 different product combinations. From the point of view of assembly they are all identical, so demand for these 400 variants would be aggregated together.

The starting point for planning is the projected demand for individual products, per time period, up to the planning horizon. This is usually called the master production schedule. The planning system is required to map projected demand onto available capacity, highlighting problems of over- or under-capacity.

Management may then take appropriate action to adjust either the master production schedule, or capacity, and feed the revised figures back into the planning system. As forecast demand becomes actual orders these changes must also be fed into the system and further adjustments made as necessary. This gives a continuous rolling plan. The process is illustrated in Figure 7.2.

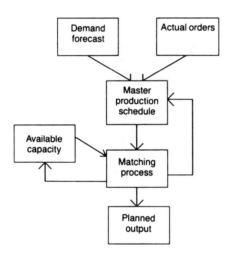

Figure 7.2   MPS planning process

Product data

In situations where there are standard products, the product data are gathered into the bill of materials file. This contains all the information necessary to allow a specific quantity of the product to be scheduled. It gives information on the raw materials and components used, and their quantities, the processes used, and the standard times required, the process sequence, and the process yield.

The bill of materials for a bottle of 100 aspirin tablets might look rather like that shown in Table 7.3. This gives all the information needed to allow an order

Table 7.3 Bill of materials data for aspirin manufacture (Batch of 100 bottles of 100 tablets)

Process stage	Plant	Standard time	Material	Quantity	Yield %
Weigh		3	Aspirin	5,000 gm	
			Starch	5,000 gm	
			Moulding		
			Agent	100 gm	
Mix	Cube blender	6			
Set press	Rotary press	10			
Press		20			98
Inspect		5			97
Pack	Autobottler	5	Bottle	100	
			Cotton wool	25 gm	
			Lid	100	
Label	Autolabeller	3	Label	100	

for bottles of 100 aspirin tablets to be converted into required machine and labour capacity, and into required raw material and component quantities. Provided the standard costs of operating the various machines is known, it also allows the standard cost of the product to be determined. Standard times are derived from work measurement data (see Chapter 6) while plant, process sequence and material requirements are part of the design specification of the product. Process yield must be obtained through observation. Obviously the accuracy of the plan depends upon the accuracy of the data. Changes in product specification, process methods, time standards and yields must be fed back into the bill of materials file.

A further complication can arise with low yield processes when the possibility of rework arises. If 35% of the aspirin tablets have to be ground up and pressed again the bill of materials must allow for this.

Capacity data

Capacity data need to be realistic. The use of standard times in the bill of materials should ensure that relaxation allowances and contingencies such as work not available and machine breakdown are taken into account, but other issues which influence labour availability include sickness, training courses, absenteeism, and holidays. A substantial change in process, or influx or new staff, will also necessitate an allowance for untrained operators. Machine availability will be determined by planned maintenance schedules.

A further complication at this stage arises from the fact that the plan is being superimposed upon an already working facility but this is usually more important in the shorter term scheduling than in aggregate planning which tends to ignore it.

Project/job planning

Unlike standard product operations, the one-off job is characterized by a high level of uncertainty. Some operations may be repeated often enough for standard times to be measured, but many others will be specific to the order or project in question, with only broad guidance available from past experience. Under these circumstances neither work measurement nor the conventional bill of materials is of much relevance, and the planning of projects is heavily dependent on subjective estimating. These issues are addressed in more detail in Chapter 11.

LINEAR PROGRAMMING

Linear programming is a widely applicable technique used for optimizing the use of resources when operating under resource constraints. As the name implies, the relationships between the factors treated must be linear. In operations management the most obvious application is in optimizing product mix when faced with capacity constraints. If these constraints cannot easily be overcome, and it is acceptable to leave some demand unsatisfied, then the object is to determine that feasible mix of output which will maximize some measure of satisfaction. This is frequently simply contribution to profit.

The technique is based upon setting up a number of simultaneous equations representing the constraints, and then solving these in a way which maximizes contribution. Where only two variables are involved (i.e. two products sharing the same resources) this can be done graphically. With more than two variables it is normal to use a purpose designed computer package. The technique is illustrated in Appendix 1.

SUMMARY

Achieving a balance between demand and capacity is essential for high utilization, and hence competitive, operations. In order to achieve this, accurate predictions of demand, and accurate and compatible measures of capacity are required. This chapter has considered the nature of demand, and in particular the distinction between dependent and independent demand, and the basic principles of demand forecasting using time series, causal and subjective methods.

Demand is characterized by variability while capacity is usually rather less flexible. The level capacity and chase demand strategies for matching demand and capacity have been described together with a number of ways of implementing them. The function of the medium-term planning system has been considered and the necessary database defined.

Occasionally there is no alternative but to leave some demand unsatisfied. In this case linear programming can make a useful contribution to identifying the mix of demand which should be satisfied.

Chapter 8 will consider the issues of material management in an independent demand situation in more detail, while Chapters 9, 10 and 11 will consider short-term planning and scheduling.

CASE STUDY: Electronic Components Ltd. II

Electronic Components Ltd. is a well established manufacturer of components for electrical and electronic assembly industries. It has a number of factories, each one specializing in the manufacture of a particular range of products. The factory in question manufactures non-linear resistors for use in surge diverters.

All the products are ceramic bodied discs, and vary in size from 20 cm diameter by 5 cm thick to 1 cm diameter by 1 mm thick. This case study concerns only the low power market, involving the smaller components.

The product

The low power product range consists of discs of 3 cm diameter and less. All have wires soldered onto their faces and are encapsulated in insulating resin.

Products are identified by a five digit product code. The first three digits identify the physical characteristics of the product (i.e. diameter, thickness, type of coating) and the last two identify its electrical characteristics. Since a given disc may make a variety of finished products, the discs and finished products are coded separately. Table 7.4 shows the range of discs and the finished products which are made from them.

The process

All the products follow the same basic process sequence: a mix of four raw materials is made and then pressed into discs on a mechanical tableting press. All mixes are composed of the same proportions of four raw materials:

SCG   silicon carbide grit
CA   finely ground clay
CC   calcined clay
PEG   polyethylene glycol

Five grades of SCG are used, the grade being determined by the electrical specification of the disc.

The mix has a shelf life of at least 4 weeks, but the discs tend to deteriorate if not fired within 24 hours of pressing. The resultant discs are fired in a kiln to a temperature of 1300°C. Following a visual inspection for mechanical defects, electrical contacts are flame sprayed onto each face of the disc, and the electrical characteristics of the disc are tested. If the disc is within specification wires are then soldered to the faces and the assembly is coated with an insulating paint. The assembly is colour coded to indicate its electrical specification, retested to confirm that it is still within tolerance, given a final visual inspection and packed for despatch.

Rejects at inspection face a variety of possible fates. Physically damaged or out of tolerance discs are always scrapped. Damaged or defective coatings can sometimes be reclaimed either by stripping off the original coating (PVC coated products) or by coating over the original defective coating (silicone coated products).

Discs which are out of specification electrically may be reclassified into an adjacent specification (i.e. a 401/01 may become a 401/02 and vice versa), or, if they are a low resistance reject, they may be reclaimed by heat treatment. This process is never 100% successful and usually results in further physical damage. High resistance rejects which cannot be reclassified are scrapped.

Final assemblies which are out of specification electrically can only be reclaimed into other electrical specifications. For example a high resistance 602/01 could become a 602/02 by recoating it. Assemblies coated in PVC can be recoated in either PVC or silicone after removing the original PVC, but assemblies coated in silicone can only be recoated in silicone since the silicone paint cannot be removed.

The plant

- **Mixing** A 15 kg mix is made using one of three z-blade dough mixers. A 5 kg mixer is available for the occasional small order. Quantities of less than 5 kg cannot be made.
- **Pressing** The company has one Matsubishu 12 stage rotary press, two Friedland single stage presses, and two Komada single stage presses. Disc type 401 can be produced on either the Matsubishu or Friedland presses, type 402 on the Friedland only and the others on the Komada only. The presses are all automatic, but setting and tool changing require the services of a skilled setter. Supervision during operation is left to a semi-skilled worker who is responsible for topping up the feed hopper with mix, ensuring that the mix is flowing smoothly, and checking the physical quality of the discs. One operator will usually mind two machines.
- **Firing** The discs are placed on top of larger components in a continuous tunnel kiln. The firing cycle is fixed at 6 hours, but the firing itself can be considered as effectively free.
- **Flame spraying** This is a semiautomatic process. Discs are fed automatically into jigs, an operator then loads the jig into the automatic flame spray booth where brass contacts are sprayed onto each face. The process consumes brass wire, propane and oxygen. The jigs are automatically unloaded but are then manually cleaned before reuse.

- **Electrical test**   401 discs are sorted on an automatic sorter of which there are two. Because they frequently jam they need supervision. All other discs are sorted manually.
- **Assemble and coat**   This is done automatically except for disc type 406. Tinned copper wire is cut, preformed and loaded into jigs, a disc is inserted between each pair of wires, the assembly is dipped in flux, then in solder, then in cleaning fluid, and finally, after a pause to allow the cleaning fluid to dry, into the appropriate coating. The jigs are then loaded by hand into a curing oven. After an initial cure (2 minutes for silicone, 4 for PVC) the assemblies are colour coded either by dipping in up to three different colours of paint, or by hand painting up to two spots on one face. This is followed by a further cure. All processing of rework is done manually.
- **Final test**   This is done manually for all products.

The market

The annual demand at present is:

Type	Quantity (K)
601	2
602	4,000
603	250
605	40
606	16
610	8
611	2.5
613	3
614	18

Five major customers account for the bulk of the demand with another 12 customers accounting for the remainder. Contracts have been negotiated with four customers as follows:

- **Customer A**   130K type 602 per month, and 12K type 603 per month with the option of a ±40% variation at 2 weeks' notice.
- **Customer B**   An average of 25K type 602 per month, actual requirements being called off on one month's notice.
- **Customer C**   An average of 20K type 603 per month, terms as Customer B.
- **Customer D**   An average of 15K type 602 and 18K type 603 per month, terms as Customer B.

Despite the contractual specifications, changes are often demanded at very short notice.

Other customers order as required, and the company quotes a 10 week delivery. Order size varies between 500 items and 25K items. There is no minimum order size, but there is a minimum order cost.

Questions

Set up a structure for the planning database for this product range.

Table 7.4 Electronic Components Ltd: low voltage product range

Disc Assembly	401/ 01	401/ 02	401/ 03	402/ 01	402/ 02	402/ 03	404/ 02	404/ 03	404/ 04	405/ 01	406/ 03
601/01	x										
602/01	x										
602/02		x									
602/03			x								
603/01	x										
603/02		x									
603/03			x								
605/01				x							
605/02					x						
605/03						x					
606/04					x						
606/11				x							
610/01							x				
610/03								x			
611/05									x		
613/01										x	
614/02											x

Chapter 8

Inventory control

In Chapter 7 it was shown that inventory can play a major role in enabling a manufacturing organization to operate effective capacity planning, through allowing it to absorb variation in demand. Also although service cannot be stocked, the goods which sometimes form part of the service transaction can be stocked, therefore inventory is often an essential element of any service transaction – for instance in retail distribution. There are many other sources of inventory, for example spares, stationery, consumables, which are common to all organizations. Inventory also plays a major role in the internal organization of the scheduling system adopted by the organization as will be shown in Chapter 9.

Inventory is central to the efficient and effective operation of most enterprises. Its high cost makes accurate planning and control essential.

In this chapter consideration will be given to the various categories of inventory and their purpose, the costs involved in obtaining, retaining and using inventory and the means of reconciling these costs. Finally some of the more common methods of managing inventory and the circumstances in which they are used will be considered.

INVENTORY TYPES

Raw materials

A general term which can be taken to include all bought in goods which become part of the finished product. In manufacturing, extensive work may be done to transform the raw material into a finished product, whereas in distribution little more than display and repackaging may take place. The principles governing management are the same. Raw material stocks are held for the following reasons:

- supply is unreliable;
- it is more cost effective to buy in periodically than operate from hand to mouth;
- extensive acceptance testing is required;

- security (many operations managers and buyers become very uncomfortable if stocks are not available).

Finished product

Finished product describes stocks ready for supply to the customer. The main reason for holding these is to decouple manufacturing from demand, so that an unpredictable, or predictably variable market can be supplied without varying capacity excessively. Other reasons include:

- **Cost effectiveness**   It may be better to make a large batch even when immediate demand is small.
- **Mistakes**   Goods over made, or made to the wrong specification, or made for cancelled orders are likely to end up as finished goods stock.

Work in progress

There is always going to be some work in progress stock since it will always take a finite time to convert the raw material into finished product. What is of concern is work in progress over and above this minimum due to:

- Delays in carrying out work, due to the scheduling rules applied, or long interstage transport (one of the first assembly operations carried out at Morgan Cars is to fit the wheels to the chassis since the vehicle travels so far between operations).
- Setting up intermediate stockholding points to help buffer bottlenecks, or to permit a more rapid response to demand for finished product (the use of cook chill, or pre-cooked frozen portions and the microwave oven allows the catering industry to stock its product much nearer the end stage and respond much more rapidly to demand).

Consumables

Consumables are materials used in the operation of the organization, but not forming part of the finished product, for instance, stationery, cleaning materials, lubricants, etc. These are normally treated in the same way as raw materials.

Spares

Spares for a firm's own products, held as a service to its customers, are best treated as finished goods stock. The only risk with this is that they may be stolen by production. Spares for a firm's own plant may be held on site or they may rely upon the supplier or his agent. These issues are considered further in Chapter 13.

Strategic stocks

Strategic stocks are held for other than strictly operations purposes. Stocks of a raw material may be built up because suspected industrial unrest at the suppliers, or political unrest in the supplying country, might disrupt supplies in the future, or to damage the competition. (An attempt was made a few years ago to influence the price of silver by building up large stocks. It failed.) No general rules can be given for this area and it is, strictly speaking, outside the operations manager's remit.

COSTS OF INVENTORY

There are three major sources of cost associated with carrying inventory, apart from the cost of the inventory itself. Given that the materials will be used, and would therefore be purchased regardless of the inventory policy, this cost is irrelevant.

Stockholding cost

Probably the most obvious cost is stockholding cost, which has three components:

- **The cost of the capital tied up in inventory**.   This obviously depends upon the cost of money at the time.
- **The cost of storage, including space, equipment, labour, services, etc.** This is usually expressed as a percentage of stock value, so that it is compatible with the cost of capital. It is likely to be somewhere between 5 and 10% of stock value per annum.
- **Stock losses**. These occur for various reasons, both legitimate and otherwise. Theft is always a problem (the food industry uses the term 'grazing rights'), but losses also occur through accidental damage, through stock exceeding its shelf life, and through stock becoming obsolete. The level of loss depends upon the nature of the goods, but it will never be zero.

The total cost is invariably expressed as a percentage of stock value, and is likely to lie between 15 and 30% per annum.

Cost of acquisition

There is a cost associated with acquiring goods quite independent of the cost of the goods themselves. When making for stock, there is the cost of setting up machines, and the cost of raising the paperwork to authorize the manufacture of the items. For example, in injection moulding plastic kitchenware, it may take a skilled setter an hour to set up the press, during which he might waste 5 kg of material in trial settings. After the run, the press must be stripped down and the tooling cleaned and inspected. The set up cost includes labour costs of the order of £30, material wastage of say £10, loss of production capacity of at least one hour, and the cost of producing the paperwork of say £25. The total set up cost is at least £65 regardless of whether 5 or 5,000 items are made.

Purchasing for stock incurs the administrative costs of raising the order, the goods receipt procedure, and the invoice processing routines. There may also be delivery costs, particularly if the order is small. It is more difficult to work this out accurately, but if all labour and overhead costs are taken into account it is unlikely to cost less than £50 to raise a single order.

Purchasing for stock on an *ad hoc* basis is of course not the only way of acquiring bought in goods. Long-term contracts may be arranged with suppliers with regular deliveries (with Just in Time supply these may be several times per shift), or a contract to buy a certain quantity in say a year, to be called off when required, may be entered into. These approaches complicate the costing of acquisition since they introduce two levels of cost namely, the cost of setting up the contract, which is likely to be rather more than the £50 quoted above, and the cost of processing each consignment, which will be somewhat less. However the average cost per consignment can still be determined.

Cost of stockout

Stock is held for various reasons, but, whatever the initial reason, systems using stock eventually come to depend upon it. If a shortage of raw materials occurs in manufacturing, production might be rescheduled to make something else, stopped altogether, or steps might be taken to arrange an emergency supply. All of these have determinable costs, but generalization is impossible. A car assembly line which runs out of body panels (or even paint) must stop, a canning plant which runs out of beans could perhaps transfer to tomatoes.

If there is a stockout of finished goods, or if the stockout of raw materials or consumables is severe enough to affect the customer (not unusual in restaurants where menu items are deleted as materials are used up) then the situation is far less clear cut. Custom may be lost immediately through cancelled orders or departing clients, and it may be lost in the longer term through customers becoming dissatisfied with the service. In essence goodwill is being lost and its financial value is incalculable.

COST RECONCILIATION

The simpler approaches to inventory management allow the input and output sides of the system to be separated out. It is assumed that on the supply side receipts are instantaneous and intermittent. Where they are progressive the maths is somewhat more complex, but such situations are less common and the errors introduced by the simple approach are very slight.

On the demand side, the assumption is that individual issues from stock are small relative to the total usage. In other words, if 1,000 widgets per annum are used, they are used in several lots of 50 or less rather than say three issues of

300. Where occasional large discrete issues are made, a Material Requirements Planning approach is more appropriate (see Chapter 9).

The economic order quantity

It is self-evident that, for a given level of usage, an organization could, at the extremes, purchase or make occasional large consignments, or frequent small consignments. The former would lead to a low acquisition cost and a high stockholding cost, while the latter would lead to a low stockholding cost but a high acquisition cost. The Economic Order Quantity (also known as the Economic Batch Quantity, or the Economic Lot Size and usually abbreviated to EOQ) seeks to balance these two costs in the optimum order size.

Mathematically we have:

Cost of stockholding = $E \times P \times S/200$
Where E = Order quantity
P = Unit price
S = Stockholding cost per annum (%)
($E \times P/2$ is the value of the average stockholding, assumed to be half the order quantity.)

Cost of acquisition = $A \times C/E$
Where A = Annual usage
C = Cost of ordering (or set up)
(A/E is the number of orders placed in a year)

Total cost = $E \times P \times S/200 + A \times C/E$

This is shown graphically in Figure 8.1.

The minimum total cost occurs with an order size which exactly balances the cost of stockholding with the cost of acquisition and is given by the equation:

EOQ = $\sqrt{(200 \times C \times A/P/S)}$

Figure 8.2 shows the effect of different order costs on the EOQ while Figure 8.3 shows the effect of different holding costs. Both are calculated on the basis of an annual usage of 1,000 units at a unit price of £20.

Limitations of the EOQ

The most obvious limitation of the EOQ is that it does not necessarily give round numbers – it is unreasonable to order 341.7 widgets, 350 is far more sensible. The demand figures should always be expressed in units of supply, not units of issue. Overstocking is often caused by someone forgetting that goods are bought by the gross but used by the dozen.

Order quantities should never exceed storage space availability, nor should they exceed what is affordable (it is not unknown for public sector bodies to buy stationery in small quantities, retail, towards the end of the financial year

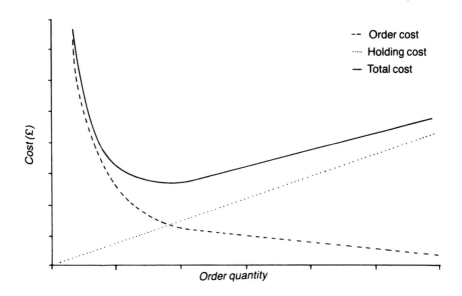

Figure 8.1   Economic order quantity

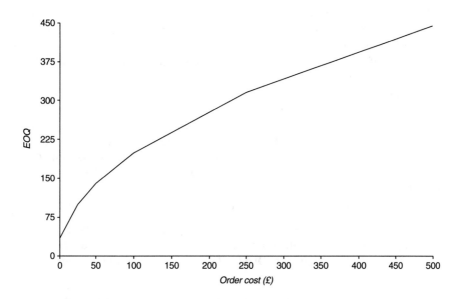

Figure 8.2   Variation of EOQ with order cost

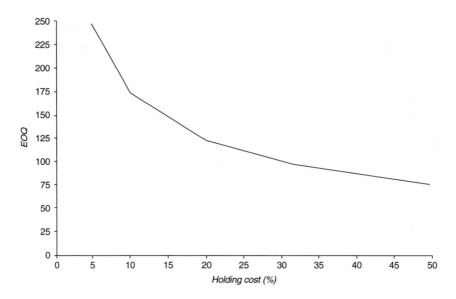

Figure 8.3 Variation of EOQ with holding cost

because the budget is exhausted), nor should an order be greater than the amount which will be used during any shelf life limitations. The EOQ is a starting point and it may be necessary to purchase less.

The EOQ does not take account of price breaks. Here the value of the discount must be balanced against the additional stockholding cost and more should be bought only if it is cheaper overall. All the above limitations still need to be taken into account.

The most serious limitation is the quality of the information used. The whole approach is based on the assumption that the true variable costs are known. In other words, if fewer orders are placed £50 per order will actually be saved. If smaller quantities are purchased warehousing costs will be saved (proportional to stock value) as well as capital costs. It is almost impossible to determine the true variable cost of ordering or stockholding, so at best moderately good estimates are being used.

These fundamental flaws are not as serious as they would appear at first sight.

The Economic Order Quantity is surprisingly insensitive to error, and provided the cost and demand figures are of the correct order of magnitude they will give an Order Quantity which is quite accurate enough.

The poor quality of the data does however suggest that more elaborate mathematical procedures, and there are many, are probably not worth considering, since their presumed improvement over the simple approach described is measured using this same poor quality cost data. Figure 8.4 shows the effect of error on the performance of the EOQ formula. If any combination of values is in error by the factor shown the increased cost of stockholding and ordering due to using the incorrect figure will be as indicated. For example, if the true cost of ordering is twice (or half) the value actually used, the acquisition and holding cost will increase by only 6%.

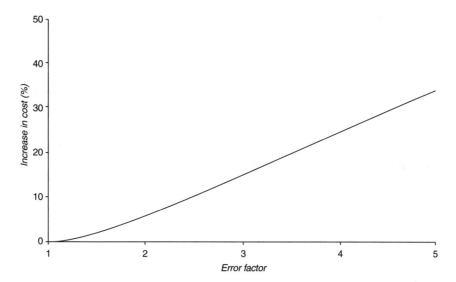

Figure 8.4   Sensitivity of the EOQ

The safety stock

Stockout may arise because replenishment is delayed, or because usage is higher than expected. If both usage and replenishment are absolutely predictable, stockout is not a matter of concern, all that is required is to order the EOQ at an appropriate time. The resultant stock movement pattern is shown in Figure 8.5.

In reality both usage and replenishment are usually unpredictable, and the situation shown in Figure 8.5 would result in a stockout in 50% of the replenishment cycles. To reduce the risk of a stockout a safety stock is introduced as shown in Figure 8.6.

The safety stock is intended to absorb the likely excess demand and lead time.

Lead time in stock control is the time between the requirement for replenishment arising and the new consignment being available for use. It includes delays in detecting the need for replenishment, the time required to

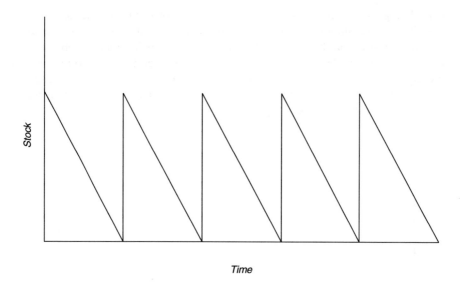

Figure 8.5 Stock movement, no variability

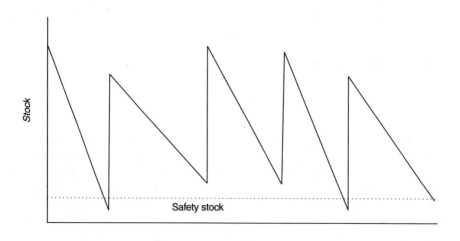

Figure 8.6 Stock movement, variable demand

process paperwork, the actual time required to obtain or produce the goods and the time in goods inwards and quality control.

No system can guarantee to have enough stock to cope with all eventualities so it is normal to specify a service level. This is the probability that stock will be available to meet demand, and it is the setting of the service level, usually by discussion and negotiation, that balances the imponderable costs of stockout with the additional cost of holding the safety stock.

The accurate calculation of safety stocks requires detailed knowledge of the distribution of demand and lead time. If both are normally distributed (see Appendix 1), the formula for safety stock is given by:

$$\text{Safety stock} = z\sqrt{(LD_v + D^2L_v)}$$

Where L = mean lead time
D = mean demand
L_v = variance of lead time
D_v = variance of demand
z is the standard normal deviate. A value of 1.6 will give a service level of 95% and a value of 2.3 will give 99%.

Lead time in particular rarely follows the normal distribution, and treatment of other distributions is beyond the scope of this book, but the formula does show that reduction in the size and variability of lead time will reduce safety stock. Since much of the lead time is often under the control of the purchaser, lead time analysis, with a view to reducing both of these, is always worth considering.

CONTROL SYSTEMS

Given variable demand and/or lead time, it is obvious that a fixed quantity of stock can be ordered at a variable time, or a variable quantity of stock at a fixed time, but quantity and time cannot both be fixed. The fixed quantity systems have the advantages of resulting in lower stocks, and being better able to cope with excessive demand changes. The fixed time systems have the advantages of easier management. Orders can be scheduled to suit the convenience of the organization (i.e. all processed at the same time, orders to a particular supplier consolidated, etc.).

Fixed quantity systems

Based upon the EOQ, these systems all generate orders for replenishment when stock falls below a predetermined level. This level, the reorder point or reorder level, gives them their name.

The reorder level is the mean demand during the mean lead time, plus the safety stock, or mathematically:

$$\text{ROL} = DL + z\sqrt{(LD_v + D^2L_v)}$$

A frequently used rule of thumb is ROL = $1.5DL$, i.e. the safety stock is half the mean lead time usage.

At the simplest, the two bin system requires only that the reorder level be indicated visually. Two bins, of equal size, are used for storage. When one becomes empty, an order for one binful is raised. This will (usually) arrive and be placed in the first bin before the second bin becomes empty. When the second bin becomes empty an order is again raised and so on. Provided proper stock rotation is practised and no issues are made from one bin before the other is empty, the system works well with little administrative effort.

Where this is inappropriate, the system depends upon the maintenance of a stock record showing issues, receipts and balance. Where this is a paper based system, there will be delays in checking stock against the reorder level (sometimes this is only done weekly) and this must be allowed for in the safety stock. Automatic systems where goods are issued by computer, or systems where goods are checked out by an on-line system (i.e. supermarket code-reading point of sale terminals) have the potential for raising orders immediately the stock falls below reorder level.

Given such an automatic system, the inclusion of a demand forecasting routine which updates the demand figures used in calculating the reorder level and order quantity gives a fully adaptive stock control system.

Fixed time systems

The simplest system, requiring almost no administration, is to estimate the requirement for the coming year, order it, and forget about it. This is obviously only suitable for items of little value and low bulk.

Other systems depend upon setting a maximum stock level. They are usually referred to as reorder cycle systems since, at the appointed time (the frequency of ordering can be based upon the EOQ), the current stock is subtracted from the maximum stock to give the amount to be ordered. This is shown in Figure 8.7.

The maximum stock is the mean demand during the cycle time plus the safety stock, but the safety stock must allow for the fact that an increase in demand at any time could give rise to a stockout (with the reorder level system only an increase in demand during the lead time can give rise to a stockout). The time at risk, for which the safety stock must offer protection is thus L (the lead time) + T (the cycle time) and the formula for the maximum stock level becomes:

$$\text{Max stock} = D(L + T) + z\sqrt{((L + T)D_v + D^2L_v)}$$

The penalty paid for the convenience of this approach is an increased safety stock. A further disadvantage lies in the response of the system to changes in demand. With the reorder level system, the average stock remains much the same whatever happens to demand, and while rising demand would increase the risk of a stockout, there would at least be an outstanding order to chase when stock was exhausted. With the reorder cycle system increase in demand could

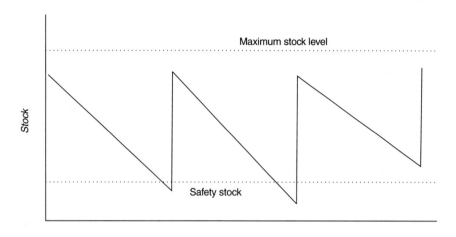

Figure 8.7   Reorder cycle system

result in a stockout before the re-order time had been reached, while a reduction in demand actually results in an increase in stock as shown in Figure 8.8.

Some authors have suggested that these problems can be overcome by introducing a conventional reorder level and a 'do not order unless below' level,

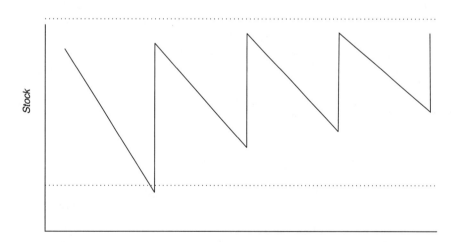

Figure 8.8   ROC system, reduced demand

but such complexity not only greatly increases the risk of error, but undermines the administrative convenience which is the method's greatest advantage.

CHOOSING A SYSTEM

Five systems have been identified. They are, in order of increasing complexity:

1 Annual demand;
2 Two bin;
3 Reorder cycle;
4 Reorder level;
5 Adaptive reorder level.

No system will satisfy all requirements, and many organizations use a combination of systems. The choice between a fixed quantity and fixed time approach depends upon the balance of risk of unforeseen demand change against the value of the convenience of being able to schedule replenishment. In addition, the increased safety stock penalty of the fixed time systems will become prohibitive as the value of stock usage increases and the variability of demand increases. In general, fixed time systems are best suited to stock items with fairly stable, or predictable demand patterns with a moderate to low value of usage.

Issues of risk and security must also be considered. In general optimizing stock for those items with the highest usage value will prove most cost effective, since they are incurring most of the costs, but items of lower value and usage may be critically important (i.e. spares for production equipment), and all items are at risk from theft. An important security device is a set of accurate stock records which will allow theft to be detected and act as an important deterrent. This suggests that items of high value or high importance should not be controlled using a two bin or annual usage system since these offer little security.

A useful way of classifying stock items is Pareto, or ABC analysis (sometimes called the 80/20 rule). All stock items are ranked in descending order of their usage value and then a cumulative frequency curve is plotted (see Figure 8.9, plotted from the data in Table 8.1).

Table 8.1   Usage of stock items, Company XYZ

Stock number	Unit price	Usage	Usage value	Cumulative % usage value
1053	12.47	5,287	65,911	35.71
1116	37.00	735	27,195	50.44
1215	14.72	1,713	25,217	64.10
1050	3.80	5,379	20,440	75.17
1092	6.07	1,591	9,650	80.40

1187	9.44	740	6,987	84.18
1232	12.10	560	6,776	87.86
1202	16.30	359	5,853	91.03
1178	0.47	6,975	3,290	92.81
1098	5.61	497	2,790	94.32
1049	13.55	197	2,668	95.77
1151	15.28	170	2,597	97.17
1145	18.75	107	2,006	98.26
1175	15.63	86	1,344	98.99
1110	10.93	75	820	99.43
1191	18.48	31	572	99.74
1090	18.03	19	342	99.93
1042	7.71	8	61	99.96
1101	1.67	32	53	99.99
1239	7.52	3	22	100.00

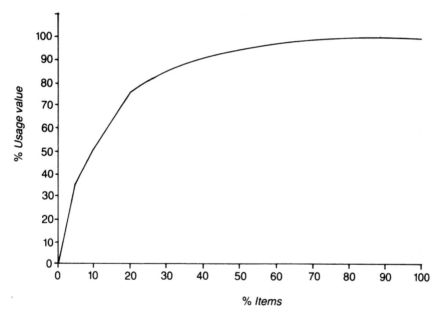

Figure 8.9   Pareto curve

It is often found that about 80% of the usage value is accounted for by only 20% of the items, and these might be controlled with an adaptive system, perhaps with continuous monitoring. The next 30% of items might account for 15% of value and could be controlled using a reorder cycle system, while the remaining 50% could be managed with a two bin or annual demand system. These three groups are often referred to as A, B and C hence the term ABC analysis. Pareto analysis allows us to identify where the effort of control is best spent, but it does not take into account the criticality or the security issues mentioned above. It should be noted that Pareto analysis does not always produce such clear cut results.

MONITORING PERFORMANCE

Two measures of performance are commonly used, reflecting the two areas of concern. Stockout is measured simply by looking at the proportion of demand actually satisfied compared with the specified service level. Stockholding cost is more usually measured by monitoring stock turn (annual usage divided by average stockholding), or coverage (stockholding times 12 months, or 52 weeks, divided by annual usage). What is acceptable varies with the industry. A stock turn of two may be acceptable in heavy engineering, while a stock turn of 20 may be considered poor in retail distribution. Individual stock items should be monitored, and those which are be considered slow moving can be investigated.

SUMMARY

In this chapter the purpose of inventory, the costs associated with carrying inventory, and some of the simpler systems for managing inventory to minimize cost have been considered, as have the criteria for selecting a particular inventory control system. Of course not all materials are necessarily carried in stock. This may be due to their perishability as in the case of some foodstuffs or a heart available for a heart transplant, or it may be due to the sheer volume required. In Chapter 9 some alternative approaches will be considered.

CASE STUDY: National Discount Appliances

NDA is a chain of discount warehouses supplying electrical and electronic household goods. It currently has 38 stores with an average turnover of £7,000,000 per store. From the outset NDA decided that it would compete on customer service as well as price and in order to maintain control over this, it was decided that all repairs would be done in house. At present the 12 largest stores each has a maintenance workshop attached. These are supplied with components from three regional warehouses, one serving the South East, one the West Country, Wales and the West Midlands, and one the East Midlands and the North. The 12 workshops fax requirements to their local warehouse, which then provides same day despatch with guaranteed next day delivery. (The transport company used is changed from time to time as rates and service vary.)

As a matter of policy, each warehouse is supposed to operate to a 95% service level on all stock items.

The system

Each warehouse is responsible for ordering its own stock, though invoicing and payment are handled by Head Office.

While there is some seasonal variation, a typical workshop will receive 17 items for repair each day. Each item will require an average of ten new components, including fasteners (clips, washers, self-tapping screws, etc.). When items arrive, they are allocated to a service engineer, who diagnoses the fault, and prepares a parts list. The clerk prepares a composite order each day which is faxed to the area warehouse by 2.30 pm. Occasionally additional orders are sent after this time.

There are 12,400 current stock items, and this is growing at a rate of 3% per year. A random sample of 50 items is shown in Table 8.2.

While fairly straightforward in theory, the system is showing signs of malfunction. Management feel that stock levels have been climbing rapidly recently, and that the company can no longer afford the investment in stock.

Workshops meanwhile, are increasingly complaining that they are not getting the service required. Unofficial stocks have been developing at workshops. This is partly because there is no provision for the return of unwanted components to the central warehouse, but also due to engineers ordering items in anticipation of future needs when shortages have occurred in the past. It has even been known for a workshop to ring round other workshops in the area seeking a component that the central warehouse cannot supply immediately. The use of local stock, or stock from other workshops does not, of course, prevent the order being placed with the central warehouse.

Table 8.2   National Discount Appliances, stock list

Stock number	Annual usage	Unit price (p)	Delivery time (weeks)	Usage value (£)
10913	79	213	1	168
13669	0	874	1	0
15828	159	62	1	99
16196	20	39	1	8
17547	223	2	8	4
18219	0	141	1	0
18840	13	61	1	8
19250	88	185	1	163
19301	0	658	1	0
23435	46	258	11	119
23605	0	4,525	2	0
23768	31	1,477	1	458
25612	26	111	4	29
25802	0	323	8	0
25823	10	413	8	41

Table 8.2   (Continued)

Stock number	Annual usage	Unit price (p)	Delivery time (weeks)	Usage value (£)
26429	151	1,494	1	2,256
28588	74	247	3	183
28649	34	187	4	64
29258	18	138	6	25
30172	185	65	1	120
32823	11	3,394	2	373
33205	19	343	1	65
33718	121	33	1	40
38887	1	286	1	3
39687	0	635	1	0
39843	0	683	1	0
41466	0	33	13	0
48105	105	499	1	524
50777	49	451	2	221
53145	56	18	10	10
54762	0	984	1	0
56745	2	25	1	1
59810	187	53	8	99
60633	0	95	1	0
61171	3	178	1	5
62685	27	464	14	125
64377	0	1,694	7	0
64832	1	18	15	0
65167	324	1	1	3
66597	0	913	1	0
68069	2	24	2	0
68164	53	139	1	74
68771	7	874	2	61
73025	159	199	1	316
73325	0	242	1	0
73753	61	4,507	13	2,749
74537	32	4	11	1
85522	19	366	1	70
98740	0	208	1	0
98875	121	59	4	71

Questions

1 Identify the changes in the organization of NDA's spares provision system that are feasible, and consider their advantages and disadvantages.
2 Given the data in Table 8.2, what stock control systems would you recommend?

Chapter 9

Planning and control 2 – Batch scheduling

In Chapter 7 the overall objectives and operation of the planning and control process were considered, while Chapter 8 addressed the contribution of inventory. Aggregate planning does not, however, address the issue of how when and by whom the work is actually going to be done.

For planning to be useful, i.e. implementable, it must lead to specific statements of when, and by whom, particular operations should be carried out.

This process of planning is usually known as scheduling. The associated control process must ensure that the planned activities are actually carried out correctly, and that any deviation from plan is fed back as quickly as possible so that corrective action can be taken. These issues will be addressed in the next three chapters.

There are three distinct approaches to the production of a schedule. The first, which will be considered in more detail in this chapter, is based upon the fairly logical process of scheduling the first operation and using the completion time of that to determine the start of the second operation and so on. Scheduling is done in process sequence. This is sometimes known as push scheduling since orders are pushed through the system from the first stage. It tends to stress high utilization as the dominant aim in producing a schedule.

Financial and competitive pressures have recently led to a reconsideration of the overall aims and constraints of the operations system. This has led to the development of scheduling approaches driven to a much greater degree by market demand, with a stress on output rather than utilization. These approaches, sometimes known as pull scheduling since the shipment of finished goods actually pulls demand through the operations system, are considered in Chapter 10.

Project operations, which are characterized by the need to co-ordinate a whole range of activities under conditions of high uncertainty, present their own particular scheduling problems and a distinct set of techniques has been developed to solve these. Project scheduling is considered in Chapter 11.

This chapter considers the characteristics of batch, or sequential, scheduling and introduces the Gantt chart. Some approaches to simplifying the enormous complexity of typical batch scheduling are also considered.

Batch scheduling frequently treats demand for raw material and components as independent since, although the demand for individual products is variable, the demand for common components may be fairly smooth. Where this is not the case Material Requirements Planning (MRP) and Manufacturing Resources Planning (MRP II), which treat demand for components and raw materials as dependent, may be used. MRP and MRP II are described later in this chapter, together with the approach sometimes known as Optimized Production Technology (OPT).

SEQUENTIAL SCHEDULING

The underlying assumption behind sequential scheduling is that materials for a particular product, or customers undergoing a particular service, always follow the same sequence of operations, or process route. This is embodied in the bill of materials which also specifies the time and materials required for each operation. The process is consistent and reproducible. It is also assumed that the process stages are discrete, that an operation cannot commence until the previous operation has been completed, but there is no requirement for the next operation to commence immediately. Delays between stages are permitted. In batch scheduling it is usually assumed that a batch will move as a single unit and will not progress onto the next stage until the whole batch is completed at the current stage. Exceptions to this might arise if two operations are so closely coupled that they can be considered as a single stage. The following example illustrates the process of preparing a simple batch schedule.

A plastics moulding company producing kitchenware has a four stage process. The requisite materials are mixed, then injection moulded. The moulded articles are then trimmed and inspected and finally packed. Batches are based upon the actual product and its colour. The batch size is determined by the cost of setting up the injection moulding press.

Consider three orders as follows:

A   200 Yellow 250mm cutlery trays
B   150 Red 300mm cutlery trays
C   250 Red dish drainers

with the following work contents in standard minutes:

	A	B	C
Mix	10	13	13
Mould	28	33	30
Trim	17	14	21
Pack	8	7	10

The Gantt chart provides a convenient and simple means of developing, and displaying a schedule for these tasks. It consists of a horizontal time scale, with a row to represent each required resource. If the row is blank, the resource is assumed to be available. Assuming that no other work is in progress, the starting point for producing a schedule for these orders is the chart shown in Figure 9.1.

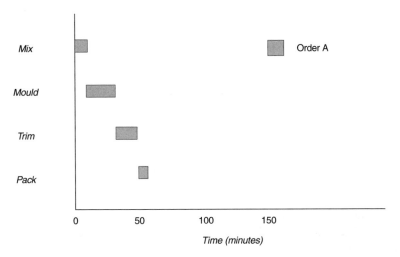

Figure 9.1   Gantt chart, start

If order A is scheduled to start first, then the requisite time is blocked off in the mixing row. Once mixing is completed then, and not before, moulding can commence and so on. Orders B and C can then be scheduled to follow on from A. The completed schedule is shown in Figure 9.2.

This is a feasible schedule, but not necessarily the best schedule: 'Best' is frequently defined as that schedule leading to the highest utilization of resources. Alternatively the schedule leading to the earliest completion of all batches might be considered best, but high utilization and early completion are usually compatible.

Assuming that these three batches go through each process stage in the same sequence then there are 3! (= 6) possible schedules. The only procedure guaranteed to find the best schedule is trial and error.

In general the number of possible schedules is given by $(N!)^M$ where N is the number of batches and M is the number of process stages. This allows for the possibility that not every product follows the same process sequence.

The quite modest problem of scheduling 20 batches in a 10 stage process gives rise to 7.27×10^{183} possible schedules. Even if the sequence is assumed to remain constant there are 2.4×10^{18} schedules.

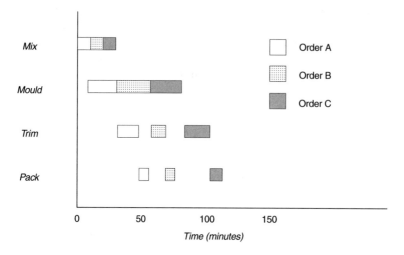

Figure 9.2   Gantt chart, completed

Selecting the best schedule by trial and error under these circumstances is impossible even with powerful computer assistance, so the usual aim is to produce a feasible solution quickly, and then if time permits to look for obvious improvement potential.

There are a number of variants on the simple Gantt chart. The magnetic planning board, where strips of magnetized material stick to a steel board, allows easy movement of activities to investigate alternative schedules. Slotted wallboards have a slot for each resource and cards are inserted into the slots to indicate when that resource is involved with a particular batch. Graphic computer displays can be used in the planning process. Access to alternative displays makes the planning process more convenient, but does not address the basic problem of excessive complexity.

The Gantt chart also allows progress to be monitored. A vertical line is used to indicate the current time. If activities are removed from the chart as they are completed then anything to the left of the vertical line is overdue.

PRACTICAL BATCH SCHEDULING

With the number of alternatives available in batch scheduling, even simple trial and error becomes a daunting task, and assumptions are usually made which reduce variety while leading to more, rather than less, desirable schedules.

Work content scheduling

Where there is a wide variety in the work content of the batches to be scheduled, those batches with the highest work content are scheduled first. This is likely to

leave a schedule with substantial gaps into which the batches with low work content can be fitted.

Priority based scheduling

A simple first come first served schedule has the advantage of being easy to construct and is seen to be 'fair'. It will not be efficient, and it ignores commercially significant issues such as the customer delivery requirements, the profitability of the order, and the importance of the customer. If priorities are pre-assigned, usually by sales, then high priority batches can be scheduled first. Anything more complex than two, or at most three, levels of priority becomes unworkable.

There are several disadvantages with this approach. It does not lead to efficient utilization, since it is driven solely by the need for early completion of high priority orders. It is often difficult to get complete agreement on priorities. Low priority orders may be pushed back to make room for more recent high priority work. This may lead to a situation where some work is never actually completed. Alternatively if long waiting times lead to an increase in priority to overcome this, a situation may be reached where all work is of high priority. (The author has witnessed a batch based factory where 85% of scheduled batches were first priority, 15% second and none third.)

Bottleneck scheduling

Where the capacity of consecutive stages is unbalanced, then the aim must be to maximize utilization of those processes where demand most closely approaches capacity, i.e. the bottlenecks. Time lost at a bottleneck is lost forever, whereas time lost at an under-utilized stage is probably of little significance. Producing a schedule which only considers the bottlenecks is rather easier than producing a schedule which considers every process stage, and more time can be devoted to trying to optimize the schedule. It is assumed that the presence of surplus capacity at other process stages will ensure that they can meet the requirements of the schedule.

It should be noted that while unbalanced capacity may well make scheduling easier, it would be more cost effective in the long run to seek to balance the production facility.

Separation of scheduling and loading

From the scheduler's point of view it is not always necessary to specify the precise time, and the precise equipment, which will be used to carry out a task. In the example of the plastic moulding plant, there may be several mixing machines and presses which could be used, and there will be several process operators who could carry out the tasks. All that is of interest to the scheduler is the overall capacity within a given time period. If a weekly time unit is used for planning, then with two mixers and three presses, the total capacity on mixing would be 80 hours, and on pressing 120 hours. Batches with a total work content of 80 hours can be scheduled in any one week, but provided these batches are not scheduled for pressing until the following week the sequence in which they are done is of no interest to the scheduler. The task of scheduling is now a simple broad brush approach, which can be carried out quickly and efficiently.

The task of loading, the actual allocation of individual batches to individual machines/operators at specific times is left to the first line supervision. This approach is frequently used, but has a number of disadvantages. The most important is the cost associated with stockholding. Since the minimum throughput time is one week per process stage, batches such as those illustrated above would be in progress for four weeks even though the total work content is only an hour or so. Large quantities of work in progress are generated with resultant investment in space and in the stock itself. Other problems follow in the form of loss, damage and general confusion resulting from the large quantities of part finished work. The long throughput time also leads to poor service in terms of quoted delivery times. Sales rarely abides by the constraints imposed by this type of schedule, so it is frequently necessary to accelerate batches. This leads to the task of progress chasing. Progress chasers seek out batches which are to be accelerated, persuade first line supervision to complete them early then move them onto the next stage ahead of schedule. This disrupts the schedule for everything else and tends to lead to the need for even more progress chasing.

Algorithm based scheduling

There is a simple procedure for arriving at the best schedule where only two process stages are involved. Unfortunately this situation is very rare. Johnson's algorithm is easier to illustrate than explain. Table 9.1 shows a set of batches to be scheduled, with their work contents. The schedule in this case is simply the

Table 9.1   Work content for ten batches

Batch	Stage A	Stage B
1	20	13
2	23	22
3	11	18
4	23	13
5	23	11
6	18	15
7	21	17
8	14	23
9	12	28
10	16	17

sequence in which they are to be carried out, and the best schedule is assumed to be the one which leads to the earliest completion of all tasks since this also leads to the lowest idle time.

First the tasks are ranked in ascending order of shortest operation time, regardless of whether this is the first or second operation. This gives the following result.

Table 9.2   Ten batches ordered by shortest operation time

Batch	Stage A	Stage B
3	11	18
5	23	11
9	12	28
1	20	13
4	23	13
8	14	23
6	18	15
10	16	17
7	21	17
2	23	22

A sequence is now constructed, by working down this list assigning each batch in turn to a position in the sequence. If the first operation time is the shorter the batch is assigned to the earliest available position while if the last operation time is shorter it is assigned to the latest available position, i.e. since the stage A time for batch 3 is shorter than the stage B time it is assigned to the first position in the sequence while batch 5 is assigned to the last position since its stage B time is the shorter. The completed sequence is:

Optimal schedule of ten batches

Sequence	1	2	3	4	5	6	7	8	9	10
Batch	3	9	8	10	2	7	6	4	1	5

A variation on Johnson's algorithm treats multi-stage processes as if they were two stage processes and has been found to produce good, if not optimal, schedules. A number of artificial two stage problems are created, and Johnson's rule is applied to each. The total elapsed times of the resulting schedules are then calculated, and the best is chosen. The artificial problems are created by adding adjacent stage times, for example in a six stage process, the following schedules would be determined;

Stage 1 and stage 6
Stage 1 + stage 2 and stage 5 + stage 6
Stage 1 + stage 2 + stage 3 and stage 4 + stage 5 + stage 6

This approach satisfies the requirement of producing a good schedule reasonably efficiently. In this six stage problem, only three schedules out of a possible 720 are considered.

MATERIAL REQUIREMENTS PLANNING

Where raw material and component lead times are short relative to the total planning horizon, it is possible to arrange the purchase of materials so that the quantity required for a particular batch arrives when required. This would appear to have considerable merit in reducing stockholding costs and space requirements, though possibly at the expense of increasing procurement costs, compared with a stock based system using the economic order quantity.

Material Requirements Planning, usually simply called MRP, is intended to ensure that this happens. In effect scheduling is extended to embrace the procurement function.

For MRP to function a number of additions must be made to the data in the bill of materials database. At the very least these are the individual process lead times, and the supplier delivery lead times. It is customary to produce a tree structure for each product, and to identify subassemblies and components by level within the tree, level 0 being the finished product, level 1 being final stage assemblies and so on. Table 9.3 shows part of a (highly simplified) structure diagram for a portable radio. Only the tuner circuit board is shown to level 3.

Each item at each level requires a lead time which will be the supplier lead time for bought in items and the standard manufacturing lead time for that level for other items.

Table 9.3 Structure diagram for portable radio

Level				Description
0				Radio
	1			Case back
		2		Front moulding
		2		Scale
	1			Case back
		2		Back moulding
		2		Handle
	1			Tuner assembly
		2		Aerial
		2		Switches (3)
		2		Tuner circuit board
			3	Tuner PCB
			3	Tuner components
	1			Loudspeaker
	1			Amplifier assembly
	1			Power supply

At its simplest an MRP procedure will take the master production schedule, which is in effect the level 0 demand and process this against the bill of materials to produce a purchase order schedule and the input demand data for the aggregate planning process. It does not concern itself with scheduling, and effectively assumes infinite capacity. Even this is a complex task when applied to a real situation with perhaps 100 products and ten or more levels. MRP is always carried out using a computer, usually with one of several proprietary packages.

The assumption that stock can be reduced to zero is rarely justified for the following reasons:

- Orders are cancelled and demand patterns change and stock is affected.
- Processes and suppliers may not be reliable enough, and safety stocks are necessary to allow for this.
- The lead time accepted by customers is rarely enough to allow all the demand to be made to order, therefore the master production schedule is based upon forecast rather than actual demand. Stocks of finished goods must consequently be held.

As a result, all MRP packages have provision for holding stock records of all components at all levels. The required quantities of sub-assemblies and components are adjusted to take account of the available stock and minimum stock levels. Where different finished products share common sub-assemblies or components, it is necessary to consolidate output requirements to avoid the absurdity of sending several small orders to the same supplier on consecutive days, or setting up manufacturing plant for several small batches when one large batch would be more efficient. This further complicates the MRP program.

MRP is complex, and a full MRP run may involve several hours of expensive computer time. MRP runs are not done frequently and some packages save time by allowing net changes to be processed rather than the full master production schedule, though a full run is required periodically to correct cumulative errors.

Since, at least in theory, MRP is designed to reduce stock levels to a minimum, its successful operation is critically dependent on accurate and complete data. The bill of materials data must be up to date, and the stock data must be accurate. The transition from simple batch based scheduling, with independent demand raw material stock control, large amounts of work in progress, progress chasing and a high degree of pragmatism, to the discipline of MRP can be traumatic. Successful transfer depends as much upon thorough training of both process operators and management as upon appropriate computer facilities.

MANUFACTURING RESOURCES PLANNING

The greatest drawback of MRP is its lack of reference to capacity. If the master production schedule is well matched to available capacity this may not matter, but a frequent result of an MRP run is an aggregate plan which does not match capacity. If capacity cannot be adjusted then the master production schedule must be changed and a further expensive and time consuming MRP run carried out. Manufacturing Resources Planning (MRP II) overcomes this problem by introducing a rough cut capacity planning stage before the full MRP stage. The overall sequence is shown in Figure 9.3.

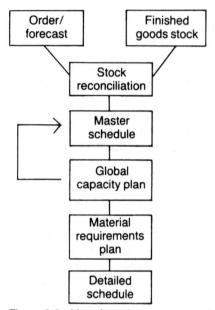

Figure 9.3 Manufacturing resources planning

This has the effect of ensuring that the output from the MRP process is usually feasible. MRP II usually produces a detailed capacity plan as well as the material requirements, and thus effectively includes the aggregate planning and scheduling stages.

The American Production and Inventory Control Society defines MRP II as:

> a method for the effective planning of all resources of manufacturing company. Ideally, it addresses operational planning in units, financial planning in dollars, and has simulation capability to answer 'what if' questions. It is made up of a variety of functions, each linked together: business planning, capacity requirements planning, master production scheduling, material requirements planning, and the execution of support systems for capacity and material. Output from these systems would be integrated with financial reports such as the business plan, purchase commitment report, shipping budget, inventory projections, etc.

It is doubtful if any implementation of MRP II actually achieves all of this, but there is no doubt that, while even more complex and expensive than MRP, MRP II is more efficient and does give more comprehensive capacity planning and scheduling. The demand for accurate data is even greater than for MRP and MRP II is most suitable in situations where continuous on-line collection ensures up to date and accurate data.

SYSTEM OPERATION

However sophisticated the planning system, it will not result in useful production unless the plans are communicated effectively to the shop floor, while control demands that accurate feedback on progress is received from the shop floor. A simple manual system will require a batch or job control sheet which identifies the batch, the product and possibly the customer order if the batch is not being made for stock. It will also list the process stages in sequence with planned quantities and scheduled dates. On completion of a stage, the time and the actual quantity produced are recorded and the batch, with its documentation, is sent to the interstage buffer store before the next stage. This document identifies the batch and its schedule and acts as an authority to carry out the work specified.

The batch control sheet does not provide feedback, so it is accompanied by a set of job cards, one for each process stage, together with cards that requisition materials and components from stores. The cards contain the same basic information as the batch control sheet for that process stage, but provide space for the operator to report quantities and times. These cards are completed by the operator and returned to production control when the batch proceeds to the next stage, thus providing feedback on progress.

Where a planning board is used this can then be updated. The cards may be forwarded to accounts for costing purposes and to payroll if some form of performance related payment system is in operation.

There are, of course, difficulties with shop floor data collection. Cards are wrongly completed, completed out of sequence or simply lost. These errors can be reduced by automating the data collection system, and several commercial systems based upon bar codes and optical scanners are available. Each batch, stage, and operator has a unique bar code so that when a batch arrives, and leaves, the fixed data can be entered on the workstation or section terminal. The operator keys in the variable data, usually only quantities, on a keyboard. While substantially more expensive, such systems do give greater accuracy and more rapid feedback.

OPTIMIZED PRODUCTION TECHNOLOGY

Traditional batch scheduling tends to be based upon maximizing utilization. Maximum utilization is assumed to mean minimum cost, and therefore, through the use of fixed lead time scheduling, and the Economic Batch Quantity, stock is effectively used to ensure that facilities need never be idle.

Optimized production technology (OPT) is a proprietary scheduling system, based upon the principle that maximizing throughput, and hence revenue, is the correct way to maximize profit. The traditional approach of maximizing utilization, while reducing unit costs, does not necessarily lead to revenue. OPT is essentially a development of the long established principle of scheduling bottlenecks described above, however the philosophy behind it goes rather further in addressing flow and balance rather than utilization, and its implementation requires substantial revision to management attitudes and to control systems. For example traditional costing systems, which recover the total costs of a process against units output from that process, encourage manufacture for utilization since this appears to reduce unit costs. In an OPT system, this is unacceptable.

A further effect of this approach is to change the derivation of batch sizes. A traditional approach considers the cost of all lost time during set ups, or more commonly the lost time at the longest set up in the process. OPT considers that time can only be lost at bottlenecks since there is surplus capacity at other stages, so batch sizes are based upon bottleneck set up costs. Since optimal batch sizes at bottlenecks do not necessarily lend themselves to efficient processing elsewhere in the process, the movement of work is often governed by transfer batches whose size, dictated by demand and scheduling constraints, is often smaller. In effect batch identity no longer holds throughout the process and stocks are built up after bottlenecks.

In essence OPT is a comprehensive computer based scheduling and loading system which concentrates upon identified bottlenecks. At its heart is an algorithm developed by Eliyahu Goldratt which approaches optimality in loading bottlenecks. The surrounding software manages the master production schedule, stocks and procurement in much the same way as MRP II.

SUMMARY

In this chapter the basic operation of batch scheduling systems has been considered. The considerable complexity of the batch scheduling problem has been described. The solutions to this problem include separation of scheduling and loading to reduce the number of sequence alternatives considered, scheduling large work content jobs first, using priority based scheduling, and using Johnson's algorithm. None of these gives an optimal solution, and none is universally applicable.

Batch scheduling frequently assumes independent demand of materials since this leads to very simple systems. Where this is inappropriate MRP can be used to schedule orders for bought in components and materials to correspond with the production schedule. While this theoretically leads to the elimination of stock, in practice stock is usually required, but must be monitored and controlled with much greater accuracy. The drawbacks of MRP are those of the cost of computer facilities, the need for a high level of accuracy, and the problems that can arise because the MRP is constructed from the master production schedule before the aggregate plan is matched to capacity.

MRP II overcomes the problem of MRP not considering capacity by introducing a rough cut capacity planning stage before the MRP stage, but at the expense of even more sophisticated computer facilities and even more accurate data requirements.

OPT rejects the goal of utilization implicit in batch scheduling and aims for high output. It achieves this by identifying, and optimizing, the scheduling of bottlenecks in the process, but is otherwise a similar high cost high technology solution to the problem of efficient scheduling.

The simpler systems are best suited to environments which do not have a history of high technology and accurate reporting. Before MRP, MRP II or OPT can be introduced a discipline of accurate reporting, particularly for stock, must be developed.

Given this, MRP is suitable for an organization where the master production schedule is fairly well matched to capacity, and MRP II is appropriate where this is not the case. OPT would be a valid alternative to MRP II where bottlenecks exist.

This chapter has shown that batch scheduling is complex and has described a number of high technology approaches to its management. In the next chapter, the rather simpler and more pragmatic approach of Just in Time will be considered.

CASE STUDY: Electronic Components Ltd. III

Using the information provided in the description of this case in Chapter 7, determine the relative advantages and disadvantages of conventional batch scheduling and MRP.

Chapter 10

Planning and control 3 – JIT

In Chapter 9 a long established approach to planning and scheduling was considered. This is based upon converting demand into appropriate discrete units, batches or orders, and then assigning the work to available capacity in sequence starting with the first stage. The problems which arise are traditionally solved by using stock. This may be in the form of raw material stock, finished goods stock, and interstage buffer stocks. The practice of block scheduling, so that each process stage takes a week or a month or whatever time unit is considered appropriate generates large work in progress stocks. MRP, intended to substantially reduce stocks, rarely does so in practice, while OPT depends upon buffering bottlenecks through stock. The driving force behind these approaches is the desire to maintain high utilization and thus low unit costs, but the effect is often to drive up the costs associated with stockholding to the point where unit costs are even higher. In addition the lack of responsiveness brought on by the inertia of the system can adversely affect competitive advantage – an organization with three months' raw material stock, three months' finished goods stock, and a twelve week throughput time, requires nine months to respond to market changes. Until the 1950s demand largely exceeded supply, and stockholding was relatively inexpensive, however, since then we have seen the development of global competition with ever more capacity and an ever more discerning market. In addition the true cost of stockholding has become increasingly apparent.

The need for greater responsiveness, and the ever increasing pressure on price generated by the change from under- to over-capacity, can be seen as the driving force behind the development of MRP and OPT; an example of the 'Scientific Management' school depending upon technology for the solution of problems. In Japan the response was rather different. Post war Japanese manufacturing could afford neither the stock nor the technology. The result was a manifestation of pure pragmatism which is commonly called Just in Time (JIT), but is heavily intertwined with those other manifestations of Japanese pragmatism, kaizen and Total Quality.

In this chapter the alternative definitions of JIT will first be considered, followed by a discussion of its function and implementation. The chapter will then go on to consider developments in kaizen and 'delayering', before considering the benefits and disadvantages of the approach.

JUST IN TIME

There is some confusion over whether Just in Time (JIT) is a material supply system, a scheduling system, or an operations philosophy. Three alternative definitions can be given:

1 Delivery of materials/components to the point of use precisely when needed.
2 A technique for improving productivity and reducing waste.
3 An operations philosophy based upon the principle of continuous improvement.

Definition 1 is often seen as applying only to bought in materials and components and is sometimes translated as 'Forcing your suppliers to hold your stock'. Since the stock still exists, there is little or no advantage to anyone from this interpretation. If applied throughout the process, however, it becomes indistinguishable from the third definition.

Definition 2 very much reflects the Western management approach of implementing solutions to problems. JIT is to be implemented in much the same way as MRP II, and if it doesn't work, go on to the next panacea. It is certainly possible to implement some elements of JIT in this way, but the long term benefits will certainly be missed.

Definition 3 is the one which, at least potentially, confers the greatest benefit, although it also makes the greatest demands upon both management and labour. It is the one which will be assumed throughout this chapter.

The approach originated in the Japanese motor industry after World War II, and was in some ways accidental. The industry modelled itself upon Detroit, then the home of the most successful motor manufacturers, but found that it could not afford the required investment in inventory. This simple failure of capital led to the perception of inventory as waste, and a drive towards waste free manufacture. The aim of JIT can be described simply as:

Instant manufacture (or service) with zero waste.

This may well be unattainable, but the underlying philosophy is one of continuous development and improvement. Waste can always be reduced further, as can lead times. JIT does not permit of any arbitrary limit to improvement.

Unlike OPT and MRP, JIT is not something which can be bought and installed and then left to operate. It is a programme which requires continuous attention at all levels of the organization. The benefits are substantial, and successful implementations have led to reductions in process throughput time to less than twice the work content. This may well represent a reduction from 10 weeks to 3 days. This has a proportional effect on stockholding, and stock turns are increased from three or four times per annum to 30 to 50 times per annum. The release of space and capital is also substantial.

Waste, in JIT terms, can be defined as any asset or activity which is not directly contributing to meeting customer needs.

The list of possible sources of waste is quite extensive:

- **Scrap and rework** These are waste by any definition, but JIT does not accept the argument that it may be more cost effective to tolerate scrap than to eliminate it. The aim is zero defects.
- **Idle plant or labour** The two main sources are set up, when neither plant nor labour are engaged in producing output, and lack of balance (i.e. bottlenecks) which necessitates non-bottleneck resources being idle.
- **Under utilized space** This is fairly obviously waste, but may be disguised as flexibility. It is also a by-product of stockholding, since the space occupied by stock is not productive. In the service sector, waiting customers are analogous to stock, and space used by queues is obviously wasted.
- **Transport** Moving goods (or customers) between stages is not directly productive, and the aim should be to minimize transport. This will result in part from the elimination of under utilized space, but it will also release the space occupied by conveyors, corridors, etc.
- **Inventory** is defined as any material (or customer) not actively being worked upon. All inventory is waste and includes:
  - Raw material and finished goods stock, customers waiting for service.
  - Work in Progress stock set up to buffer the schedule, waiting periods between stages in a multi-stage service.
  - Large batch sizes which inevitably lead to large work in progress.
  - Long process times. In services this might be a desirable part of the service – most people would see the reduction of a three hour play to ten minutes as undesirable – but the process itself must be a positive benefit to the customer.
  - Long process routes – goods are in stock while being moved, customers moving from stage to stage are not undergoing a productive aspect of the service.
  - Bottlenecks, which generate stock (or queues) through their effect on utilization.

It is noteworthy that traditional manufacturing would not necessarily see these as waste. Stock is seen as an asset in accounting terms, and as an aid to flexibility and high utilization. Large batches are an essential part of the concept of economies of scale, and the Economic Batch Quantity optimizes set up and stockholding costs. Bottlenecks are essential to the successful implementation of OPT.

JIT IMPLEMENTATION

The successful implementation of JIT will result in a continuous flow of material or customers through a balanced production facility with no pauses or stockholding points. Such a system is very vulnerable, since without stock, any delay at any stage will stop production completely. Because of this, the recommended procedure for the implementation of JIT begins by seeking to minimize the risk of interruption. It is illustrated in Figure 10.1 where it is shown as a closed loop since it is an ongoing process.

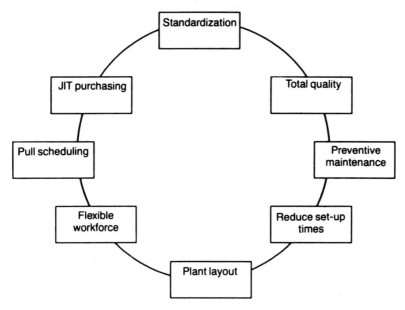

Figure 10.1   JIT implementation sequence

In detail the steps are:

- **Standardization** Ease of manufacture is essential for success. Any difficulties, inconsistencies, or frequent changes in the process will give rise to unacceptably high risks of delay. In some ways the approach here is similar to that of Group Technology. Production units are set up to produce a small range of very similar products, an approach sometimes referred to as focusing. This may require the division of a large high variety production unit into a number of independent smaller units. It may also require rationalization of the product range and a degree of redesign to maximize common elements.
- **Total quality** Obviously defective materials or components will stop production if no buffer stock is present, so it is necessary to ensure that the occurrence of defects is very rare if not non-existent. These issues are addressed in Chapter 12.

- **Preventive maintenance**   As with quality, machine failures are intolerable, so an effective preventive maintenance programme is a necessary prerequisite. This is covered further in Chapter 13.
- **Plant changes**   JIT does not ignore the economic constraints of production, so substantial redesign of the production facility may be required before, for example, batch sizes can be reduced. A determination to operate with a batch size of one does not alter the principles behind the Economic Batch Quantity. The focusing of production will give rise to substantial changes and it may be necessary to invest in several smaller machines rather than one large machine. This is likely to reduce set up costs but further work will be necessary. A common approach is to off-line as much of the set up as possible so that it does not interfere with the operation of the machine, however this does not eliminate the waste of productive time (and space) involved in setting up off-line, so the aim is to eliminate the need for significant set up.
- **Layout**   JIT gives rise to a continuous flow process without interstage buffers and this dictates plant layout, but flexibility of labour, and high visibility require that the plant area should be compact, and all process stages should be visible to each other. This is usually achieved by designing a U shaped line which minimizes the distance between stages.
- **Flexible workforce**   Ideally all operators should be able to carry out any operation on any product. Total quality also demands that the operators take responsibility for the quality of their work. In fully developed JIT environments process operators also take responsibility for the maintenance of their machines and for cleaning the work area. In the event of a failure leading to the stoppage of production, operators should first determine whether they can contribute to the solution of the problem, and if not, should go on to maintenance or cleaning. This results in a very high labour utilization, but is likely to be one of the most difficult areas to implement. It involves the removal of boundaries between skilled, semi-skilled and unskilled operatives, and while those at the lower end of the hierarchy may be happy to assume more responsibility and a higher income, those further up are likely to protest the loss of differentials.
- **Pull scheduling**   At a casual glance, JIT may look very similar to a conventional flow line. The key difference lies in the fact that the flow of work in a JIT system is demand driven, whereas conventional scheduling pushes material through from the first stage. The final stage in a JIT process is only activated in response to a demand for finished product. The use of material by the final stage generates demand for material from the penultimate stage and so on back to the suppliers. The processes which control this are usually referred to by the Japanese word *kanban*. The *kanban* may be a card which is used to authorize production. When it is received by the final stage, that stage assembles the product from the components it already has and, having used those components passes a *kanban* on to the

preceding stage as a request for more components. Alternatively the *kanban* may be a physical container for the components, or a space between stages. An empty container or space provides the necessary authority for work to be carried out.

One effect of the *kanban* system is that problems are immediately apparent. If any process stage ceases to operate the whole line stops because subsequent stages will have no material, and preceding stages will have no *kanbans*. It is not possible for the front of the line to continue to build up material for stock since it will not receive the authority to manufacture. Problems must be solved rather than bypassed.

A difficulty with this approach is that the line must already be primed with the necessary components to produce what is required. If the final stage is holding the components to assemble a blue deluxe widget, then it cannot make a standard green widget whatever the *kanban* requires. The mix of different products must be set in advance, and cannot be changed within the process lead time.

- **JIT purchasing** All too often seen as the first and sometimes the only stage, purchasing should be the last aspect of JIT to be implemented. The elimination of raw material stocks may seem attractive, but if this is simply a way of forcing suppliers to hold more stocks then there is no overall cost saving. The aim is to have suppliers deliver to the point of use several times per shift. This requires total reliability of delivery, and total reliability of quality. There is no scope for goods inwards inspection, or any other form of quality assurance.

  This requires a degree of mutual trust between supplier and customer that has been unusual in the West. It implies single sourcing, and close liaison with suppliers to the extent of providing them with up to date master production schedules, and consulting them about future plans. Suppliers must be seen as partners rather than adversaries. The more successful implementations of JIT take a pragmatic view of JIT supply and only use it where suppliers are geographically close, with good communication links and proven reliability. Where these do not apply, supply cannot be guaranteed and the holding of raw material stocks is more prudent. Frequent small deliveries imply road transport, and moves towards costing road transport according to its environmental effects, as well as increasing congestion, are beginning to call the whole issue of JIT supply into question. Japanese industry in particular, where the approach was invented, is beginning to question the value of JIT supply when this means forcing yet more delivery vans onto already crowded and polluted roads in order to make ever slower journeys. The constraints of the Economic Order Quantity still apply, and delivery costs can outweigh all the benefits of operating without stock.

JIT is neverending, it is not implemented then forgotten. Most of the steps described above are actually continuous processes. The organization gradually develops and learns the skills necessary to reduce or eliminate set up, to work flexibly, to achieve progressively better quality and greater reliability of plant. The principle is one of continuous improvement rather than sudden change.

APPLICATION AND LIMITATIONS OF JIT

Viewed as an approach to operations based upon continuous improvement and waste reduction, JIT can be applied in any circumstances, but in its more common manifestation as continuous flow manufacture without stock, its application is more limited. In principle a JIT manufacturing system should be extremely responsive, since lead times are very short and there is no backlog of stock to work out of the system. In practice the short lead times are only achieved by very carefully balancing the production facilities with the market requirements, and a commitment of stability with suppliers. JIT as described only works well where demand is stable and predictable.

JIT does not address the problems of seasonality, and it leaves little scope for a chase demand approach. This means that, whatever happens on the shop floor, it may well be necessary to hold stocks of finished goods. Unfortunately the presence of a full warehouse at the end of a JIT production line does not encourage the correct attitude of waste reduction, so it is not uncommon for JIT manufacturers to have quite separate finished goods warehousing, or even to subcontract warehousing by selling on goods to agents who then handle the distribution.

The paradox of JIT is that, by eliminating stock – ideally throughout the whole supply chain – it introduces the possibility of a highly responsive and flexible operation, however the full benefits are only easily obtainable within a low variety, high stability, market.

The ultimate criticism of JIT is, perhaps, that it is based upon continuous improvement. Once started, it is incremental in nature, and will therefore not lead to dramatic changes in performance after the initial implementation. There is a limit to the extent to which improvement can be achieved if it is constrained by the starting point.

The alternative course of action which is sometimes proposed is that of Business Process Re-engineering (BPR). This seeks to redefine the organization, or that section under consideration, in terms of its objectives without reference to its present state. In other words it seeks to impose an optimal structure. This is, of course, no different from the Systems Engineering approach of the 1960s, and it suffers from the same drawbacks namely:

- **Design skills**   Incremental change of something which works is unlikely to lead to catastrophic failure. A completely new design may well fail completely.
- **Resistance to change**   Imposed change is rarely as acceptable as change arrived at through negotiation and involvement. The resistance can be great enough to render the change unworkable even if theoretically sound.

- **Rate of learning** Even with the active support and co-operation of staff, a completely new organization will take time to settle down.

Incrementalism is, in any case, only a criticism of JIT applied at a purely operational level. If the idea of waste reduction, in the broad definition used, and continuous improvement is applied strategically, it will result in dramatic change in many organizations.

KAIZEN

It is debatable as to whether there is any real difference between JIT, kaizen and Total Quality. All are essentially approaches based upon the principle of continuous improvement using all the resources of the organization.

Kaizen is generally seen as the use of small, empowered teams to continuously improve product, service and process. It is aimed at maximizing customer satisfaction – an explicit objective of Total Quality, but also an implicit objective of JIT, since a dissatisfied customer is also 'waste'. It is also aimed at minimizing cost, thus reducing waste in whatever form it arises – the key objective of JIT.

Where kaizen differs from traditional management is in its recognition of the human resource. Traditional scientific management, as exemplified by Taylorism, requires that managers manage and workers obey orders. It is based upon a command and control structure with more or less rigid divisions of function. Kaizen proposes that those nearest the issues probably have the most to contribute, and this tends to mean the machine operators on the shop floor or the customer contact personnel as much as management or technical specialists.

A kaizen team would have a working team leader (i.e. not a purely supervisory leader) and would not only manage the way it planned and carried out its designated work, but would be charged with the responsibility of continuously improving the work situation. This may of course involve liaising with other teams and calling upon technical expertise, and the team would be entitled to do this. Control and co-ordination are obviously necessary, and are achieved through the normal management structure and through setting up multi-disciplinary teams as well. This approach can be seen as an extension of the JIT principle of waste reduction extended to the idea of not wasting human skills and capabilities. It has also contributed to the concept of de-layering. Where decision making and responsibility are delegated to the lowest possible level, a situation which kaizen encourages, then much of the routine command and control function of management is eliminated. It is no longer necessary to have chargehands, foremen, superintendents, etc. between worker and manager. The difference between the flexible team working in a JIT production facility, and kaizen, is perhaps slight, but increasingly JIT is seen as a *manufacturing* approach. In this light, perhaps kaizen might be seen as an approach suitable for service industries.

SUMMARY

In this chapter an alternative approach to scheduling has been considered. In contrast to MRP and OPT, JIT, originating in Japan, adopts a low technology approach to the problem of scheduling, and maintains that the first step is to develop a balanced high utilization process with maximum flexibility of labour. Since there are no bottlenecks all that is required is to load the production facility in a pattern corresponding to the proportions of different products required by the market and allow the material to flow through the system. By adopting pull scheduling the approach ensures that problems are immediately apparent, and scheduling requires no more technology than is embodied in a piece of card. This approach brings with it a whole host of pre-requisites designed to ensure that there is no interruption to production, including total quality, flexibility, compact plant, low set up costs, etc. It is this stress on efficiency, and a refusal to accept constraints, that gives JIT its great advantage when applied in appropriate circumstances. The parallel, but somewhat less prescriptive, approach of kaizen has also been described.

These are not panaceas. JIT is too often seen merely as a stock reduction programme, and in keeping with the push scheduling attitude of most manufacturing, tends to be implemented at the front of the process with raw materials. The full benefits of JIT are likely to be seen only in the case of stable markets with relatively few product variations. OPT and MRP are more flexible in their demands on production and the market, and do not require such a wholesale shift in attitudes, but both are expensive, and OPT depends on unbalanced production facilities. Neither lead to the corporate zeal for waste reduction that can be an outcome of JIT.

CASE STUDY: Kitchen Components II

Kitchen Components are a well established manufacturer of plastic kitchenware. Their product range is shown in Table 10.1. The standard range of kitchenware is available in four basic colours with contrasting trim. The premium range is similar except that six colours are available, and the plastic mouldings are 10% thicker.

The process

All products follow the same process. A batch of plastic is mixed with the addition of an appropriate quantity of pigment. The mix is then transferred to an injection moulding press already fitted with the appropriate moulds. The press setter carries out a trial pressing and checks the dimensions of the moulding. If necessary adjustments are made to the press before it is handed over to the operator to complete the pressing of the batch. Once pressed, the batch proceeds to trimming and inspection before going into store. Typical batch sizes are 100 components.

Table 10.1 Kitchen Components: product range

Item	Number of components
1 Pedal Bin	4
2 Swing Bin	3
3 Rectangular bowl	
4 Round bowl	
5 Dish drainer	
6 Cutlery drainer	2
7 Small vegetable rack	3
8 Large vegetable rack	4
9 Bucket	2
10 Soap dish	2
11 Small plastic box	set of 4
12 Large plastic box	set of 3
Sets	
13 Drainer set	one each of 5 and 6
14 Sink set	3 or 4 plus 5, 6 and 10
15 Small kitchen set	1 and 7
16 Large kitchen set	2 and 8

Finished products are assembled by drawing the appropriate components from store, labelling them, assembling them into sets and packing them.

The present equipment consists of two 50 kg capacity mixers and two 25 kg capacity mixers. There are eight presses available, in two sizes. While the capacity of the presses is expressed in terms of the maximum pressure they can apply, the company rates them in terms of the surface area of product. Three presses are able to produce up to three square metres per cycle and the remaining five up to one square metre. Process times and costs (pence) for a typical product (rectangular bowl) are:

Mix

	50 kg at 190 p/kg	9,500
	0.15 hours at 1,700 p/hour	255

Press

Setting	0.50 hours at 2,000 p/hour		1,000
Pressing	1.45 hours at 1,100 p/hour		1,595
Yield	Standard		96%
	Premium		86%

Finish

	1.35 hours at 700 p/hour	945
Total Cost		13,295
Cost per unit		
	Standard	138
	Premium	155

Current demand and stock positions

A downturn in sales over the past three months has led to a substantial increase in stocks prior to assembly and packing, and management are concerned about the implications of this for cost and profitability. The managing director has heard of JIT, and believes that this could be used to eliminate the intermediate stockholding prior to assembly and result in substantial cost savings. Table 10.2 shows the current stock position while Table 10.3 shows overall demand over the past twelve months. Demand for individual items has remained fairly constant as a proportion of the total.

Table 10.2　Current stock position

		Stock value (£ cost)
Pedal bin	Base	3,200
	Lid	1,700
	Pedal	1,600
	Lever	1,600
Swing bin	Base	5,100
	Surround	1,700
	Lid	1,800
Rectangular bowl		3,100
Round bowl		3,500
Dish drainer		3,300
Cutlery drainer	Outer	1,600
	Inner	1,600
Vegetable rack basket		1,200
Bucket	Body	3,300
	Handle	1,200
Soap dish	Inner	1,800
	Outer	1,900
Small box		1,600
Large box		2,683

Note selling price is typically 2.3 times cost prior to final assembly.

Questions

1 What impact would the implementation of JIT have on the organization? Would you recommend it?
2 Develop an implementation plan for the proposal.

Table 10.3 Demand for products

Month	Sales (£)
1	42,700
2	43,100
3	42,500
4	41,600
5	42,300
6	41,100
7	41,100
8	42,500
9	40,700
10	39,400
11	36,000
12	34,000

Chapter 11

Project planning and control

The particular problems of project scheduling were briefly mentioned in Chapter 9. The first main issue which must be addressed by a successful technique is the uniqueness of the project. Projects are by their very nature unique. The construction of a hospital, or the development of a new product, will have important similarities with previous construction or development projects, but the differences will be considerable. Batch and flow manufacturing are characterized by the fact that each consecutive product is virtually identical in its demands for material and resources. In a project based operation neither the precise requirements for material and resources, nor the precise sequence of operations will remain the same from one project to the next. Because of this, a high level of uncertainty will exist about the structure of the project and its resource needs. This of course gives rise to difficulties when an organization is called upon to quote prices and delivery dates.

The second major difference between project operations and batch and flow operations is the tendency for projects to break down into a large number of more or less interrelated activities. It is, to a limited extent, a characteristic of some batch and flow operations that a number of different sequences of activity come together at an assembly stage, but in project operations sequences of activity branch out and back again throughout the project in a way that is not always immediately apparent. Project operations are thus characterized by complexity and uncertainty. The complexity is handled by using a network as the main planning tool, while the uncertainty is dealt with by using subjective estimating backed up by records of past performance and a team approach to maximize input and consensus.

The family of techniques developed to deal with these issues are known variously as Network Analysis, Critical Path Analysis (CPA), Critical Path Method (CPM) and Project Evaluation and Review Technique (PERT). While PERT has a number of additional facilities they are all essentially the same.

In this chapter the construction of the basic network will first be considered, followed by the issues involved in the determination and analysis of duration. The planning of resource usage and the disposition of any flexibility remaining in the schedule will then be discussed together with the control of the project once underway.

PRODUCING THE NETWORK

A project network is designed to show the sequence of activities which must be completed in order to complete the project. Some of these activities will follow in a logical sequence one after the other while others may well be carried out simultaneously. The initial steps in project planning involve the project team breaking down the project into discrete and clearly identifiable activities and then working out their interdependency. The use of a team is essential if activities are not to be omitted or wrongly sequenced. The activities and their relationships are shown on the network which is usually sketched while the analysis of the project is taking place. There are two networking conventions, which are unfortunately diametrically opposed. These are the Activity on Arrow convention and the Activity on Node convention.

Activity on arrow

The activity on arrow network uses the two symbols shown in Figure 11.1: the arrow which is used to represent any activity, and the node, a circle, which represents an event, the beginning or end of an activity. Arrows have duration while nodes are instantaneous.

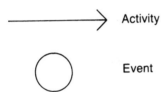

Activity

Event

Figure 11.1   Network symbols

The nodes are used to indicate interdependence. Figure 11.2 shows an example where activity B depends upon activity A and activity D upon activity C, but there is no interdependence of A or B with C and D except in as much as all must be completed for the successful completion of the project. In order to avoid any ambiguity, projects are always shown with a single starting point and a single finishing point.

A brief description or identification is written above the arrow and the duration of the activity, when determined, below the arrow. Sequence is assumed to be left to right, and where this is the case, arrowheads are sometimes omitted. No attempt is made to time scale the arrows, they are as long as is necessary to join the required nodes. Crossing arrows are not forbidden but should be avoided where possible to reduce the risk of confusion.

Nodes are numbered sequentially from left to right. This assists in identifying and locating activities in large networks since an activity can be identified by its

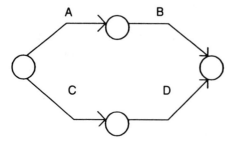

Figure 11.2   Basic network

starting and finishing node numbers, which means that unique names are not required. This convention generates a requirement for dummy activities. These are activities which require neither duration nor resources but are required to eliminate ambiguity. Occasionally situations arise which can only be represented by the use of dummy activities.

Figure 11.3 illustrates the use of a dummy to represent the situation in which B depends upon A, C depends upon A, D depends upon B and C.

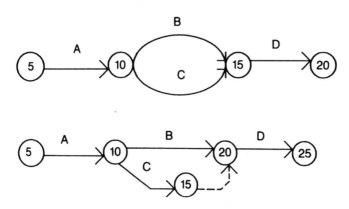

Figure 11.3   Use of dummy activity

The case of Mega Enterprises illustrates the process of drawing a network.

Mega Enterprises is planning the launch of a new product and has identified the following activities.

A   Source components
B   Order components and await delivery

C Set up assembly and packaging facilities
D Design packaging
E Source packaging
F Order packaging and await delivery
G Advance publicity to dealers
H Prepare advertising campaign
L Conduct advertising campaign
M Assemble and pack first consignments
N Ship product

Discussion has led to identification of the following dependences:

B depends upon A
F depends upon E which depends upon D
H depends upon D (the publicity will illustrate the package)
L depends upon H
M depends upon B, C, and F
N depends upon G.

The advertising campaign will continue after launch, but a minimum must take place before launch.

Activities which do not depend upon other activities (A, C, D, G) can commence at the beginning of the project, while those upon which nothing depends (L, N) will finish at the end of the project.

The complete network is shown in Figure 11.4.

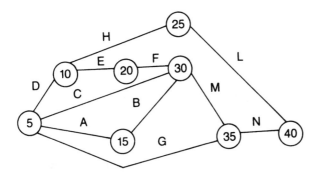

Figure 11.4 New product launch network

Activity on node

The activity on node convention is in some respects simpler than the activity on arrow convention. In particular it completely eliminates the need for dummy activities. The node is a rectangular box, and arrows are used to show the dependences. The node is divided into a number of segments as shown in Figure 11.5.

Earliest start	Latest start
Description	
Duration	Float

Figure 11.5   Node (activity on node)

Figure 11.6 shows the example used in Figure 11.3 drawn as an activity on node network. Most organizations use only one of these alternatives, and it is usually wise to follow the convention of the organization.

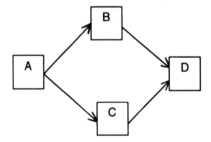

Figure 11.6   Activity on node version of Figure 11.3

Large networks

It is not unusual for a major project to involve several hundred or even thousand activities, and while these could be represented on a single network the result would be considerable confusion rather than any useful outcome. In such cases the project is best broken down into a number of substantial sub-units which can themselves be expressed as networks. For example if a project involved the manufacture of a number of different components, the project network could show the individual activities involved in the manufacture of each of these components. This would lead to a large and complex network. Alternatively the manufacture of each component could be shown on the main project network as a single activity, and a separate network could be produced for the manufacture of each individual component.

The advantage of this approach, producing a hierarchy of small networks, is that an observer can easily assimilate the information required at an appropriate level of detail. An overview can be gained by looking at the main project network, while detail can be obtained by looking at, for example, the network for manufacturing Part X. There are, of course, occasions when this is impossible, for example where the project does not break easily into discrete sections, and then a complete, detailed network must be used.

ANALYSIS OF DURATION

The determination of activities, duration and resource requirements is usually carried out simultaneously, but the use of the data is necessarily sequential. Where times can be established accurately from past records or existing time standards, then these are used, but there will always be some activities in the project for which past experience does not exist or is not considered to be a good guide. Where objective data are not available subjective data must be used, and frequently the data used in project planning are derived from the experience of department heads and their staff rather than from objective measurement. What is required is something equivalent to the standard time described in Chapter 6, an estimate of how long the activity will take under normal circumstances, given a normal level of unforeseen difficulties. Unfortunately this is not always what is given. The over enthusiastic, wishing to demonstrate competence and commitment may well give over optimistic estimates, while the more cautious, wishing at all costs to avoid blame for lateness, may give pessimistic estimates. A project plan based upon optimistic estimates will almost certainly overrun, while that based upon pessimistic estimates may well fail to be accepted in the presence of competition.

The PERT approach differs from other project planning approaches in specifically addressing this issue. PERT asks for three estimates of time:

- **the shortest likely** the time the task will take if there are no problems and everything runs smoothly;
- **the most likely** the time the task will take given a normal run of good and bad luck;
- **the longest likely** the time the task will take if almost everything that can go wrong does so.

This pre-empts both the optimist and the pessimist, and hopefully leads to everyone providing well considered estimates.

Assuming a single estimate of time for each activity, the first stage of analysis is aimed at estimating the earliest possible finish for the whole project. This is illustrated using the Mega Enterprises project.

Mega Enterprises has identified the following times for the product launch activities:

A	Source components	2
B	Order components	4
C	Set up assembly	4
D	Design packaging	1
E	Source packaging	1
F	Order packaging	2
G	Advance publicity	2
H	Prepare advert. campaign	2
L	Conduct advert. campaign	4 minimum before launch
M	Assemble and pack	2
N	Ship product	1

All times are in weeks.

The times are entered on the network and then the earliest possible time for the completion of each node is calculated. This is calculated by starting the project at time zero and calculating the earliest time at each node by adding the time for the intervening activity, thus the time at node 10 is $0 + 1 = 1$ and the time at node 20 is 1 (the node 10 time) + 1 (the duration of E) = 2. Where several activities come together at the same node, the longest time is taken since this is the earliest that the event (the completion of all activities leading in to the node) can take place. Thus at node 30, the route A, B takes 6 weeks, the route C takes 4 weeks and the route D, E, F takes 4 weeks, so the earliest that all three can be finished is 6 weeks. The analysis continues to the end of the network as shown in Figure 11.7. Earliest times are written above the node.

The earliest completion of 9 weeks can now be used to identify the critical path. The critical path is that route, or routes, through the network where there is no slack time available. This is identified by working backwards through the network determining the latest time for each node on the assumption that the project is to be completed in the shortest possible time. The activity time is subtracted from the latest time at the following node to obtain the latest time at the preceding node. Where several routes branch from a node the smallest latest time is taken otherwise that branch would then be late. Latest times are written below the node. Figure 11.8 shows the completed analysis for this project.

The critical path is that route joining nodes where the top and bottom times are the same, A, B, M, N. Although C joins nodes where this rule applies it is not

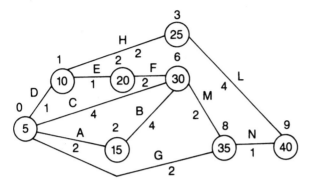

Figure 11.7   New product launch network – minimum time

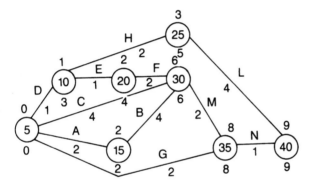

Figure 11.8   New product launch network – full analysis

on the critical path since the time available is 6 weeks and it only requires 4 weeks.

A more rigorous treatment would require the construction of a table showing earliest and latest starts and finishes for each activity together with the float, or amount by which an activity may be allowed to slip without delaying the project.

Float = latest finish – earliest start – duration.

The float analysis is shown in Table 11.1. Those activities where the earliest and latest starts are equal are on the critical path.

It should be noted that the float identified in the table is not all independent, for example the two weeks identified for activities D, E and F are the same two weeks. This is usually only the start of the process since the project time calculated is often too long for commercial acceptability, so attempts are likely

Table 11.1 Float analysis – Mega Enterprises

Activity	Duration	Earliest start	Latest start	Earliest finish	Latest finish	Float
A	2	0	0	2	2	0
B	4	2	2	6	6	0
C	4	0	2	4	6	2
D	1	0	2	1	3	2
E	1	1	3	2	4	2
F	2	2	4	4	6	2
G	2	0	4	2	6	4
H	2	2	4	4	6	2
L	3	4	6	7	9	2
M	2	6	6	8	8	0
N	1	8	8	9	9	0

to be made to shorten the overall project time. This can be achieved either by changing the sequence or by speeding up individual activities. Initial attention should be directed at the critical path. For example if A and B could be carried out simultaneously (obviously impossible in this case) two weeks could be saved. Equally if B could be shortened to two weeks, two weeks could be saved. There is no point in shortening B further since C is now also on the critical path.

Limited contraction of a network is usually fairly easy to achieve on paper, but the further this is pressed, the more routes become critical and the more difficult further contraction becomes.

The analysis proceeds in exactly the same way for activity on node networks, with the results being written into the appropriate spaces in the node. Analysis with PERT is somewhat more complex since PERT uses the three time estimates to establish a probability distribution of time. The treatment of this is beyond the scope of this book. Suffice it to say that while many organizations claim to use PERT, relatively few of them use the statistical facilities.

PERT analysis can be greatly simplified if a computer package is used. Software is available to determine the critical path and carry out float analysis and produce fair copies of the network, however, the task of determining the activities, dependences, times and resources must still be done manually.

Project scheduling

The network, and its analysis, leads to an agreed completion time for the project, and agreed resources. It does not, however, specify the starting and finishing times for activities not on the critical path. The project manager cannot leave such issues open, and the project schedule must specify the start and finish time of every activity. The key issue is the decision on how to use float.

It might be considered that activities with float should be started as early as possible since this maximizes safety margins, but since carrying out an activity usually involves cost, it also maximizes the outflow of cash and may well be unacceptable financially. Completing activities too early may also be counter-productive, for example cleaning a metal component well before it is to be used simply allows it to corrode again. The financial view would normally require that all activities which lead to cash outflow start as late as possible, but this would lead to every activity being critical and would reduce the probability of completing the project on time to an unacceptably low level.

Float is normally used to give a safety margin in those activities where there is a high level of uncertainty, or to smooth resources usage. If a major civil engineering project were allowed to proceed on an earliest start, or a latest start, basis the variation in labour requirements from day to day could be substantial. Rapid variation in labour requirement makes management and control very difficult, and a steady requirement for labour throughout the project is preferable. The use of float may help to achieve this. Float may also be used to prevent conflict for the use of scarce skills or resources.

The use of float for resource smoothing is illustrated in the following example.

Activity	Depends on	Duration	Labour
A		2	2
B		1	2
C	A	3	4
D	B	3	1
E	B	2	2
F	C, D	4	2
G	E	3	1
H	F	2	5

The completed network and analysis is shown in Figure 11.9.

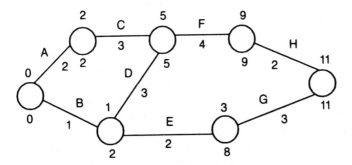

Figure 11.9 Use of float – network

An alternative way of presenting the data, once the network has been drawn and the critical path identified, is as a Gantt chart. The Gantt chart makes the float quite explicit and can be turned directly into a resource histogram. In producing the Gantt chart the critical path is plotted first since it does not involve float, and other branches of the network are then drawn using an earliest start approach, with horizontal lines showing float and vertical lines showing dependences. The resource histogram is then drawn by working from left to right along the Gantt chart totalling the resources required. Figure 11.10 shows the completed Gantt chart and labour histogram for this project.

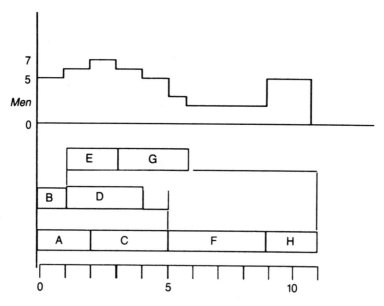

Figure 11.10 Earliest start – Gantt chart and labour histogram

It should be noted that this has been drawn on the assumption that all labour is interchangeable. If this is not the case, then a separate histogram should be drawn for each type of resource, or a stacked histogram may be drawn with appropriate coding to identify the different resources.

The histogram in Figure 11.10 shows labour requirements varying between two and seven, with a trough in the middle of the project. By starting E and G later a somewhat smoother labour requirement is obtained as shown in Figure 11.11. While not perfect, this does make labour control somewhat easier while still retaining some float on activities E and G.

Float might be used to smooth cash flow, avoid conflict for specialist equipment and services or even avoid interference between two tasks which are logically, but not physically independent, as well as to smooth labour. The

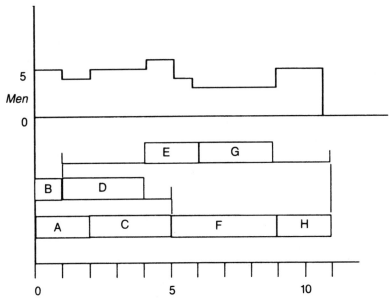

Figure 11.11   Resource smoothed activity chart

project manager must evaluate these possibly conflicting requirements and arrive at a best compromise. Having produced an acceptable schedule the precise start and finish times, and the precise disposition of resources can be published.

Project control

No matter how good the project plan, it is of little value unless steps are taken to monitor its implementation. Projects are by their very nature unpredictable, so that while the operations manager in a well organized batch or flow environment can expect things to run according to plan, the project manager must expect the plan to fail. Project control must be directed at receiving information on problems and delays as soon as possible, and considering the implications for the whole project immediately. It is common practice to use the Gantt chart as an immediate indicator of problems on the scale of whole activities. On a daily or weekly basis as appropriate completed activities are blocked in on the chart. Any activities to the left of the current date which are not blocked in are then shown to be late. Late activities should always be investigated, even if there is still float available, but more importantly, the implications for following activities and for the overall completion of the project must be considered.

If a delay is likely to push project completion out, the first step is to seek ways of minimizing this by seeking to contract the remainder of the network, by carrying out activities in parallel that were previously sequential, or by contracting individual activity times. The project network must now be re-drawn and analysed, and revised schedules published.

The earlier delays are detected, the more chance there is of minimizing their effect, so it is preferable with activities of long duration to monitor progress and enter staged completions onto the project plan. It is equally important to ensure that starts take place on time as well as finishes. Formal feedback of progress is required in projects just as in other process organizations.

If delay becomes inevitable, the issue of informing the client becomes a matter of commercial judgement beyond the authority of the operations manager. It can be argued that early warning of delay enables the client to undertake damage limitation, but there are those who would prefer to keep quiet and hope for a miracle.

SUMMARY

Project management is complicated by the uncertain nature of the project in terms of activities, the interdependence of activities, times and resource requirements. The use of network planning allows the complexity of the situation to be clearly modelled, while the use of subjective estimating is necessary in the absence of objective data on rates of work.

A team approach to project management is essential if the expertise and experience needed for effective planning is to be maximized.

Problems of estimating can be reduced by using the PERT three time estimate method, and problems of uncertainty can be addressed by using a full PERT statistical analysis, although this is not often used in practice.

Network analysis invariably shows float on some activities, which requires the project manager to specify precise start and finish times to avoid ambiguity. Float may be used to maximize safety margins, or delay expenditure, but is more usually used to smooth resource requirements. This is achieved through the use of Gantt charts and resource histograms.

The intrinsic uncertainty of project situations ensures that projects rarely run to plan. Continuous monitoring of progress is required, feeding back to the Gantt chart as an accessible means of displaying progress. Insurmountable delays require that the network be re-drawn and analysed.

This chapter concludes our consideration of planning and the control of resources. The remaining chapters address issues of quality, both of the product/service and of the plant.

CASE STUDY: Oldborough Development Plan

Oldborough Council is about to embark on a substantial redevelopment plan, involving both the city centre and the southern fringes of the town. The new university of Nether Whitton has reduced the student numbers at Oldborough Technical College to the point where the college is no longer viable. The college is next to the Police Station which is no longer adequate to meet the needs of an expanding community, and the opportunity has arisen to sell both to a developer to build a new shopping centre. The shopping centre will require a new traffic plan for the city centre. The money released from this sale will enable the council to purchase the disused railway station from BR and build a swimming pool and leisure centre to replace the facilities in the technical college. A legacy of £500,000 has been left to the council but a covenant requires that it is spent, within three years, upon measures to improve the fitness of the community, but not upon buildings. The council proposes to use this legacy to equip the new leisure centre. A long standing commitment to build a new southern relief road will allow the building of a new police station and new council offices on the southern outskirts of the town. The sale of council land near the proposed road for a private housing development will help defray the cost of the scheme. The developer will also be required to provide a new school. New pollution control regulations require the sewage treatment plant to be upgraded before any occupation of the new housing development. It is unlikely that a developer will buy the land until the sewage upgrading work has started.

In summary the activities are as follows:

Activity	Duration (months)	Cost (£M)
Build relief road	14	
Sell development land	3	−4.0
Upgrade sewage works phase 1	3	
Upgrade sewage works phase 2	18	
Build new Police Station and council offices	12	18.0
Move into new Police Station	1	
Sell College and Police Station	3	−14.0
Buy Station	1	2.0
Demolish Station	2	0.5
Build Leisure Centre	14	16.0
Equip Leisure Centre	2	1.2
Develop new traffic plan	6	0.2
Install new traffic plan	3	0.5
Developer builds shopping centre	18	
Developer builds housing estate	9 (to first occupation)	

Questions

1 Determine the earliest that the whole project can be completed and identify the critical path.

2 The borough treasurer has insisted that borrowing must be kept below £22M. Prepare a schedule to satisfy this constraint without putting out the overall

completion time. For the sake of simplicity assume that all moneys become due immediately the activity finishes. The contractors will not pay for the college, police station or new building land earlier than they need to.

3 What implication does the answer to question 2 have for the legacy?

4 The project has commenced under the schedule developed in question 2 and it is now month 14. A change of government has led to a resurgence of interest in rail travel, and BR have indicated that they may wish to reopen the railway station. What do you do?

Chapter 12

The management of quality

The specification of quality as an aspect of product/service design has already been considered in Chapters 3 and 4, and in an ideal world the presumption of operations management would be that this is correct that it is clearly and unambiguously specified. In reality this is often not the case and ambiguity of interpretation of specification is frequently a problem.

In this chapter the concern is not with design quality, but with conformance quality. Problems of interpretation have to be faced, but they are not the principal concern.

Conformance quality is concerned with the capability of the operations process to produce to the specified quality standard and with the systems necessary to ensure that this is in fact the case.

It is generally accepted that quality adds to cost, and that to produce to a higher quality standard than the market requires adds unnecessarily to cost and thus reduces profit. Failure to meet the required standard is even more expensive. It can ultimately lead to exclusion from that market altogether, but in the shorter term it can create restitution costs for the substandard goods and may also involve costs due to consequential loss. In safety critical applications these penalties can be substantial.

This chapter will consider the importance, and costs, of quality management in more detail. There are two basic approaches to quality management – the reactive approach represented by statistical quality control, which endeavours to control and contain the situation, and the proactive approach which seeks to develop and improve the situation. This approach includes total quality management, statistical process control, and quality circles. Finally, this chapter will address the issue of national and international quality standards.

QUALITY DEFINED

There is an assumption that quality is a 'good thing' and that we will recognize it when we see it, but this view greatly over simplifies a complex situation. There are at least six alternative definitions of quality, namely:

1 **Transcendent** Quality as innate excellence, a property possessed by an object, and recognized rather than identified or measured.
2 **Meeting customer requirements** The product or service meets the requirements of the customer. This is a design focused definition that presumes that customer requirements can be clearly identified and specified. Sometimes expressed as 'Fitness for Purpose'.
3 **Conformance to specification** The product or service received by the customer meets specification. This is an operations centred approach that presumes that the specification is correct.
4 **Free from errors** When applied to the delivered product/service this is equivalent to 'conformance to specification', but when applied to the operations process, it becomes a waste reduction issue. Should 'right first time' be the aim, or should inspection be used to prevent defects reaching the customer?
5 **Value for money** Quality is relative to price. A utility model approach that argues that 'good' quality is proportional to the net utility received by the buyer.
6 **Exceeding customer requirements** The 'delight' school of thought which suggests that every service experience must be better than the last if it is to justify the label high quality.

While there is some overlap between these definitions, there are wide areas of difference, and this is often a cause of confusion when quality is discussed. The issues are, perhaps, more clear cut in manufacturing than in the service sector, where the multi-faceted nature of most services, and the wide range of customer skill and experience, complicates matters still further.

From an operations viewpoint, the transcendent quality definition can be rejected as irrelevant. It treats quality as a matter of aesthetics and has little to do with specifications. It will be argued later that the 'exceeding customer requirements' definition is ultimately self-defeating, and can also be rejected. The remaining four definitions can be subsumed into three:

1 **Design quality** The extent to which the specification of the product or service meets the needs of the market. This covers both fitness for purpose, and value for money (the product or service must be designed in such a way that it can be produced at an acceptable price).
2 **Conformance quality** The extent to which the operations system delivers products or services that meet specification. This is output based, but links the design and operational quality issues.
3 **Operational quality** The extent to which the process produces products or services that meet specification without failure. This encapsulates the 'right first time' approach to quality, and is clearly different from conformance quality. Conformance quality can be maintained by inspection even when operational quality is poor.

While operations should have an input into design quality, if only to ensure that it is actually attainable, this is ultimately only a target for operations. If the specification of the product or service does not meet market needs then it is hardly a fault of operations, though it should still be a concern.

The key issues for operations are conformance quality and operational quality. With the former we are concerned with ensuring that customer satisfaction and competitive advantage are maintained, while the latter is concerned with achieving this cost effectively.

THE COST OF QUALITY

The cost of quality can be divided into costs of conformance and costs of failure, however there are differences between the costs associated with the three qualities. Failures in design and conformance quality directly affect the customer, while failures in operational quality are purely internal and may even be planned.

Failure to meet the required quality standard when quality is a market entry criterion is of course catastrophic since it will ultimately lead to that part of the business failing completely. When quality is an order winning criterion then loss of competitive advantage can be serious in the long term, while in the short term the cost is lost profit on missed orders. Once a reputation for quality is lost, it can take a considerable time to recover since customers tend to have long memories. More direct costs of quality failures which reach the customer include the cost of making restitution and consequential loss penalties.

With operational quality, the costs of failure are more readily ascertained. They include the cost of inspection, the cost of scrap, the cost of rework, and the cost of the stock necessary to sustain deliveries while inspection and rework are being carried out. There are also less tangible motivational factors since producing rubbish is thought to give less job satisfaction than producing good quality output.

Any quality failure is expensive. Despite this the cost of maintaining/improving quality can also be high and may not always be justified. High quality output generally requires high quality materials, plant and operators, all of which are likely to be more expensive. It may also require substantial changes in corporate culture.

The classic approach of a separate and independent inspection department leads inevitably to conflict, particularly where specifications are more ambiguous than they should be. When inspection maintains that a consignment is substandard and sales are anxious to ship to meet target, then considerable hostility can be generated. Likewise disputes on the shop floor between inspectors and supervisors are not unusual, particularly if bonuses are at stake. The overall culture tends to become based upon conflict with the whole issue of quality being disowned by the shop floor since it is the province of the inspection department. The attitude may become even more negative where rejection leads to rework rather than scrap since rework may be seen as acceptable since nothing is obviously lost.

Changing the culture from one of confrontation and division to one of mutual co-operation and responsibility is an essential prerequisite of any serious attempt to improve quality.

Such change is likely to prove difficult, time consuming and expensive. Figure 12.1 shows the effect upon operating costs of adopting a proactive approach to quality, but it does not include the start up costs and each situation must be judged on its merits.

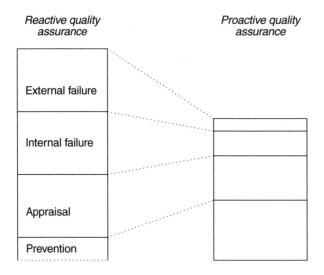

Figure 12.1   Relative costs of quality – reactive and proactive

STATISTICAL QUALITY CONTROL (SQC)

Statistical Quality Control is based upon a fundamental assumption that perfect quality is probably unattainable and certainly too expensive to be worth seeking. This is, at least in theory, true. No matter how well set up a manufacturing process, and no matter how tight its tolerance, the actual product property (i.e. weight, thickness, etc.) of concern will follow a statistical distribution, probably the normal distribution. Since the normal distribution is open ended any value is theoretically possible. Inspecting every single item produced is one possible approach to the problem of eliminating defects, but it does not guarantee zero defects. The inspection process itself is prone to failure. Consider a process that produces 5% defectives, followed by an inspection process with a 5% failure rate. This means that 5% of the defectives are not detected at inspection so 5% of

5% ($0.05 \times 0.05 \times 100$) or 0.25% defectives go on to the next stage. Even if a second inspection is introduced there will still be 5% of 0.25% or 0.0125% defectives. This is less than 1 in 10,000 which may be considered small, but it is certainly not zero.

The 100% inspection approach cannot be used under circumstances which involve deterioration or destruction of the item. Testing for breaking strain, electrostatic strength, flammability, etc. can only be carried out on a sample basis.

SQC is based upon the premise that perfection being impossible a certain level of defects must be acceptable and sampling schemes can be developed which ensure that this minimum is adhered to.

SQC is almost exclusively concerned with defects. It is not generally concerned with the cause or nature of the defect, merely with its presence. Since the issue is whether or not a component is defective, it is represented by the Binomial distribution, but since the sample size is usually relatively large and the proportion of defectives small the Poisson approximation is used.

When a batch is sampled, generally at a late stage in the process, or on receipt by the customer, there are a number of possible actions:

• accept the batch;
• take a further sample;
• reject the batch.

If the batch is rejected further alternatives are:

• 100% inspect and scrap the defectives;
• 100% inspect and either reclassify or rework the defectives;
• rework the batch;
• reclassify the batch to a lower quality specification.

Of course, the customer in receipt of a defective batch would not rework the batch, and would expect financial compensation from the supplier for any of the other alternatives.

All sampling schemes carry the risk of error. There is the risk of wrongly rejecting an acceptable batch, in statistical terms the type I error, and the risk of wrongly accepting a substandard batch, the type II error. Since the rejection of an acceptable batch carries unnecessary cost penalties for the producer it is known as the producer's risk, while the incorrect acceptance of a defective batch adversely effects the customer and is called the consumer's risk.

The key measure of the effectiveness of a sampling scheme is its operating characteristic. This is a measure of its ability to discriminate between acceptable and defective batches. It is usually represented as a graph of percentage of batches accepted against percentage defectives in the batch. Figure 12.2 shows an ideal operating characteristic for a situation where up to 5% defectives are acceptable. Such a characteristic is, of course, unattainable in practice.

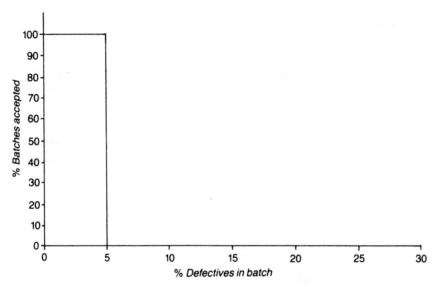

Figure 12.2   Ideal operating characteristics

Single sampling schemes

The simplest sampling scheme is one where a single sample of size n is taken from each batch of size N. The batch is accepted if the number of defectives in the sample does not exceed the acceptance number, c. Such schemes are sometimes referred to as N, n, c schemes.

Consider a situation where N, the batch size, is 1,000, and the percentage of defectives acceptable (the acceptable quality level, usually called the AQL) is 5%. In a scheme where the sample size n is 50, and the maximum permitted defectives c is 2, the operating characteristic can be determined by calculating the probability of >2 defectives in 50 for various percentage defectives in the batch. The probability of n defectives is $a^n e^{-a}/n!$. This is shown in Table 12.1.

If the sample size and the permitted defectives are increased the situation shown in Table 12.2 arises.

Figure 12.3 shows the operating characteristics.

It is obvious from both Tables 12.1 and 12.2 and the graph in Figure 12.3 that neither scheme is especially good, but that the larger sample size gives a more discriminating characteristic. Even this allows 13% of batches with 7.5% defects through, while rejecting 11% of batches with only 2.5% defectives.

The consumer's and producer's risks cannot be calculated without specifying the actual percentage of defectives expected. This is usually referred to as the process average percentage defective or PAPD. Actual batches will have percentage defectives which vary about this figure. In fact about 50% of batches

Table 12.1   1000, 50, 2 scheme

Actual % defectives	Mean (np)	P(0)	P(1)	P(2)	Proportion accepted
0.00	0.00	1.00	0.00	0.00	1.00
1.00	0.50	0.61	0.30	0.08	0.99
2.50	1.25	0.29	0.36	0.22	0.87
5.00	2.50	0.08	0.21	0.26	0.54
7.50	3.75	0.02	0.09	0.17	0.28
10.00	5.00	0.01	0.03	0.08	0.12
20.00	10.00	0.00	0.00	0.00	0.00

Table 12.2   1000, 100, 4 scheme

Actual % defectives	Mean (np)	P(0)	P(1)	P(2)	P(3)	P(4)	Proportion accepted
0.00	0.00	1.00	0.00	0.00	0.00	0.00	1.00
1.00	1.00	0.37	0.37	0.18	0.06	0.02	1.00
2.50	2.50	0.08	0.21	0.26	0.21	0.13	0.89
5.00	5.00	0.01	0.03	0.08	0.14	0.18	0.44
7.50	7.50	0.00	0.00	0.02	0.04	0.07	0.13
10.00	10.00	0.00	0.00	0.00	0.01	0.02	0.03
20.00	20.00	0.00	0.00	0.00	0.00	0.00	0.00

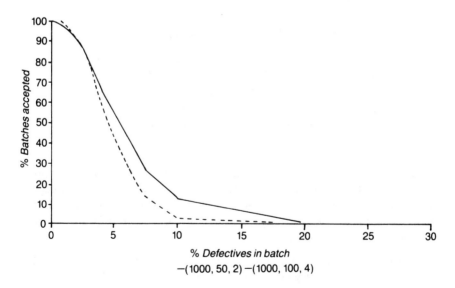

−(1000, 50, 2) −(1000, 100, 4)

Figure 12.3   Operating characteristics, single sample schemes

will exceed this, so the customer must be prepared to accept a higher figure than the PAPD in individual batches. If not then either the PAPD must be reduced or 100% inspection must be accepted. The maximum percentage defects the customer is prepared to accept in an individual batch is called the lot tolerance percentage defectives or LTPD. It may be that the customer is prepared to accept an average percentage defectives greater than the PAPD. The average percentage defectives that the customer is prepared to accept is known as the acceptable quality level or AQL. It is often assumed to be the same as the PAPD.

Figure 12.4 shows an operating characteristic with an AQL of 1.5% and an LTDP of 4%. The producer's risk is the probability of rejecting batches with less than 1.5% defectives while the consumer's risk is the probability of accepting batches with more than 4% defectives.

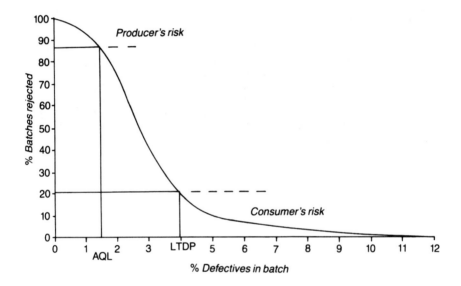

Figure 12.4   An OC with consumer's and producer's risks

Generally, the choice of scheme is based upon balancing the cost of sampling, plus the cost of reprocessing rejected good batches, against the cost of accepting batches which should be rejected. The cost of sampling and processing is usually easily determined. The cost of the consumer's risk is more difficult to specify and there are several alternatives.

1 If a batch is inspected prior to passing it to the next stage of the process, then the consequences of trying to process further an unacceptable batch can be specified.

2 If sampling prior to supplying a customer then the cost of the effect that rejection will have on future trade with the customer together with the cost of making restitution are adjusted by the probability of the customer's acceptance sampling detecting the defective batch.
3 A customer setting up an acceptance scheme is in a similar position to alternative number 1.

The specification of acceptable risks is usually a matter of judgement. Once these have been specified, and the AQL and LTPD are known the actual scheme is found by looking up the required N, n and c in published tables.

Where rejection of a batch results in 100% inspection, the sampling scheme may be based upon the average outgoing quality level or AOQL rather than the AQL. It is an interesting characteristic of acceptance sampling schemes with 100% inspection of rejected batches that as average quality deteriorates, the AOQL rises and then falls again. Initially, with perfect batches there will be no defectives. A small number of defectives will not generally be picked up by the scheme, but as the number of defectives rises, more and more batches will be 100% inspected and the residues of those batches will be almost completely defect free. The AOQL will thus rise to a maximum and then as more and more batches are 100% inspected, it will begin to fall again. This effect is shown in Figure 12.5. It is an important benefit of acceptance sampling that a maximum AOQL can be specified which is quite independent of the PAPD.

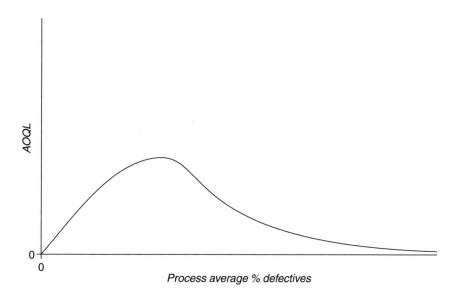

Figure 12.5 Average outgoing quality

Multi-stage sampling

If a small sample gives a clear indication that a batch is acceptable, or conversely that it is defective, then the batch is either accepted or rejected at very little cost. If the sample is inconclusive, then a further sample may be taken. The combined larger sample will be more discriminating, and should give a clear indication of acceptability. Such a scheme might operate as follows:

1 Inspect 50
2 If defects <2 accept
3 If defects >5 reject
4 If defects $= 3$ or defects $= 4$ then inspect a further 50
5 If total defects <7 accept
6 If total defects $\geqslant 7$ reject

Another alternative is the continuous sampling scheme. Here sampling, after a certain minimum is reached, continues until a clear decision is obtained. This is illustrated in Figure 12.6.

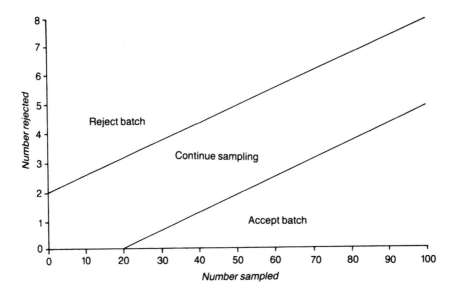

Figure 12.6 Continuous sampling scheme

While such schemes offer a good compromise between cost and discrimination, their greater complexity makes them more difficult to operate correctly, and many organizations prefer to use the simpler single stage sample.

PROACTIVE QUALITY MANAGEMENT

As quality has increasingly become an order winning criterion, and in many areas may be seen as a qualifying criterion, the pressure to improve quality actively has become irresistible. Improving design and conformance quality maintains and improves competitive advantage in markets where quality is important. Improving operational quality reduces cost.

While the Total Quality school argues that there should be no limit to quality improvement – 'quality is a journey, not a destination' – a more cautious approach recognizes that there are costs on both sides and that the law of diminishing returns is applicable. Figure 12.7 illustrates this argument, showing that there is probably an optimum quality level. Despite this, there can be little doubt that the break-even point is forever moving towards higher quality.

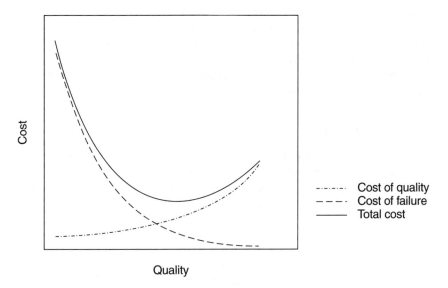

Figure 12.7 Optimal quality level

Statistical process control

Statistical process control (SPC) was developed at about the same time as statistical quality control, and is superficially rather similar. The main differences are that SPC is applied as early in the process as possible and frequently enough to prevent defects being made. It is also usually carried out by process operators, not inspectors and thus involves staff in the definition and management of the quality of their own work. It is the main formal technique associated with Total Quality Management, but, like many of the other techniques claimed by TQM it has an established independent existence.

The objective of SPC is to ensure that the process is set up to, and continues to, produce to specification.

All processes are variable, and SPC is based upon the observation that variation will be due to a combination of the intrinsic variability of the process (sometimes called common cause variation) and variation due to changes in the process or its environment (sometimes called special cause variation). By definition, nothing can be done to correct common cause variation short of changing the whole process, therefore SPC seeks to discriminate between the two so that action is taken to counteract or investigate special cause variation only.

There is an implicit assumption that the process is capable of producing to specification. Producing metal rods with a diameter of 20 mm ± 0.2 mm on a machine which produces to a tolerance of ± 0.3 mm is possible only with 100% inspection since neither statistical process control nor statistical quality control will be of any help. The first requirement is that the process tolerance (the precision with which the process can produce) must be tighter than the product tolerance (the precision required by the customer). The size of the difference between these will directly affect the difficulty of the task of process control and the size of sample required to carry it out.

Control of attributes

It is much easier to measure attributes than values. Much process control measurement is based upon simple gauges which classify the controlled dimension (thickness, weight, electrical resistance, viscosity, etc.) as acceptable or unacceptable. The statistical procedures are very similar to those described above in the discussion of the cost of quality, and rejection of a sample may well lead to 100% inspection of the production from which the sample came, but the main objective of process control sampling is to determine whether or not the process is operating correctly, and the main action in case of rejection is to reset the process. Sampling is therefore carried out intermittently at regular intervals rather than on a batch basis.

The most convenient way of representing the results of the inspection process and indicating the requirement for action is the control chart. First the tolerance within which the process is expected to operate is established. For example, if a process can produce metal rods to a tolerance of ± 0.2 mm, and the product specification is 20 mm ± 0.4 mm, then a variation in the machine setting of ± 0.1 mm, giving a finished tolerance of ± 0.3 mm, might be acceptable. The objective of process control sampling is to establish when the process has drifted outside this range.

A go no-go gauge which does not allow oversize product to enter, but allows undersize product to pass right through allows sampling by attribute. The dimensions of the gauge would be set so as to ensure that the process was set within ± 0.1 mm and a sampling scheme set up such that anything above a minimum level of rejects would lead to resetting of the process.

If the maximum level of rejects in a sample of 10 is set at 1 then the probability of a reject is 0.1. This represents a binomial distribution with a mean of 1 and a standard deviation (σ) of;

$$\sqrt{(np(1-p))} = \sqrt{(10 \times 0.1 \times 0.9)} = 0.95.$$

Two limits are now set, a warning limit at $+2\sigma$, and an action limit at $+3\sigma$. In this case these are:

Warning limit $= 1 + 2 \times 0.95 = 2.9$
Action limit $\quad = 1 + 3 \times 0.95 = 3.85$.

The procedure is now to take samples of 10 at regular intervals during the running of the process, to count the number of rejects in the sample and to record this on the control chart illustrated in Figure 12.8. If a sample exceeds the action limit, the process is stopped and adjusted. If a sample exceeds the warning limit, a second sample is taken immediately and if this also exceeds the warning limit the process is again stopped for adjustment.

Occasionally attribute control charts include lower warning and action limits as well. This may seem surprising since producing fewer rejects than expected is hardly a problem, but it may indicate an improvement in the process which warrants investigation, or it may indicate a failure of the measuring process.

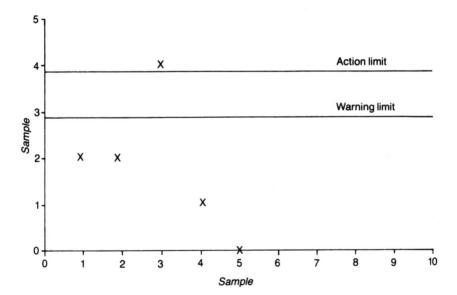

Figure 12.8 Control chart

Control of dimensions

Control by actual measurement is much more powerful and discriminating, but also much more expensive. It takes far more skill and time to measure the diameter of 10 pieces of metal rod with a micrometer than it does to feed them into a go no-go gauge. In addition the sample mean must be calculated. Unlike attribute sampling this requires a more highly skilled machine operator, or a separate inspector may be employed. The cost of sampling by measurement is often as much as twenty times greater than sampling by attribute. For this reason it is less frequently used. When it is used for routine process control, the principle is exactly the same as for attribute sampling. Control charts with warning limits at $\pm 2\sigma$ and action limits at $\pm 3\sigma$ are created. The only difference is that it is actual dimension which is plotted, and the sampler has to calculate the sample mean.

The general principles of control charts are much more widely applicable than merely sampling manufacturing process output. Common and special cause variation apply to any measurements over time, and control charts can be used to discriminate between them in any circumstances. This is particularly useful in the monitoring of service quality where precise and regular sample measurements are much less likely to be available, but it can also be applied to administrative output in order to monitor productivity. A discussion of the use of controls charts with single value, rather than sample, data is given in Appendix 2.

TOTAL QUALITY MANAGEMENT

Total quality management aims to achieve perfection in all aspects of customer service, not just in the conformance of the product to specification but also in all other aspects of the relationship; thus late delivery, incorrect quantities, or incorrect paperwork, or even just a failure to understand the customer would also be considered quality failures. While perfection is probably unattainable, and certainly cannot be sustained, TQM aims at continuous and unremitting vigilance and improvement.

TQM represents an unequivocal commitment to quality by the whole organization and involves every member of the organization, there is no separate quality department to which responsibility can be transferred.

Since the whole purpose of TQM is to gain competitive advantage it is important that quality is perceived as what the customer wants rather than what the supplying organization feels is appropriate.

The drive for quality improvement involves all those directly involved in the production and distribution of the product, as well as all other customer contact staff. Thus in addition to production, the marketing, design and purchasing departments are directly involved with the product, while sales, despatch, customer services and accounts are concerned with the quality of their customer contact. Other functions without direct interaction with customer or product are still seen as supporting the total quality direction by developing and improving the quality of their service to the rest of the organization. TQM represents a radical departure for organizations which have traditionally regarded quality as the exclusive preserve of the quality department, especially as it affects internal service functions which had previously believed that they had no connection with quality.

Since TQM is 'people' based rather than technique based its implementation requires a carefully controlled long term plan. It is implemented over a year or more rather than weeks. Equally TQM cannot be partially introduced. Any attempt to introduce TQM only for selected products or selected customers, or only in certain functional areas is doomed to failure, since success demands a constant attitude of quality first, and continuous support and reinforcement.

Detailed implementation plans depend upon the nature and starting point of the organization, but success requires that the following steps be carried out:

- **Education**, and possibly structural change, of the whole organization to develop a customer service orientation, and a positive attitude to the idea of continuous improvement. This will be most difficult in organizations with rigid hierarchical structures based around the idea of specialist functions. Such organizations usually have a problem solving orientation which does not fit well with the idea of continuous improvement. In extreme cases structural change and a certain amount of staff movement will be essential if the programme is not to be completely blocked. A common approach is for a number of members of the organization to be trained as facilitators by outside consultants. They then return to the organization as trainers.
- **Training**   Extensive training is required in a variety of techniques. Key elements in TQM are statistical process control, designed to ensure that the product is produced correctly in the first place, and quality circles, designed to harness shop floor skills and experience in the pursuit of improvement. Both require training of shop floor operatives and supervision. Customer contact staff will also require training in customer care techniques.
- **Systems**   TQM could deteriorate into little more than a collection of pious hopes without the discipline of a formal systematic base. Clear and explicit procedures must be set up and documented for all activities, and appropriate performance targets and monitoring systems implemented. Monitoring should always lead to analysis and action.

There are many approaches to the implementation of TQM, varying from a fundamental review of the structure and culture of the organization through to the toolkit approach which gives staff a set of techniques to apply.

Nicholls (1993) identified four phases through which an organization must pass to achieve comprehensive Total Quality:

Phase 1   aims at conformance to specification and uses systems based upon Quality Assurance, Statistical Process Control, ISO 9000. This is essentially a product and cost focused orientation.

Phase 2   aims at a quality definition based upon fitness for purpose and uses systems based upon a team focus and involvement. Systems are more concerned with function and with ideas such as 'right first time'.

Phase 3   aims at meeting customer requirements and uses a systems based upon value chain and customer satisfaction. The viewpoint is now outwards and the whole organization should be customer focused.

Phase 4   carries this to its limit, using a quality definition such as maximizing customer value. The organization will have been re-engineered to bring about a partnership focus, and to maximize staff empowerment. Systems should be transparent to the customer, and control should be based upon value added measurement.

It seems unlikely that any organization has fully realized phase 4 in this model, and perhaps the sacrifice of independence implicit in phase 4 makes its value questionable.

In summary, the implementation of TQM is a major strategic step for an organization, intended to bring quality in the widest sense to the centre of the struggle for competitive advantage. It involves the whole organization, and being based upon the idea of continuous improvement, it never ends.

Quality circles

Originally developed in Japan, in part as a reaction to a shortage of quality specialists, quality circles are based upon the premise that quality is everyone's business (at least on the shop floor). Quality circles are an embodiment of the participatory problem solving approach required for the successful implementation of TQM and JIT. Quality circles consist of small (5–15) groups of employees from a particular area who meet regularly to identify issues of concern in the fields of quality and productivity, analyse those issues, and produce proposals for their resolution. In Japan such groups frequently meet during unpaid overtime, an approach which has met with little success elsewhere.

Like TQM, but on a smaller scale, quality circles may require substantial changes in attitude. Shop floor operatives, used to thinking of quality as being the province of the quality control department, and problem solving being the province of management, are often resistant to this extension of their responsibilities. Equally management may find it very difficult to delegate responsibility and authority to the shop floor, and yet if this is not done quality circles will fail since there is little motivation in producing proposals only to see management reject them. Successful implementation requires commitment from management in the form of facilities, training, technical support, and a willingness to implement proposals or give a reasoned explanation of why proposals cannot be implemented.

Initially developed in manufacturing, quality circles have proved a useful device for harnessing the insight of customer service personnel into customer perceptions in service industries.

Initially quality circles should be set up in areas where there is obvious potential for improvement since early success motivates the circle members and serves to sell the scheme to uncommitted management. While some users recommend that the team is led by a member of management, others suggest that greater participation and motivation are achieved by allowing the team to select its own leader, thus confirming its independence. Whichever approach is used, the team leader will require training in leadership, team management and communication skills. Other team members will probably require training in diagnostic and problem solving skills and possibly in areas such as elementary costing and simple engineering, but such training should be offered when appropriate rather than forced upon the team at the outset. If the team leader is not a member of management then procedures for gaining access to support services (production engineering, quality control, design, etc.) must be set up.

Management need to tread a narrow line between directing the group away from areas of little potential, or excessive cost, where the probability of a successful outcome is low, and allowing the team to operate independently. As an example, a quality circle may decide to investigate a particular product which is obviously unsatisfactory at a time when management have decided to discontinue the product, but are not yet ready to announce the decision. To allow the team to continue will eventually lead to wasted effort and disillusion, while redirection will look very like interference. It is sometimes found that new quality circles need to be directed towards particular problems and even towards the most appropriate techniques to apply. More mature quality circles should be allowed more discretion.

The success of quality circles, like most activities involving the introduction of group work, is mixed and the cohesion of the group itself is frequently a key issue. Effective leadership and the conviction of management support help initially, but in the longer term the scheme requires identifiable success and concrete recognition of that success. Compulsory quality circles, in overtime, with overt management supervision will almost certainly not work, but allowing the circle to meet during normal working hours without supervision may well lead to nothing more than an extended tea break.

QUALITY STANDARDS

The increased profile of quality in recent years has led to the development of far greater concern for standard, verifiable procedures for monitoring and controlling quality. Such standards are not new, but their importance is, and in many areas it is becoming increasingly difficult to trade without some form of certification of quality. Standards have often been operated independently by major customers, for example in motor manufacture and in the defence industries potential suppliers are subject to approval and established suppliers subject to review, but increasingly national and international standards are being called for even by relatively small customers, and the possession of approval to a recognized standard is moving from conferring a competitive advantage to becoming a market entry criterion.

The certification of product quality is relatively straightforward, but time consuming since each product and each development requires individual attention, but product certification does not guarantee that standards will be maintained. This has led to the development of standards for the certification of capability and procedures. In other words the organization is validated rather than its output. The British Standards Institute have operated a certification scheme based upon systems rather than products (the System for the Registration of Firms of Assessed Capability) since 1979, its current incarnation being BS 5750. ISO 9000 is a very similar standard from the International Standards Organization.

BS 5750 and ISO 9000 do not establish quality standards, this would be impossible for a single instrument, but they set out to ensure that the certificated organization has the necessary quality control procedures and disciplines to meet the requirements of its market. This is demonstrated through the production of a quality manual specifying quality related procedures in all areas of the organization. The capability of the organization is then reviewed by approved independent auditors before certification is granted. Continued certification is subject to a periodic satisfactory independent audit.

The advantage of certification of capability is its generality and widespread recognition. Being procedure based and involving clear specifications of all quality related issues it also has the advantage of raising the profile of quality in the organization as a whole and demonstrating that quality is a core concern of everyone.

SERVICE QUALITY

Everything that has already been discussed is, of course, relevant to services, but services do present particular problems in quality management which are not generally found in manufacturing. These stem from the presence of the customer which leads to two significant problems:

- The distinction between conformance quality and operational quality is less well defined. Since quality failures occur in the presence of the customer they cannot be inspected out. To the extent that a front office/back shop approach has been taken, inspection can be applied to the back shop activities.
- The intangible nature of much of the service encounter defies specification, therefore it is difficult to arrive at clear cut service quality definitions.

Ultimately the customer is the only relevant judge of service quality which introduces a further complication in that intangibility tends to imply subjectivity.

Definitions

In services, service quality is usually taken to mean perceived (by the customer) service quality, so definitions of quality tend to be based upon what customers feel is important, and investigation and measurement is frequently an aspect of market research. Both the relative importance of different aspects of the service, and customers' perceptions of quality, are identified through attitude surveys, or focus groups.

Since services are complex, subjective and multi-faceted, several attempts have been made to break service quality down into discrete components. The most widely used approach is that embodied in the SERVQUAL model of Parasaruman *et al*. This proposes that service quality conforms to five dimensions shown in Table 12.3.

Table 12.3 SERVQUAL dimensions

Dimension	Description
Tangibles	Appearance of physical facilities, equipment, personnel and communication materials
Reliability	Ability to perform the promised service dependably and accurately
Responsiveness	Willingness to help customers and provide prompt service
Assurance	Knowledge and courtesy of employees and their ability to convey trust and confidence
Empathy	Caring, individualized attention the firm provides its customers

The model has been the subject of a great deal of research – with conflicting results, but it seems safe to conclude that it is not a universal underlying model of perceived service quality, and that the subject is probably too variable for such a model to exist. From an operations viewpoint, a marketing/customer attitude model may not be particularly useful. The present author has proposed a model based upon three dimensions which reflect the variability of the service and the relative difficulty of managing quality.

- **An outcome/process** dimension which indicates the extent to which the customer is purchasing an outcome, for example a new tyre fitted to a car, or undergoing a process, for example a visit to the cinema. Outcomes are generally more readily specified, and are far more objective than processes, and an outcome based service lends itself to a high back shop component.

- **A hard/soft** dimension which defines the extent to which interpersonal (soft) or facility (hard) issues predominate in quality perception, for example, discussing an overdraft with a bank manager is a softer service transaction than drawing cash at an ATM. Again hard services tend to be more objective and predictable.
- **An objective/subjective** dimension which defines the extent to which any measure of quality can be considered objective and reproducible. For example, whether or not a supermarket actually has goods in stock is a completely objective issue. However, whether or not the wait at the check-out is acceptable will vary between customers, and even with the same customer over time. Subjective services are intrinsically unpredictable since the customer quality perception will vary from encounter to encounter.

While this might not directly reflect customer perceptions, the service can be classified by its position on these three dimensions. The ease with which quality can be defined and managed can then be established. Ease of quality management will be far greater with outcome based, hard, objective services, and increasingly difficult with process based, soft, subjective services, but caution is necessary. Subjectivity creeps into even the most deterministic situations. The withdrawal of cash from an ATM is self-evidently an outcome based service, and hard, but when the failure rate of the service is considered, subjectivity dominates. A success rate in excess of 95% is considered acceptable by most people, but if it falls much below this customers perceive the service as unacceptably poor to the point where they might claim it is not worth bothering with because it always fails. There is no progressive relationship between performance and perception, but a sudden transition.

Along with the dimensions outlined above SERVQUAL proposes a gap model of perceived service quality. Quality is seen as a function of the gap between perception and expectation. Closing this gap will increase quality, and making it positive – i.e. exceeding expectations – will delight the customer. The elements that make up the gap are shown in Figure 12.9.

It is important to note that expectations are influenced by past experience, so the model does imply an ever increasing spiral for high quality services.

It has been suggested by several authors that a zone of tolerance exists in many aspects of service quality. Within certain limits variation in performance is not noticed, and performance is considered acceptable. Performance outside these limits will lead to a perception of poor quality, or of excellent quality, depending upon the direction of change. For example, a patient might expect to wait between four and eight weeks for a hospital consultation. A waiting time of less than four weeks will be greeted with delight, while anything over eight weeks will be seen as poor service. It is likely that the more critical quality

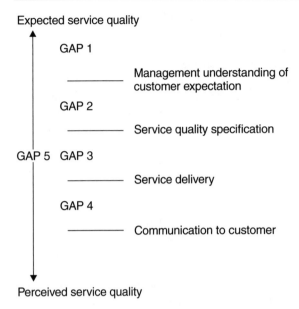

Expected service quality

GAP 1

—————— Management understanding of
customer expectation

GAP 2

——————— Service quality specification

GAP 5   GAP 3

—————— Service delivery

GAP 4

——————— Communication to customer

Perceived service quality

Figure 12.9 The gap model of service quality

elements will have a narrower zone of tolerance, and that this will narrow further as the element becomes a qualifier rather than an order winner.

The zone of tolerance is sensitive to other influences. A customer in a hurry is likely to have a lower tolerance of waiting than one who is not. In multi-stage services, poor performance at one stage sensitizes the customer to performance at subsequent stages. The hotel guest who finds that his booking has been mislaid on arrival is likely to be more critical of the room when finally accommodated. Service providers who are sensitive to customer perceptions usually go out of their way to recover a service failure because of this. The hotel might, for example, offer a free room upgrade to counteract this heightened sensitivity.

Relevance

Operational service quality has a direct impact upon costs. Scrap and rework exist in services as in manufacturing and their control is therefore important. A retail bank found that more than 12% of its direct staff was occupied with remedial work, and reduced direct staff costs by this amount as a result of implementing TQM.

While it is sometimes suggested that poor quality is always morally wrong, Design and Conformance quality are really only relevant if they confer competitive advantage, i.e. if they are qualifying or order winning criteria. It is by no means obvious that this is always the case. Where substantial barriers to change are present (even if they are only imagined by the customer), poor quality does not necessarily drive customers away, and a service provider might have difficulty in persuading the market that they really are better. Surveys of customer satisfaction with banking in the UK, generally suggest that service quality is inadequate, but few people change banks. In part this is because change is seen as difficult, but it is also due in part to the belief that all banks are the same. Only word of mouth recommendation and independent surveys overcome this prejudice.

Market research surveys frequently find that customers who have had a high quality service will express a strong repurchase intention, but there is little evidence that these intentions become reality in many cases.

The importance of word of mouth communication is seen in the development of the idea that a high quality service is one which 'delights' the customer. It is widely accepted that a dissatisfied customer will tell ten or more people while a delighted customer might tell two or three, therefore a service intending to develop through high quality needs to maximize the level of delight. Unfortunately, the gap model of service quality suggests that this will be self-defeating in the long run since the delighted customer will develop ever higher expectations.

Measurement and control of service quality

If service quality is to be promoted then it must be measured. Without measurement there can be no control or improvement.

Back shop elements are easier to measure and to control because they take place in the absence of the customer, and the criteria are more likely to be objective. Control at this level should be formal, but frequently it is left to customer service staff to manage on an informal level.

A retail bank introduced centralized decision making for all financial services. Specialist offices were set up to deal with loans, mortgages, property insurance, motor insurance, pensions, etc. Enquiries where taken at bank branches and forwarded to the appropriate office by telephone, fax or electronic data exchange. Specialist staff then dealt with the enquiry and returned the reply to the branch. Centralization was intended to give greater utilization of specialist resources, greater consistency, and better quality. Using electronic communication meant that no delay would be introduced. The service was intended to be a same day service (morning enquiries) or next morning for enquiries received later in the day.

Branch staff rapidly came to realize that the service was not fulfilling its objectives. Only about 60% of enquiries were dealt with on time, and 30% of these contained errors. In order to protect customers from poor quality service, and themselves from customer complaints, staff learned to tell enquirers that a reply would be forthcoming in two or three days, thus leaving time for late answers and corrections.

The measurement and control of quality of back shop operations should be no different for services than for manufacturing, and there is little excuse for poor quality crossing the boundary between back shop and front office. The measurement of front office quality is complicated by the intangibility and subjectivity of many of the elements. The measurement of tangibles such as waiting time, service time, availability, cleanliness, etc. through observation or inspection or even automatic recording does not ensure that they represent good quality.

The measurement of perceived service quality must depend upon the customer and is at present more appropriate to marketing than operations. In brief the methods used are:

- **Monitoring complaints (and praise)** This only yields the extremes, and gives no real indication of satisfaction. Few dissatisfied customers complain (at least to the service provider), and even fewer offer unsolicited praise.
- **Universal customer satisfaction questionnaires** Many service outlets present customers with a feedback questionnaire as a matter of course. The completion rate is usually very poor, and the questionnaires often so poorly designed as to be of little value.
- **Attitude surveys** Correctly carried out surveys of customer attitude. Usually delegated to a market research specialist. This is probably the most reliable method of collecting data, although attitude surveys are not without their problems.
- **Focus groups** A (usually constant) group of customers meets regularly under the direction of a trained convenor. The group might either discuss issues of concern to themselves or to the service provider. This avoids the restrictions imposed by a rigid attitude questionnaire, and allows a limited amount of tracking, but, of necessity, it involves small samples of customers.
- **Mystery shoppers** These are generally members of the public with limited training, to ensure that a genuine customer perspective is preserved. They use the service in a normal manner then report on quality issues. This also suffers from the small sample size of focus groups, but also has the drawback that mystery shoppers are already sensitized to quality issues and therefore not representative of the general customer.

None of these methods is completely satisfactory, which is why good service quality is, as described in Chapter 4, dependent upon management and staff commitment more than any procedural mechanisms.

SUMMARY

Quality issues can be divided into those of design, which were addressed briefly in Chapters 3 and 4 and those of conformance addressed in this chapter. The importance of quality in giving a competitive advantage, and increasingly in becoming a market entry criterion has been identified, along with the costs of failure to achieve the required level of quality. Two approaches to quality have been outlined. The reactive approach which accepts the inevitability of defects and seeks to control their level, and the proactive approach which seeks to attain perfection through a process of continual improvement.

Reactive quality management depends heavily upon inspection, either on a 100% basis to seek to remove defective components prior to further processing or shipment, or as the basis for statistical quality control. The management of quality is usually considered to be a specialist function within the organization, reducing the perceived responsibility of other departments. The derivation and use of sampling schemes to limit the number of defects to an average or a maximum have been described. Proactive quality management adopts the view that quality will only be improved, and that improvement sustained, through the involvement of the whole organization.

Limited progress can be achieved through the introduction of statistical process control, which uses samples during production to ensure that the process is correctly set. This in its turn may require design, plant and labour changes to ensure that the process is capable of producing to the required tolerance, but does ensure that shop floor operatives recognize their responsibility for quality.

Quality circles can further develop the involvement of shop floor and customer contact staff in the solution of quality problems. This may involve substantial cultural change to persuade management to relinquish, and operational staff to take on, responsibility for problem identification and solution. Ultimately proactive quality management involves the whole organization in a disciplined approach to providing quality in all customer contact transactions, and ensuring the necessary quality of support to those engaged in customer critical tasks.

The increasing profile of quality in most transactions has led to the development of moves towards certificating the quality capabilities of organizations. BS 5750 in the UK is presented as an example of this approach.

Service operations present particular difficulties due to the presence of the customer, and the intangibility and subjectivity of many elements of service quality.

Several models of service quality have been discussed, and their relevance to operations outlined. It has been suggested that the relevance of service quality depends upon the frequency of use of the service and the perceived barriers to change. The methods currently available for measuring service quality and their limitations have been briefly described.

CASE STUDY: Electronic Components Ltd. III

Introduction

Electronic Components Ltd. is a well established manufacturer of components for electrical and electronic assembly industries. It has a number of factories, each one specializing in the manufacture of a particular range of products. The factory in question manufactures non-linear resistors for use in surge diverters.

All the products are ceramic bodied discs, and vary in size from 20 cm diameter by 5 cm thick to 1 cm diameter by 1 mm thick. This case study concerns only the low power market, involving the smaller components, which is described in more detail at the end of Chapter 7.

The product

Type 401 discs are assembled into type 601, 602 and 603 final assemblies. They represent, at 4,250,000 units a year, the bulk of the low power market. The discs are 1 cm diameter with a thickness of 1 mm ± 0.1 mm. They are produced on the Matsubishu 12 stage rotary press or occasionally on a Friedland single stage press. The press is set at the beginning of a batch by a skilled setter who adjusts pressure and depth of fill of the die to give the required thickness and density. This is tested by weighing and measuring 10 discs. The nominal weight is 6 grams and the nominal thickness 1 mm. Once the press is set the operator checks 10 discs every 15 minutes using a go no-go gauge set at 0.9 and 1.1 mm. The presence of any out-of-tolerance pieces would lead to the press being stopped and the setter called. The physical dimension of the final assembly is not, in fact, critical and the main reasons for exercising control over the thickness of the disc are:

- to avoid wasting material;
- to avoid problems with the automatic sorter, and the metal spraying stages, both of which are intolerant of excessive size variation;
- to avoid breakage which is more common with discs under about 0.9 mm thick.

After firing and flame spraying brass contacts onto the faces, the discs are sorted on an automatic sorter. Typical yields are as follows:

401/01	low resistance rejects	15%
	OK	70%
	in 401/02 range	15%

401/02	in 401/01 range	10%
	OK	77%
	in 401/03 range	13%
401/03	in 401/02 range	10%
	OK	75%
	Scrap	15%

The low resistance rejects from 401/01 batches are heat treated and give a further yield of:

401/01	32%
401/02	18%
401/03	12%
Scrap	38%

After final assembly batches are tested on an acceptance sampling basis to the following scheme:

$N = 10,000$
$n = 100$
$d = 4$

The process average defectives is about 2.5%. About 10% of batches are rejected which leads to 100% inspection. Although reclamation of some rejects is possible by re-coating, the cost is such that they are usually scrapped.

Opportunities

At present all 601, 602 and 603 assemblies are sold to an electrical tolerance of $\pm 10\%$. Since this leads to a small overlap in specification, it maximizes the possibility of cross classification and thus yield. There is some evidence of demand for a $\pm 5\%$ tolerance range, for which a premium of 60% on price would be paid, but as the current process operates to a standard deviation of about 9%, the resultant reject rate would not make this a cost effective proposition.

Since electrical resistance should be proportional to thickness, the senior applications engineer has collected the data shown in Table 12.4 to see whether or not a tighter dimensional tolerance could lead to a better electrical tolerance. If the case is proved, a Matsubishu Hytol could be obtained for £130,000. This is claimed to operate at a tolerance of ± 0.03 mm.

Questions

Assume that the current Matsubishu produces with a standard deviation of 0.03 mm and the Hytol would produce with a standard deviation of 0.01 mm. The average current selling price of 601, 602 and 603 assemblies is 30 pence and

Table 12.4   Electronic Components Ltd: tolerance data

Thickness (mm)	Resistance (% of nominal)
0.95	90.40
0.95	91.93
1.02	105.67
1.03	109.37
1.00	95.91
1.01	95.20
0.91	84.98
0.99	99.62
1.02	105.49
0.99	97.93
1.01	104.99
0.96	96.28
0.96	90.55
0.94	91.33
1.01	105.11
0.97	99.04
0.96	89.10
0.95	87.31
0.97	90.49
1.02	94.98
1.00	98.58
1.02	103.28
1.06	114.98
1.00	100.12
1.00	104.93
1.01	105.59
1.01	99.01
1.01	96.03
1.03	104.42
1.00	101.79
1.04	110.02
1.01	106.91
0.98	100.01
1.02	102.63
1.01	103.67
0.98	86.76
0.97	90.09
0.98	98.63
1.04	107.90
0.99	97.69
0.97	93.92
0.95	89.38
0.96	83.99
0.98	97.03
1.00	100.01
1.01	108.25
1.03	109.52
1.01	100.13
1.02	106.60
0.97	94.84

the direct manufacturing cost is 12 pence. The cost at the disc sorting stage is 4 pence.

1 Does the data in Table 12.4 support the view that a tighter physical tolerance would lead to a tighter electrical tolerance?
2 Given the answer to question 1, under what circumstances, if any, would the company be justified in buying the Hytol press?

Chapter 13

Plant maintenance

All production and most service operations depend upon the availability and correct function of necessary equipment. Failure of equipment may lead to loss of production, loss of customer goodwill, wastage of materials and capacity due to substandard operation, or even injury or death in safety critical applications. All of these consequences carry cost penalties, which can usually be determined fairly easily, although their severity will vary with the situation. The failure of an item of production equipment in a batch processing environment is likely to be inconvenient but not particularly damaging to the schedule because of the relatively high levels of stock, whereas a similar failure in a JIT environment will lead to the total cessation of production. Similarly an engine failure on a milk float is rather less serious than on a passenger airliner.

All organizations have a *de facto* maintenance policy since breakdowns occur and are dealt with. It would seem reasonable for organizations to address the risks and costs involved and set up a formal maintenance policy. The utility of such a policy will increase with the amount of equipment used, the cost of failure, and the safety criticality of the situation.

The objective of a maintenance policy is to minimize the sum of the cost of failure and the cost of maintenance.

There are two basic approaches to maintenance – reactive and proactive – and these are considered in this chapter. The issue of who should be responsible for maintenance, and the specification of a maintenance policy is also considered.

REACTIVE MAINTENANCE

Reactive maintenance is based upon the principle of non-intervention until problems arise. In other words it addresses breakdowns, while proactive maintenance works towards anticipation and prevention. Proactive maintenance is sometimes referred to as planned maintenance, but this is a misnomer since both require careful planning if they are to be successful.

While safety critical applications cannot reasonably be left to reactive maintenance policies, in most other cases the choice is based upon the relative costs.

Failure of plant will result in the following costs:

- the cost of lost of production capacity;
- the cost of wasted material, either through damage if the failure is violent, increased scrap if the failure only results in a deterioration in performance, or the loss of material awaiting processing if it is perishable;
- the costs associated with rescheduling to enable other parts of the process to continue;
- the cost of the repair;
- if the failure affects the customer, the cost of lost goodwill.

Against this, removal of plant from service also carries costs, including:

- the cost of loss of production capacity while plant is being overhauled;
- the cost of the overhaul;
- the value of the remaining useful life in any replaced components.

If it can be assumed that the more frequent the overhaul the less likely in service failure is, a cost function such as that illustrated in Figure 13.1 will arise. It may well be more economical in some cases to overhaul very infrequently if at all, hence the reactive approach to maintenance can be more cost effective.

On a small scale little planning may be required. If the office typewriter or word processor breaks down, the simplest approach may be to telephone the nearest dealers and have a replacement delivered. In the long term this may well

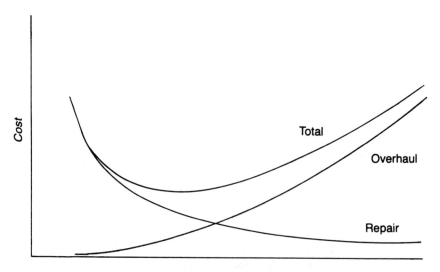

Frequency of overhaul

Figure 13.1   Cost of maintenance

be more satisfactory than trying to arrange maintenance contracts for small quantities of low price equipment. On a bigger scale, a large production unit would probably require its own maintenance department and would certainly require an assured supply of spares.

Maintenance stocks

Spares can be held on site as stock items, in which case the methods described in Chapter 8 are appropriate, however a major disadvantage of holding spares stocks is that they may never be used. The cost of stockholding will be higher for spares stock than for stocks of direct and indirect materials because of the larger contribution of obsolete stock to the total. A further difference arises when the cost of stockout is considered since this is directly related to the cost of lost production during the time taken to obtain spares. If orthodox stock control methods are to be applied to spares stocks then the costs need to be separately evaluated first. An alternative provided by some equipment suppliers or distributors is a guarantee, to a specified service level, to supply spares within a particular time period, usually 24 hours. The decision on policy is again a matter of balancing costs. Will the cost of a 24 hour delay outweigh the cost of holding spares in stock?

In cases such as air transport, the issue of spares stocks is of considerable significance. The easiest way to get an airliner with a defective engine back into service is to replace the engine with a spare. The cost of spare engines is, of course, substantial, but so is the cost of an out of service plane. Rather than using basic inventory theory, airlines invest considerable effort in developing specific simulation models to optimize the holding of major spare components.

If stockholding is adopted, the cost can be reduced considerably by standardization of plant. Purchasing plant from one maker rather than several means only one set of spares instead of many, it also means greater familiarity and skill on the part of maintenance personnel and thus faster and cheaper repairs.

Stand-by facilities

In critical applications, any delay may be unacceptable, so some form of backup must be provided. In manufacturing this generally amounts to surplus capacity. A known need for six lathes could lead to the purchase of seven so that one is available in the event of a breakdown. There are two difficulties with this approach, one being the expense of holding surplus capacity, the other being the risk of more than one failure. No amount of spare capacity can guarantee coverage. If the probability of failure of one machine is 0.01 (1%) then the probability of the failure of two is 0.01^2 (1 in 10,000) and of three 0.01^3 (1 in 1,000,000), etc. While the risks become very small, they never become zero. Examples of this approach are found with some major computer users (i.e. banks, building societies) where the 'hot stand-by' approach is used. A complete duplicate computer system is held ready to take over instantly in the event of a failure of the main system. The very high cost of this approach may be offset by subcontracting the provision of backup to a third party who may hold one computer system in readiness for several clients.

The design of safety critical systems may include duplication. The US space shuttle has three identical guidance computers so that, should one fail, correct performance is still possible.

While the provision of stand-by facilities is obviously relevant where reactive maintenance is practised and breakdowns are expected, it is also used with proactive maintenance since failures are still possible.

PROACTIVE MAINTENANCE

Where the cost function in Figure 13.1 shows a minimum well to the right of the origin, or where the application is safety critical, then the objective of the maintenance function should be to reduce the risk of breakdown or failure to as low a level as is reasonably attainable. This is achieved primarily through the practice of regular overhauls coupled, where appropriate, with the use of diagnostic monitoring. The skill lies in establishing an appropriate frequency and level of overhaul for each item of plant, for example minor overhauls, or at least diagnostic checks, might be carried out every week, and major overhauls once a year. A regular programme of maintenance activity must be established so that equipment is checked at appropriate intervals and the results logged for control purposes. This preventative maintenance plan must be constructed in such a way as to minimize disruption to the production of the product or service and is usually scheduled along with other production activities to ensure an absence of interference. Data on necessary frequency is gathered by observing and recording the condition of components during overhaul and recording the frequency of breakdowns. In some cases it may be possible to incorporate gauges to indicate undue stress or wear, and in areas where statistical process control is used, an increase in the frequency of readjustment might indicate a need for overhaul.

A general indication of likely frequency of overhaul can be gained by studying the variation of failure rate through the life of a piece of equipment. The so called bathtub curve, shown in Figure 13.2, represents the failure pattern of many products and systems. A high initial failure rate may be associated with defective or ill fitted components, inadequate installation or the unfamiliarity of operators. After this settling in period a fairly consistent, low level of failure should be observed, rising towards the end of the product's life as it begins to wear out. The initial high failure period is sometimes avoided by 'running in' the product before use, and the escalation of failure towards the end of its life may

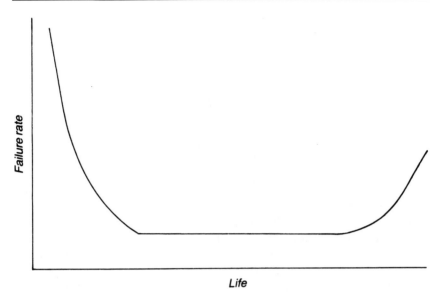

Figure 13.2   Failure rate

be dealt with by replacement. In the absence of these strategies the frequency of diagnostic checks and overhauls will need to be greater in the early and late stages of the life of the product/system.

Replacement theory

A mathematical approach to preventative maintenance has been developed in the form of replacement theory. Replacement theory is applied to components which wear out and considers the probability of failure as a function of life. At any particular time, there is a risk of the component failing, and if it is replaced before failure the costs of failure in use are avoided, however the remaining useful life of the component is wasted, together with the costs of excessive maintenance. The application is best illustrated by a simple example.

A ceramics company employs a conveyor system to transport unglazed porcelain between kilning and painting. The conveyor belt wears out and it takes 3 hours to replace it. This could be done at weekends when the belt is not in use, but if done during normal working hours the cost in lost output would be £1,000. If the belt fails in use then the product on it would be irreparably damaged at a cost of £200. A new belt costs £1,000 including replacement labour and has an average life of 20 weeks. Records of past failures suggest the following probabilities of failure:

Time (weeks)	Probability
5	0
7	0.05
10	0.1
12	0.15
15	0.2
17	0.25
20	0.45
22	0.8
25	0.95

If belts were replaced after five weeks of service, there would be no risk of failure in service, but the £1,000 cost of replacement would be incurred every 5 weeks giving a total cost of 1,000/5 or £200 per week. If belts were replaced after 7 weeks of service the risk of failure before replacement would be 0.05 or 5%. Since the cost of failure in service is £200 damaged product, £1,000 lost production time and £1,000 to replace the belt the cost of this policy in terms of failure in service would be £2,200. However only 5% of belts would fail in this way so overall the cost would be $0.05 \times 2,200$ or £110 per belt. If we assume that the belt would fail just before replacement, this works out at 110/7 or £15.71 per week. A total of 95% of belts will be replaced at 7 weeks but before failure and the cost of this is $0.95 \times 1,000$ or £950 per belt which is £135.71 per week. Thus the total cost of replacing belts at 7 weeks comes to 15.71+135.71 or £151.42 per week.

As the period between replacements is increased, the cost of failure in service will increase, for example if replacement takes place at 10 weeks, the cost of £15.71 per week due to failure at 7 weeks will still arise (since belts will still fail at 7 weeks), but there will be an additional cost due to the additional failures between 7 and 10 weeks. If it is assumed that this failure occurs just before 10 weeks, then the cost per week is $0.05 \times 2,200/10$ or £11. On the other hand the cost of replacement while still in service will be reduced to $0.9 \times 1,000$ or £900 per belt, and the belt will last 10 weeks so the cost per week of replacing good belts becomes £90.

The costs per week of both elements for various replacement strategies are:

Replace after week	Cost of replacement Failed	Good	Total cost
5	0	200.00	200.00
7	15.71	135.71	151.42
10	26.71	90.00	116.71
12	35.88	70.83	106.71
15	43.21	53.33	96.54
17	49.68	44.12	93.80
20	71.68	27.50	99.18
22	106.68	9.09	115.78
25	119.88	2.00	121.88

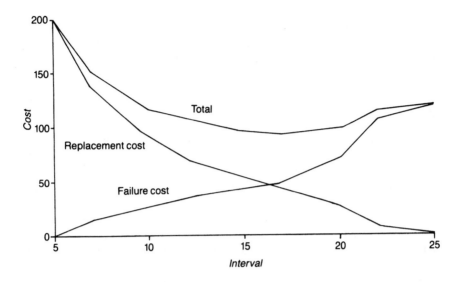

Figure 13.3 Replacement costs

This is shown graphically in Figure 13.3. The most cost effective solution, given the available data, would be to replace the belt on failure or after 17 weeks, whichever is the sooner.

The above example is a very simple model of the situations in which replacement theory can be applied. Costs are rarely so straightforward, and probability distributions rarely so simple, but the basic principle is to evaluate the total cost of each alternative and select that with the lowest cost. Where there are a large number of alternatives, a representative range can be evaluated and the minimum selected graphically. Where costs and probabilities obey defined mathematical functions it is sometimes possible to set up a single equation and solve it for minimum cost.

If this were a safety critical application (if there was a risk of the belt breaking under tension and injuring or killing operatives) much more detailed treatment would be needed since the probability of failure is never, in practice, zero. It would therefore not be possible to adopt a policy of replacing after five weeks to guarantee no failures and the cost analysis methods used would require a financial evaluation of loss of human life. In practice the problem in this example would be avoided by enclosing the conveyor with a cage, but in many areas (public transport for example) the risk cannot be so easily eliminated.

A variation on this approach, called group replacement, is used when the cost of the components replaced is small compared with the cost of labour. For example, if a machine is being stripped down for overhaul, it is usual to replace all wearing components (bearings, seals, etc.) even if they have not reached the end of their life. The major cost is the cost of removing the machine from service and stripping it down compared with which the value of the remaining life of these components is small.

MAINTENANCE POLICY

The specification of a maintenance policy is essential in any organization where interruption to production, or service, carries significant risk to life or property, or significant cost penalties. The policy should clearly specify responsibilities and reporting routes, and where a proactive policy is in force, it must also specify records systems.

An important policy decision is whether or not the organization should carry out its own maintenance. Users of small numbers of specialized plant would normally be advised to obtain a maintenance contract either with the suppliers or with an organization which has the necessary expertise. This is likely to prove more cost effective than trying to build up and retain the necessary expertise in house.

If an organization chooses to carry out its own maintenance then this will usually be the responsibility of a central maintenance function, but even here there is room for variety. The difficulties with a central maintenance function lie with the inevitable delay in responding to a call and the issue of how usefully to occupy the machine operator while repair is underway. These issues are addressed in a Just in Time environment by making the operators themselves responsible for some, or all, of the maintenance activities thus avoiding delays and idle staff.

SUMMARY

Two approaches to maintenance have been described. The reactive approach which takes the view that maintenance is an activity carried out when something fails, and the proactive approach which seeks to prevent, or at least reduce, the incidence of failure in service. The choice between the two is determined on economic and safety grounds. Where a failure in service gives rise to high costs due to consequential damage, loss of output, etc. or carries a serious risk of injury or death then preventative maintenance is indicated. Otherwise it may be just as cost effective to wait until something fails.

The operations research approach of replacement theory has been briefly described, and its application to preventative maintenance outlined.

CASE STUDY: Electronic Components IV

This case concerns the maintenance of the tunnel kilns described in Electronic Components II.

The kiln is 10 metres long by 2 metres square and is heated by 12 gas burners, 6 on each side. A D-sectioned fireproof tunnel 10 cm wide by 8 cm high runs through the length of the kiln. The kiln is illustrated in Figure 13.4.

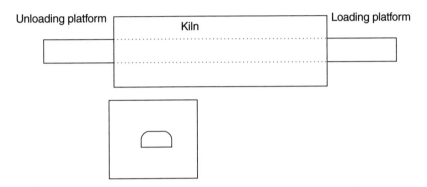

Figure 13.4   Kiln: plan view and entrance

Work to be kilned is loaded onto ceramic plates 10 cm by 20 cm which are pushed through the kiln by a hydraulic ram. Every 30 minutes the ram is released so that a further four plates of work can be added thus maintaining a continuous stream of work through the kiln.

The kiln may not be switched off because thermal shock will crack the fireproof tunnel, necessitating a complete rebuild. As a result of this the kiln must be manned 24 hours a day seven days a week. During the Christmas and summer holidays (when the rest of the factory closes for two weeks) scrap is kilned when any backlog of work has been finished.

The basic cost of operating a kiln including labour is £31 per hour.

Burner failure

Burners fail periodically and need replacing. At present the two man kiln crew turn off the failed burner and turn down the kiln temperature by 200 degrees to reduce thermal stress caused by the unbalanced heating. They then summon the emergency maintenance team, a charge-hand and two fitters, who replace the faulty burner. At best this operation takes 30 minutes, but at night, weekends or holidays it can take four hours to assemble a maintenance team. If the burner is replaced within 45 minutes the kiln can be restored to temperature within a further 30 minutes, and the work in the kiln will still be fit for use. If the burner is out of operation for more than 1 hour, the kiln must be raised back to temperature more slowly and a proportion of the work in the kiln will be scrapped.

Table 13.1 shows the life of burners.

Table 13.1 Electronic Components Ltd: burner life

Time to failure (hours)	Proportion failing
800	0.03
1,000	0.05
2,000	0.05
3,000	0.07
4,000	0.10
5,000	0.20
6,000	0.20
7,000	0.13
8,000	0.07

Tunnel replacement

The fireproof tunnel fails periodically which necessitates a complete rebuild of the kiln. This takes 8 days and costs £5,800. A further two days are required to bring the kiln up to temperature, during the second day scrap must be fired to prevent distortion of the new tunnel.

Table 13.2 shows the tunnel failure rate.

Table 13.2 Electronic Components Ltd: tunnel life

Time to failure (hours)	Proportion failing
7,000	0.10
8,000	0.13
9,000	0.20
10,000	0.25
12,000	0.20
15,000	0.10

Questions

1 What alternative approaches to the burner failure problem are available to the company? How would you evaluate them?
2 Current company policy is to replace the tunnel only when it fails. Evaluate the alternative of replacing the tunnel during the summer holiday.

Further quantitative techniques

STATISTICAL DISTRIBUTIONS

Statistical distributions describe the behaviour of quantitative information which is influenced by chance. The use of appropriate distributions allows predictions to be made, and the likely errors in those predictions to be determined. This overview is intended to refresh the memory of those who already have some knowledge of statistics; it is not a substitute for prior study. There are three statistical distributions relevant to operations management.

Binomial distribution

This distribution models the behaviour of situations where there are precisely two alternative outcomes to a particular event. Applications in operations management include quality control, where a component is either defective or not, and labour absenteeism, where a worker is either present or not. The following data are required:

The probability of the outcome of interest $= p$
(i.e. the mean proportion of defects)
The number of events $= n$
(i.e. the number inspected)

The probability of a particular number of occurrences of the outcome of interest (r) occurring is given by:

$$^nC_r p^r (1-p)^{n-r}$$

where $^nC_r = n!/r!/(n-r)!$

Poisson distribution

The Poisson distribution describes random events, i.e. accidents, arrivals at a service point, breakdowns, etc. The Poisson distribution also approximates to the binomial distribution when n is large and p small. This is the normal situation in quality control applications and since the Poisson distribution is easier to use under these circumstances it forms the basis for most SQC sampling schemes.

The only statistic required is the mean (a). If deriving this from the binomial distribution then $a = np$.

The probability of a particular number of occurrences of the outcome of interest (r) occurring is given by:

$$e^{-a}a^r/r!$$

Normal distribution

The normal distribution describes the behaviour of continuous variables, but it is not as universally applicable. For example, the variation in output of a process is likely to be normally distributed, as is the demand for a product, but other variables such as variation in lead time may well follow different distributions. In general, if the observed values are more or less symmetrically distributed about the mean, the normal distribution can probably be used safely. It is used in process control since process variability is almost always normally distributed. Its use in stock control is less secure since lead times in particular – which are subject to an irreducible minimum, but an infinitely extensible maximum – are unlikely to be symmetrically distributed. The statistics required are the mean μ and the standard deviation σ. These are used to calculate the statistic z where:

$$z = (x-\mu)/\sigma$$

where x is the value of interest.

Probabilities are looked up in tables which usually give the probability of values $>x$ arising. An outline table is given below.

Normal distribution probabilities

z	p
0.0	0.5
0.5	0.3085
1.0	0.1587
1.5	0.0668
2.0	0.0228
2.5	0.0062
3.0	0.00135
4.0	0.00003

On occasion, when calculating with normally distributed variables, the variance is used instead of the standard deviation. The variance is the square of the standard deviation.

QUEUING THEORY

The most common queuing situation is one in which arrivals are random and therefore obey the Poisson distribution, and service times follow the exponential distribution (in effect departures are also random).

The basic parameters are:

A = mean arrival rate
S = mean service rate per service channel
N = number of service channels
T (traffic intensity) = $A/(SN)$

T must be less than 1 (i.e. the service capacity must be greater than the demand otherwise the queue would simply build up indefinitely).

Single channel queues

For a single channel queue, the following equations can be derived:

Average number in queue = $T^2/(1-T)$
Average number in system = $T/(1-T)$
Average number in service = T

Since the rate at which the queue diminishes is S then:

Average time in queue = $T^2/(1-T)/S$

The proportion of time that the service facility is idle = $1-T$.
The probability of any number (n) being in the system is given by:

$P(n) = (1-T)T^n$

Multichannel queues

The formulae for multichannel queues depend upon knowing the probability of no one being in the system. This is given by:

$P(0) = 1/(1+ T+ T^2/2!+ T^3/3!+ \ldots T^{N-1}/(N-1)!+ T^N/N!(1-T/N))$.

The other formulae are

Average number in queue $(Q)= P(0)T^{N+1}/(NN!(1-T/N)^2)$
Average number in system = $Q + T$
Average number in service = T
Average time in queue = $Q/(SN)$

$P(n) = T^n P(0)/(N!N^{n-N})$ where $n>N$

Note that when $n \leqslant N$ all customers in the system are in service.

Constant service time, single channel

Where arrivals are random but the service time is constant the average number in the system is given by:

$$T + T^2/(2(1 - T)).$$

Other models

The mathematical treatment of other models becomes increasingly complex, and the most usual method of obtaining results is by simulation, rather than the solution of equations. Such situations are common and include those where priorities are assigned, where queues arise at successive stages in a process, and where appointments or schedules are used to control the situation. The treatment of simulation is beyond the scope of this book.

LINEAR PROGRAMMING

Linear programming is a widely applicable technique used for optimizing the use of resources when operating under resource constraints. As the name implies, the relationships between the factors treated must be linear. In operations management the most obvious application is in optimizing product mix when faced with capacity constraints. An alternative application which occasionally arises in product design is the optimization of a mix of raw materials to satisfy constraints on minimum content, for instance the blending of raw materials to give an animal feedstock which satisfies legal requirements for nutritional content. Here the objective would be to minimize cost.

The following example illustrates the use of the technique.

A company manufactures two products A and B using a three stage process. The process times in hours per unit, capacities in hours per week, contributions in £ per unit and maximum demand in units per week are as follows:

| | Process | | | Contribution | Demand |
	X	Y	Z		
A	3	2	4.5	140	10
B	4	1	3.5	100	18
Capacity	60	30	70		

The first step is to establish the objective function, which in this case is to maximize contribution, given by:

140A + 100B

Next the constraints are established. These represent the maximum possible output from each process, and the maximum demand.

Process X	$3A + 4B \leqslant 60$
Process Y	$2A + 1B \leqslant 30$
Process Z	$4.5A + 3.5B \leqslant 70$
Demand	$0 \leqslant A \leqslant 10$
	$0 \leqslant B \leqslant 18$

It is necessary to specify that negative production is not allowed.

With problems such as this, involving only two variables, a graphical approach can be used. The limiting values of each constraint are plotted on a graph of A against B as shown in Figure A1.1. This identifies the feasible solution area which is that area which lies within all the constraints. A line representing the objective function is then plotted. This is moved away from the origin (increasing its value) until it just leaves the area of feasible solutions. The point of last contact represents the mix of A and B which maximizes contribution.

In this case, the point of maximum contribution is either A = 9 and B = 8 or A = 10 and B = 7, the graph not being precise enough to allow a clear decision. It is a simple matter to determine that A = 9, B = 8 gives a contribution of £2,060 while A = 10, B = 7 gives a contribution of £2,100 hence the latter is the optimal product mix.

Since the optimal solution is bound to lie on the boundary of the feasible area it is often easier simply to calculate the value of the objective function for each corner of the feasible area and choose the one which gives the optimal value.

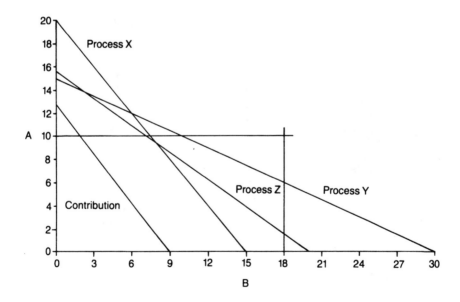

Figure A1.1 Linear programming

Problems with more than two variables cannot be solved graphically. The approach still requires that the objective function and all the constraints be identified and expressed algebraically. These are now treated as a set of simultaneous equations and solved, though the computation involved is so extensive that this is invariably done using a purpose designed linear programming computer package.

SEASONALITY IN FORECASTING

Decomposition depends upon identifying the trend in a set of data and then correcting the data for trend to reveal the underlying seasonal and cyclical movements. Provided the trend is linear and fairly constant, the most obvious method of trend identification is linear regression. The regression line is the straight line of best fit for the data and thus represents any constant growth or decay.

Once the rate of growth is known, the actual data can be corrected to that value which it would have had if there were no growth. The remaining variation is seasonality and random variation. Seasonality can be extracted by averaging.

The following example illustrates the process. It is based upon quarterly sales, but the technique could be applied to monthly, weekly or even daily figures if required.

First the periods must be numbered consecutively so that the regression equation of sales on period can be calculated.

Year	Quarter	Period number (x)	Sales (£K) (y)
1988	Spring	1	95
	Summer	2	113
	Autumn	3	145
	Winter	4	136
1989	Spring	5	94
	Summer	6	135
	Autumn	7	142
	Winter	8	115
1990	Spring	9	129
	Summer	10	145
	Autumn	11	151
	Winter	12	147
Mean		6.5	128.92

$\Sigma xy = 10{,}530$

σ (standard deviations)   3.45   19.16

r (correlation coefficient) $= \dfrac{\Sigma xy - N \bar{x} \bar{y}}{N \sigma_x \sigma_y} = 0.60$

The constants for the equation $y = ax + b$ where y is sales and x is the period number are given by:

$$a = r\sigma_y / \sigma_x = 3.32$$
$$b = y - ax = 107.35$$

a is the trend.

The regression equation is now used to calculate the base sales for each of the 12 quarters. These are then subtracted from the actual sales to get individual differences, which are then averaged to obtain the seasonal factors as follows:

Seasonal factors

Quarter	Actual	Regression	Difference
1	95	110.67	−15.67
2	113	113.99	−0.99
3	145	117.31	27.69
4	136	120.63	15.37
5	94	123.95	−29.95
6	135	127.27	7.73
7	142	130.59	11.41
8	115	133.91	−18.91
9	129	137.23	−8.23
10	145	140.55	4.45
11	151	143.87	7.13
12	147	147.19	−0.19

Averages

Spring (quarters 1, 5, 9)	− 17.95
Summer (quarters 2, 6, 10)	3.73
Autumn (quarters 3, 7, 11)	15.41
Winter (quarters 4, 8, 12)	− 1.24

To produce a forecast for 1991 the regression equation is used to produce a base sales for each quarter and the seasonal correction is then added.

Spring	$3.32 \times 13 + 107.35 - 17.95$	$= 132.56$
Summer	$3.32 \times 14 + 107.35 + 3.73$	$= 157.56$
Autumn	$3.32 \times 15 + 107.35 + 15.41$	$= 172.56$
Winter	$3.32 \times 16 + 107.35 - 1.24$	$= 159.23$

In this example an additive approach has been used in that the seasonal adjustments have been calculated as actual sales figures and added to the base sales. As an alternative, the seasonal adjustments can be expressed as a percentage of the base sales giving a multiplicative approach. The best method is the one which produces the most accurate results though the differences will be slight unless fairly rapid growth or decay is taking place.

This is only one of many approaches to time series decomposition. Its main drawback is the possibility that the trend will change, invalidating the results of the regression line.

An introduction to control charts

Control charts were developed by Walter Shewhart in the 1930s as a basis for understanding time series data and have not been bettered since. They are the basis behind much of TQM (Deming in particular acknowledges his debt to Shewhart), and all of Statistical Process Control. While associated with manufacturing, they can be applied in any situation which generates time series data (i.e. numerical values which are collected at intervals).

No meaning without context

Data are meaningless without a context, and the quality of meaning is not only no better than that of the data, but even more depends upon the quality of the contextual information. Shewhart proposed two rules to ensure adequate context:

Rule 1
Data should always be presented in a way that preserves the evidence in the data for all predictions that might be made from it.

Graphs should be supported by tables (and vice versa) and answers to the questions:

- Who (collected it)?
- When?
- Where?
- How?
- What (do the values represent)?
- What (computational procedures have been used – if any)?

should be present.

Rule 2
Whenever data is compressed, as an average, histogram, range, etc., for presentation, this should not mislead the user into taking any action which would not have been taken if the data were presented as a time series.

Compression obscures trends.

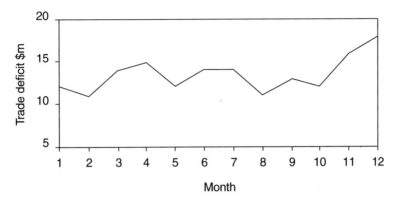

Figure A2.1   Trade deficit with time

An example

The graph in Figure A2.1 shows the trade deficit of a country for the past 10 months. The press predict disaster when the month 12 figure is published. Are they justified?

Trend and noise

Trend represents real changes in the underlying situation about which knowledge is always useful. It may even lead to action to restore the situation, or to preserve an improvement if the change is in the correct direction.

Noise is the underlying random variation within the situation. It cannot be predicted or controlled and any action to compensate for it will usually make matters worse. Trend and noise correspond to common and special causes of variation. Common cause represents the natural variability of the situation and cannot be changed without fundamental changes to the process (i.e. new plant capable of operating to a tighter tolerance). Special causes are identifiable events which can, with knowledge, be anticipated and prevented.

Action and blame

Many control systems use fixed, or predetermined, targets. These are often arbitrary, i.e. they lack context. The main result of this is to encourage people to avoid blame.

The effective outcome of a control system should be the investigation of causes of variation with a view to improving control, however this is only feasible if there is a cause. It is necessary to distinguish between trend and noise.

The control chart

Control charts distinguish between trend and noise simply, visually and in context. Discrimination can never be perfect, but the control chart establishes an appropriate balance between the two errors of losing trend values in the noise, and treating noise as trend.

A control chart simply plots actual values, in sequence, on a graph with lines representing the average, and the upper and lower limits. Variation within the limits is treated as noise, while values outside are seen as trend. The graph is the context, and sustained variation in one direction only might be interpreted as trend even if it is within the control limits. The trade deficit example, with limits is shown in Figure A2.2.

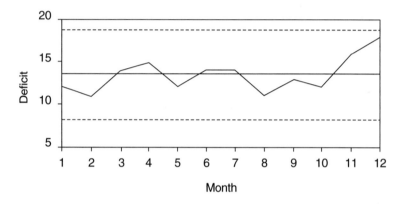

Figure A2.2 Trade deficit with limits

Control charts require a history of data to establish their parameters. Where this is not available, the values can still be plotted, but interpretation will be subjective. Once enough values have been generated the average and control limits can be fitted retrospectively and this might still lead to useful insights.

Calculating the limits

While the theory of control charts is firmly based upon conventional statistical theory, the practice has been simplified so that little statistical, or mathematical, competence is required. Statistical process control charts, using measurements taken from samples of output, usually use control limits based upon the standard error for the sample size, and limits of $\pm$ 2 or 3 standard errors might be used. This approach is not appropriate for situations where single values only are being considered (i.e. inventory this month, percentage shipped on time this week, spend relative to budget, etc.).

Here the control limits are based upon the moving range – the difference between values on consecutive time periods.

Consider the following data for on time shipments:

Month	1	2	3	4	5	6	7	8	9	10	11	12	Mean
% on time	92.1	91.6	91.8	91.5	91.1	91.1	90.1	89.2	89.9	90.8	91.2	91.2	90.97
MR		0.5	0.2	0.3	0.4	0	1	0.9	0.7	0.9	0.4	0	0.48

The moving range is calculated by subtracting the value for a particular month from the value for the previous month. Direction of change does not matter, so all values are positive. The moving range gives another control parameter. While a particular monthly figure may itself be within limits, the rate of change could still be excessive.

The limits for the control charts are computed as follows:

Individual value chart (called the X chart)
   Upper limit = Mean value + 2.66 × Mean moving range
   Lower limit = Mean value − 2.66 × Mean moving range

Moving range chart ((XmR chart)
   Upper limit = 3.27 × Mean moving range

The charts are shown in Figures A2.3 and A2.4.

While the moving range remains well within limits, the X chart clearly shows that the figure for month 8 was exceptional and warranted investigation. The same cannot be said, however, for months 7 and 9.

In reality, the control limits would be based upon several years' data and could well have been tighter (or wider) than shown. Control limits should be continuously updated as new data become available. However, if the underlying process changes then they should be scrapped and the calculation started anew. Control limits must reflect the underlying variability of the *current* situation to be of any value.

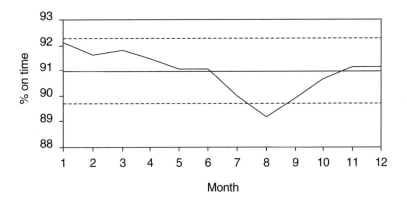

Figure A2.3   X chart

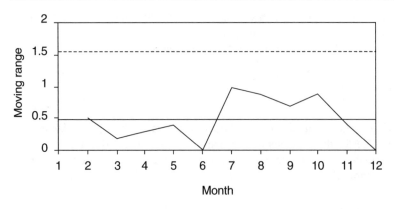

Figure A2.4   XmR chart

Use

Any time series data can be plotted on a control chart. The issue of usefulness depends upon the ability to take action. In a business context figures such as productivity, absenteeism, reject rates, total sales, expenditure to budget, stockholding, transactions per day could all usefully be subject to control charts. There are three objectives in doing this:

1 To avoid wasting time investigating causes when the change is simply random variation.
2 To find the cause of adverse variation with a view to preventing its recurrence (the aim is prevention, not blame).
3 To find the cause of favourable variation with a view to encouraging it in future.

A history of key operations concepts

4000 BC	Egypt	Concepts of planning and control. The idea that a plan must be developed and then monitored to ensure success is central to operations management.
1100 BC	China	As above.
600 BC	Chaldean Empire	Production control systems and incentive payments. The first recorded example specific to production.
500 BC	China	Standards of performance and systems of measurement. Principles of specialization. The precursors of all manufacturing systems up the 1960s.
400 BC	Cyprus	Motion study, material handling and layout. Re-invented in the nineteenth century as part of the scientific management movement.
AD 15th century	Italy	Part numbers, standardization of parts, assembly lines, inventory control – all aspects of modern operations management. Recognition of the value of interchangeable parts. Hand-crafted parts are highly variable, interchangeability depends upon standardization so that a particular component will fit no matter who made it. An essential prerequisite for any form of mass production (the Venetian arsenal could turn out a war galley in 24 hours).
18th century	Adam Smith	Specialization in manufacturing (again).
	Eli Whitney	Scientific method. The application of the principles of the scientific method, in particular observation, recording, reproducible and precise measurement to the design and management of manufacturing work.

19th century	Joseph Jacquard	Numerical control – the jacquard loom.
	James Watt	Standard procedures, standard times. Facilitates planning and control.
	James Mill	Analysis of human motion. Leading into the whole area of work study.
	Charles Babbage	Division of labour, motion and time study.
20th century		
1900s	Frederick Taylor	Scientific management – method study, time study, functional structure, need for co-operation between labour and management. Bringing together most of the developments of the previous century into a coherent discipline.
	Frank Gilbreth	Motion study.
	Henry Gantt	Gantt charts, need for training labour.
1910s	F.W. Harris	Economic Lot Size. One of the first applications of mathematical modelling to manufacturing operations.
	Henry Ford	Large scale development of the assembly line, extreme manifestation of the division of labour.
1910	W.H. Leffingwell	Scientific management in the office. An extension of the work in manufacturing to non-manufacturing activities.
1920s	Dodge and Romig	Statistical Quality Control. Probably the first example of stochastic modelling in operations.
1930s	Walter Shewhart	Statistical Process Control. Control charts for discriminating between common and special causes.
	Mary Follett	Group approach to problem solving. Not at this time of much relevance to operations, but widely used latter in approaches such as kaizen, TQM, JIT.
	P.M.S. Blackett et al.	Operations research. The integration of existing mathematical models, into a unified discipline of mathematical modelling. The most widely used models in operations are, inventory, queuing, forecasting, linear programming.
1940s	Norbert Wiener Claude Shannon	Systems analysis. Again little used in operations management at this time, but a precursor of Business Process Re-engineering.

1950s	Armband Feigenbaum	Total Quality Control. The first manifestation of the need to compete on quality. Until the late 1940s manufacturing was operating in a situation characterized by under capacity, but the stimulus of the 1939–45 war, and the subsequent rebuilding of the German and Japanese industrial base led to over-capacity and the need for real competition. A broader and more discerning market led to quality being one of the areas of competition.
	Japan	Total Quality Management. TQC was mainly design and manufacturing focused. TQM developed out of the Japanese attempts to improve quality and expanded to include all functions and personnel.
	Japan	Just in Time. Initially arising out of the Japanese motor industry's inability to finance adequate stocks, it became associated with the idea of stockless production in the West, though a broader meaning of continuous improvement through waste reduction is more appropriate.
	Japan	Kaizen. An aspect of JIT using small, empowered, workplace teams as the basis for day to day management and continuous improvement.
1960s	Douglas McGregor	Theory X and Theory Y. It can be argued that manufacturing operations management, up to this time, had been predominantly Theory X – workers had to be commanded and controlled to produce reasonable output. The more recent group approaches are, of course, ostensibly Theory Y.
	Martin Co.	Zero Defects. Developed initially for high risk defence manufacture, but widely adopted as a concept throughout manufacturing.
	USA	Service operations concepts emerge.
1970s		Material Requirements Planning. High technology computer based solutions to the problems of production scheduling. Developed into Manufacturing Resources Planning.
	Eliyahu Goldratt	Theory of Constraints. Also Optimized Production Technology and Synchronous Manufacture. The use of throughput rather than utilization as the driving force behind scheduling.

| | Simultaneous Engineering | Developing, in part, out of systems analysis. The simultaneous design of product and process shortens the time to market and increases the chance of success. Later expanded to include the use of supplier skills in the design process. |
| 1980s | Business Process Re-engineering | The application of systems analysis to the whole organization. A reaction against the progressive nature of JIT, TQM, Kaizen. Based on the assumptions that a substantial jump in performance will only be achieved by a radical redesign of the organization so that its structure matches market needs. |

Bibliography

Armistead, C.G. and Killeya J.C. (1984) 'Transfer of concepts between manufacture and service', *International Journal of Operations & Production Management* 3 (3).

Galloway, R.L. and Whyte, G.A. (1989) 'The internal information systems function as a service operation', *International Journal of Operations & Production Management*, 9 (4).

Lyth, D.M. and Johnston, R. (1988) 'A framework for designing quality into service operations', in Johnston, R. (ed.) *The Management of Service Operations* IFS Publications.

Nicholls, J.R. (1993) 'Customer value in four steps', *TQM Magazine*, December.

FURTHER READING

General

Cole, W.E. and Mogab, J.W. (1995) *The Economics of Total Quality Management*, Blackwell.

Schonberger, R.J. (1986) *World Class Manufacturing*, Free Press.

Slack, Chambers, Harland, Harrison and Johnston, (1997) *Operations Management*, Pitman.

Vandermerwe, S. (1993) *From Tin Soldiers to Russian Dolls*, Butterworth-Heinemann.

Service operations

Normann, R. (1991) *Service Management*, Wiley.

Schmenner, R.W. (1993) *Service Operations Management*, Prentice-Hall.

Strategy and design

Harrison, M. (1993) *Operations Management Strategy*, Pitman.

Hill, T. (1989) *Manufacturing Strategy*, Irwin.

Hollins, G. and Hollins, B. (1991) *Total Design*, Pitman.

Lorenz, C. (1986) *The Design Dimension*, Blackwell.

Quality

Caplan, R.H.A. (1982) *Practical Approach to Quality Control*, Business Books.

Crosby, P. (1979) *Quality is Free*, McGraw Hill.
Gaster, L. (1995) *Quality in Public Services*, Open University Press.
Ho, S.K. (1995) *TQM: An Integrated Approach*, Kogan Page.
Oakland, J.S. (1992) *Statistical Process Control*, Heinemann.
Wheeler, D.J. (1993) *Understanding Variation*, SPC Press.

Scheduling and material control

Lockyer, K.G. (1984) *Critical Path Analysis and other Project Network Techniques*, Pitman.
Tooley, D.F. (1985) *Production Control Systems and Records*, Gower.
Vollman, Berry and Whybark (1984) *Manufacturing Planning and Control Systems*, Irwin.

Index

ABC analysis, for stock optimization
118–20
acceptable quality level (AQL) l70–2
access, and layout design 64
acquisition costs 108–9,110–11
activity sampling 7–5; *see also* work study
adaptive stock control systems 116, 118
administrative costs 109
aggregate planning 98–101
algorithm-based scheduling 128–9
annual demand system of inventory
control 118
AOQL see average outgoing quality level
AQL see acceptable quality level
assurance 181
attitude survey 185
attribute control l74–5; *see also* statistical
process control (SPC)
automatic assembly process 74
automatic inspection and test process 74
automatic stock control systems 116
automation 18–19, 25, 71, 73–5
availability: of goods or services 21, 22 fig;
of labour 60, 63; of premises 61
average outgoing quality level (AOQL)
171
averages: exponentially weighted moving
93–4; moving 92–4

banking 45, 47, 59, 61; automation in 73;
and service quality 183, 184–5
batch production 12–13, 24; batch size
125, 127; control systems 133; plant
failure in 166; scheduling 123–35
bespoke tailoring 9, 20
bill of materials data 99–100, 130–1
binomial distribution 167, 201
bottleneck scheduling 127, 133–4

brainstorming 38–9
British Standards Institute: standards for
quality control capability 180; time
study rating scales 82
buffer stocks 95, 96, 106, 107: *see also*
safety stock
business process re-engineering (BPR) 142

capacity 57–70, 80, 91–102, 121; service
45, 47–8; surplus 9–10, 45, 58, 97–8,
168; *see also* volume
capital costs: of automation 73, 74; in
inventory 108
capital utilization 97
case studies; batch scheduling 135;
capacity investment 69–70; capacity
planning 102–5; inventory control
120–2; JIT 144–6; maintenance
199–200; operations strategy 28–9;
product design 40–2; project planning
160–2; quality management 187–90;
service design 54–6; task design 86–90
casual labour 97
causal methods of forecasting demand 94
centralization 16, 62–3
change, technological 32, 35, 38–9, 71
charts: control 175–6, 208–12; flow 78, 79;
from–to 67–8; Gantt 124–6, 158–9;
movement 67–8, 78; travel 68; two-
handed 78
chase demand strategy 96–7
civil engineering 9, 11, 20, 97
clothing industry 97
clustering, industrial 60
common cause variation 174, 209
competitiveness 4, 21–3, 26–8
components, numbers and variety of 33,
34–5

computer numerical control (CNC) 74
conformance quality 164
consumables 97
consumer's risk 167, 168, 170
continuous improvement 137, 143
continuous process production 13
continuous sampling scheme 172
control: automated systems 74; inventory
   106–20; project 159–60; quality
   163–86; of service quality 184–5; of
   variety 34–6; see also planning
control charts 175–6, 208–12
core business 14, 16–17, 23
corporate strategy 16–18, 57–8
cost reconciliation 109–15
costing 102–3, 133, 125; standard 90; time
   based 81
costs: acquisition 108–9, 110–11;
   administrative 108–9: automation 73–4;
   capital 73, 74, 96, 102; of customer
   waiting time 10–11, 58–9; energy 26;
   idle capacity 58; inventory 108–9,
   110–11; labour 60; maintenance 192;
   pollution 31; of quality 165–6, 173;
   sampling 170; set-up 108; standard
   product 90; of stock losses 106; of
   stockout 109, 115, 168; of stockholding
   108, 110–13, 120, 129, 193; transport
   60; of variety 2–30; warehousing 108
criminal justice system 3
critical path analysis (CPA) 148–56
critical path method (CPM) see critical
   path analysis
custom manufacturing 9, 20
customer: confidence 50; defining needs of
   20, 45; expectations 45, 52; involvement
   9, 28, 44; as labour 48; and machine
   interface 48, 64; satisfaction 19–20,
   45–6, 49; waiting 9–11, 58–9, 95, 97–8

data: bill of materials 99–100, 130–1;
   capacity 80, 98–9, 100–1; and MRP 130;
   progress 122; work 76–85; see also
   estimating; measurement
demand 91–8; and capacity 98,101; chase
   demand strategy 96–7; dependent
   101–2; and differential pricing 11, 95;
   forecasting 91–5; and inventory control
   116, 118; level capacity strategy 95–6;
   for raw materials 92; seasonal 45, 95;
   for services 11, 45, 58; variations in 11,
   45, 95–8, 106, 107

design: product 30–42; and quality 33,
   35–6, 46, 49–53; quality, 164; service
   43–56; task 62–76; work 75–6
differential pricing 11, 95
dimension control 176
dispersion see multiple site operations
distributions, statistical 201–2; binomial
   167, 201; normal 105, 201; Poisson
   58–9, 167, 201–2
drift, in operating procedures 77, 80, 81
dummy activities, in project planning 150
duration, of projects 153–6

economic batch quantity (EBQ) see
   economic order quantity
economic order quantity (EOQ)
   110–13,140
economies of scale 24, 62
education, in quality control 177
efficiency 4, 13, 20, 24, 46
electronics manufacturing 30, 33, 36, 74
empathy 181
energy costs 31
engineering see civil engineering; heavy
   engineering
environment 31; hostile working 71
ergonomics 76
errors: as finished goods stock 107;
   reworking 100, 138, 167; see also
   failures
esteem value 38
estimating 11, 148, 153; see also data;
   measurement
European Airbus 25, 61
exchange value 38
expectations, customer 45–6, 52

failures: of components 36; of new
   products 30–2; of plant 191, 192,
   194–7; of quality 165–6; in service
   44–5; see also errors
Fiat 18
finished goods stock 107, 138
fixed quantity inventory control systems
   115–16
fixed time inventory control systems
   116–18
flexibility 11, 13, 72; and automation 74,
   75; in capacity 96–7; of labour 48, 97,
   140; and layout 64–5; multiple site
   operations 62; and production process
   13, 24; of supply 21

flexible manufacturing cell 74
flexible manufacturing system (FMS) 74
flexible transfer line 74
float analysis 155–6
flow production *see* mass production
flow charts 78, 79
focus group 185
focusing, in JIT 139
Ford, Model T 20
forecasting: demand 91–5; long term 49;
    seasonal 94, 196–7
four phases of total quality management
    178; *see also* total quality management
from–to chart 67–8
front office/back shop services 47
furniture industry 9, 22

Gage's twelve steps in value analysis 38
Galloway, L. and Whyte, G.A. 50
Gantt charts 124–6, 158–9
gap model of service quality 182–3
go/no-go gauges 174
Goldratt algorithm 134
Goldratt, E. 134
goodwill 58, 99, 191, 192
group loyalty 76
group replacement 197
group technology 66, 139

health care services 10, 20, 21, 45
heavy engineering 9, 21
hot stand-by 168
human capabilities 71–3
human relations school of work design 76

industrialization, of services 46–9
information flow 5–6
infrastructure 60
inspection procedures 53, 168–72; *see also*
    monitoring
insurance company 3
integration, vertical 16
International Standards Organisation (ISO)
    180
ISO 9000 180
inventory 106–8, 110–13, 138; *see also*
    stocks
inventory control 34, 106–20; adaptive
    systems 116; annual demand system
    116, 118; automatic 116; cost
    reconciliation 109–15; fixed quantity
    system 115–16; fixed time system

116–18; monitoring 119, 120; reorder
    systems 116–18; stock record system
    116, 118; two-bin system 116, 118
investment 18, 34, 57–70, 73–5

Japan: and JIT 136–41; jobs for life policy
    97; quality circles 159
JIT see Just-in-Time
job production *see* project production
job satisfaction 76
Johnston, R. *see* Lyth, D.M. and Johnston, R.
Johnson's algorithm 128–9
Just-in-Time (JIT) 63, 109, 136–43, 191

kanban see Just-in-Time (JIT); pull-
    scheduling
kaizen 143
Korea 60

labour 18, 25, 47–8; casual 97; costs 60;
    flexible 47, 97, 140; human or machine
    71–3; and location decisions 60; multi-
    skilled 11; outwork 97; overtime
    working 96–7: part time 47–8, 97, 98;
    training 47, 71, 72; turnover 47;
    utilization 13, 34
layout 11–13, 64–8, 140
level capacity demand variation strategy
    95–6
linear programming 101, 204–6
location 25, 58, 59–63
lot tolerance percentage defective (LTPD)
    170–1
Lyth, D.M. and Johnston, R. 52–3

machine or human labour 71–3
mail order retailing 9, 59, 61
maintenance 80, 191–8: and JIT 140, 198;
    proactive 194–8; reactive 191–4
make-or-buy option 97
management: proactive 26, 173–6, 194–8;
    see also control; corporate strategy:
    planning
manufacturing 6, 8–9, 33, 34–5, 73–5;
    small scale 28
manufacturing resources planning (MRPII)
    124, 131–3; *see also* material
    requirements planning (MRP)
market entry criterion *see* qualifying
    criterion
market needs and product design 32–3
market proximity, and location 59

marketing strategy 19–23, 26–9
mass production 13, 24, 75
master production schedule 99, 130
material flow 8–11, 78, 139, 140
material requirements planning (MRP)
  124, 130–1
measurement: of service quality 184–5;
  stopwatch 82–3; time as 81, 82–3, 98;
  work 80–5, 90; see also data; estimating
method study, SREDIM methodology
  77–80
models of service quality 181–3
monitoring: inventory control 119, 120;
  performance 53, 157; production
  progress 10, 126, 128, 159; see also
  inspection procedures
Morgan cars 97
motivation 66, 72, 76
motor industry: manufacturing 18, 20, 74,
  97, 125; retailing 19–20
movement chart 67–8, 78
moving averages 92–4
moving range 211
multi-stage sampling schemes 172
multinationals 62
multiple site operations 25, 61, 62–3
mystery shopper 185

National Health Service 108
network analysis 148–56; activity on arrow
  convention 149–50; activity on node
  convention 152; large networks 152–3
Nicholls, J.R. 177
Nissan 60
normal distribution 105, 201
numerical control (NC) 74

obsolescence: of plant 33; of stock 108
operational quality 164
operations function 1–14
operations management, defined 1–4
operations strategy 15–29
operations tetrahedron 7, 19
optimized production technology (OPT)
  133–4
order winning criterion 21–3, 165
orders 110–3
organization and methods see work study
overtime working 96–7

PAPD see process average percentage
  defective

Parasuraman et al. 181
Pareto analysis and inventory optimization
  118–20
part time labour 48, 97, 98
perishable stock 9
PERT see project evaluation and review
  technique
petrochemical industry 13
planning 25; batch scheduling 123–35:
  capacity 91–102; Just-in-Time 136–43;
  manufacturing resources (MRP II)124,
  131; material requirements (MRP) 99,
  124, 130–1; optimized production
  technology (OPT) 133–4; project/job
  101, 148–59; see also control
plant: failure 191, 192, 194: and JIT 140;
  standardization of 193; utilization 34
Poisson distribution 58–9, 167, 201–2
pollution costs 31
predetermined motion time systems
  (PMTS) 83–4
price breaks 112
price competition 21
price differential 11, 95
priority-based scheduling 127
proactive management: of maintenance
  194–7; quality 173–6
process average percentage defective
  (PAPD) 168, 170
process routes, and layout design 57
processes 11–14, 24, 33, 34–5; see also
  batch production; mass production;
  project production
producer's risk 167, 168, 170
product: finished 97; improving 33; life
  cycle 17–18; new 30–2; shelf life 95,
  108, 112; standard cost of 90
product design 30–9
product development strategy 17–18
product layout 13, 65–6
product mix 65, 98, 101
production: batch 12–13, 24, 123–35, 191;
  continuous process 13; mass 13, 24, 75;
  master schedule 99; optimized
  production technology (OPT) 133–4;
  project 11, 24, 148–59
profiling 26–8
progress chasing 128
project evaluation and review technique
  (PERT) 148, 153
project production 11, 20, 148–60
project scheduling 11, 123, 156–9

projects: duration of 153–6; and
    uncertainty 148, 156
public policies, on location of industry
    60–1
pull-scheduling 123, 140–1
purchasing 141
push-scheduling 123

qualifying criteria 21–3
quality 20–1, 163–86 ; and JIT 139; and
    product design 33, 35–6; and production
    processes 12–13, 24; and services 44,
    45–6; standards 179–80
quality control 166–72; acceptable quality
    level (AQL) 170–1; average outgoing
    quality level (AOQL) 171; lot tolerance
    percentage defective (LTPD) 170–1;
    process average percentage defective
    (PAPD) 168, 170; quality circles 178–9;
    statistical quality control (SQC)
    166–72; total quality management
    (TQM) 136, 139, 176–9
queuing and queuing theory 9–11, 58–9,
    95, 97–8, 202–6; multi-channel 203;
    single channel 203

raw materials: accessibility of 59; demand
    92; stocks 106–7, 138
regression analysis 94, 206–7
relevance of service quality 183–4
reliability 181; of product 22, 33, 35–6; of
    supply 18
reorder level 115–16
reorder systems of inventory control
    116–18
replacement theory 191–97
resource usage 148, 156–8
responsiveness 181
restaurant 2–3
reworking errors 100, 138, 167

safety: and layout 63; and maintenance
    191, 194, 196–7; and stand-by facilities
    193
safety stock 113–5, 116, 118, 131
sampling: activity 84–5; continuous 172;
    costs of 170; multi-stage 172; single
    stage 168–71; in statistical process
    control 175–6
satisfaction questionnaire 185
scheduling 123–34: algorithm-based
    128–9; bottleneck 127, 133–4; priority

based 127; project 123, 156–8; pull
    123,140–1; push 123; sequential 124–6;
    work content 126–7; and work in
    progress 128
seasonality 39, 94, 95, 97, 181–2
self service 47–8
sequential scheduling 124–6
service 7, 9–11, 19–20, 43–56;
    environment 52; industrialization of
    46–9, 73; inspection procedures 53;
    product 52; quality 49–53, 180–5;
    structure 50–2; variable demand 9, 45,
    58
SERVQUAL 181
set-up costs 108, 140
shelf life 95, 108, 112
Silicon Glen 60
Silicon Valley 60
single sampling schemes 168–71
single site operation 61, 62
single-channel queuing theory 203
sites, single or multiple 61–3
space: and layout 64–5, 66; storage 111
spares stocks 107, 193
specification: capacity 50–1; and product
    design 33; of services 45–6
special cause variation 174, 209
SREDIM methodology 77–80
stand-by facilities 193–4; human 72
standard cost of product 100
standard times 100–1
standardization 18, 20, 24, 34–5, 168: and
    JIT 139; in service industries 47
statistical process control (SPC) 173–6;
    attribute control 174–5; dimension
    control 176
statistical quality control (SQC) 166–72;
    multi-stage sampling schemes 172;
    single sampling schemes 168–71
special cause variation 174
stock losses 106
stock record system of inventory control
    116, 118
stock turn 120; under JIT 137
stock out 109, 113, 115–16, 120, 168
stockholding 9, 20, 29; costs of 108,
    110–13, 120, 130, 168; under JIT 137
stocks 8–9; acquisition costs 108–9,
    110–11; buffer 95, 96, 106, 107, 138;
    finished goods 107, 120, 138; maximum
    levels 116; minimum levels 130–1; raw
    materials 9, 106–7, 138; safety 113–15,

116, 118, 131; spares 107, 193; strategic
107–8; work in progress 107, 138; *see
also* inventory
stopwatch measurement 82–3
storage 106, 111, 112
strategic stocks 107–8
subcontracting 11, 16, 23, 97
subjective estimating 11, 148, 153
subjective methods of forecasting demand
95
subjectivity 181, 182
supply and suppliers 7, 8–9, 34, 59–60;
Just-in-Time 109, 137, 141
surplus capacity 9–11, 58, 97–8, 193
synthetic methods of work measurement 84
systems engineering 142
systems, operations as 2–3

Taiwan 60
tangibles 181
task allocation 71–3
task design 71–89
teamwork 37–8, 148, 176–9
technology changes 32, 35, 38–9
technology push 32
television manufacture 2
three dimensional model of service quality
181–2
three time estimates method 153
time: and measurement of capacity 7–1,
88; and measurement of work 72–3
time series methods of forecasting demand
92–4
tolerances 36, 174–6
total quality management (TQM) 176–9;
four phases of 178; and JIT 139; *see
also* quality; quality control
training: labour 48, 71, 72, 96; and TQM
177
transfer line 74
transport 5, 9–11; costs 60

travel charts 58
turnover, labour 48
two-bin system of inventory control 116,
118
two-handed chart 78
two-tier services 10–11
Tyneside 60

uncertainty 24, 101, 123, 148, 156
usage value of stock 118–20
utilization: capital 97; labour 13, 34, 65;
low 66; maximizing 91, 96–8, 123, 125,
127, 138; plant 11, 34; of services 46;
surplus capacity 11

value analysis 37–9; and Gage's twelve
steps 38
value engineering *see* value analysis
variation, common and special causes 174,
209
variety 20, 24; control of 34–5
vertical integration 16
volume: of production 20, 24, 66; *see also*
capacity

waiting *see* queuing
warehousing costs 112
waste, JIT concepts of 138
Whyte, G.A. *see* Galloway, L. and Whyte,
G.A.
work: content 82, 126–7; design 6–7;
organization 11–13
work cells 56
work in progress: stocks 97, 138; and work
scheduling 128
work study 76–85; measurement 80–5, 90;
predetermined motion time systems
(PMTS) 83–4; time study 82–3
work force *see* labour

zone of tolerance 182